Worker Cooperatives
In America

Worker Cooperatives In America

EDITED BY
ROBERT JACKALL
AND
HENRY M. LEVIN

Berkeley

Los Angeles

London

UNIVERSITY OF CALIFORNIA PRESS

University of California Press
Berkeley and Los Angeles, California
University of California Press, Ltd.
London, England
Copyright © 1984 by
The Regents of the University of California

Library of Congress Cataloging in Publication Data
Main entry under title:

Worker cooperatives in America.

Includes index.
1. Producer cooperatives—United States. 2. Producer
cooperatives—United States—History. 3. Employee
ownership—United States. 4. Employee ownership—United
States—History. I. Jackall, Robert. II. Levin, Henry M.
HD3134.W67   1984   334'.6'0973   84–61
ISBN 0-520-05117-3

Printed in the United States of America

1 2 3 4 5 6 7 8 9

For our children
Yuriko Hirota Jackall
Mia, David, and Jesse Levin
Joshua Levin-Soler

CONTENTS

PREFACE

This book had its immediate origins in earlier research on workplace democracy carried out by both editors but in different contexts—Levin focusing on industrial democracy in Europe while Jackall was concentrating on self-management in the United States. Our earlier work had suggested that worker cooperatives, that is, businesses owned and managed by their workers, might improve employment opportunities and work productivity, as well as alleviate some of the discontents of modern work. The Center for Studies of Metropolitan Problems of the National Institute of Mental Health* agreed to support a project that focused on these issues. Our subsequent surveys, fieldwork, and analytical studies provided the basic understanding of the worker cooperative phenomenon that is the substance of this book. All of the essays in the book are original and derive from specific work commissioned as part of the overall research design. There are, therefore, common themes that run through all the essays; we have tried to articulate these in the first and last chapters as well in the brief introductory remarks to each section.

We are deeply indebted to a large number of people and organizations. We are especially grateful to the members of the worker cooperatives cited in the book who gave us the opportunity to learn about their work and their lives. Bill Behn, Kathy Wilcox, Robert Margolis, and Allen Graubard, who all participated in the research, deserve special mention for their important contributions to our thinking. We are grateful, too, to the other authors of this book, both for their essays and for the insights that their research provided. We would like to thank Michael Reich, Eliot Freidson, and Janice Hirota, who all read portions of the manuscript and made many valuable suggestions.

We also wish to thank Hal Vreeland and Elliot Liebow of the National Institute of Mental Health for their strong encouragement

*Our work was funded under the Work and Mental Health program of the Center for Studies of Metropolitan Problems; this program was subsequently transferred to the Center for Prevention Research of NIMH.

and support. Many thanks, too, to Stan Holwitz and Shirley Warren of the University of California Press for their work on the manuscript. Finally, we want to express our deep appreciation to those who assisted us in producing the manuscript through its many revisions—Stephanie Evans and Catherine O'Connor of Stanford University, and Rosemary Lane, Donna Chenail, Louise Gilotti, and Eileen Sahady of Williams College.

R. J.
H. M. L.

PART I

Introduction

1

Work in America and the Cooperative Movement

ROBERT JACKALL
AND
HENRY M. LEVIN

———————

This book addresses the history, dynamics, challenges, and potential of a remarkable form of enterprise, the worker cooperative. Worker cooperatives are productive firms that are democratically owned and managed by their workers. In an age of unparalleled bureaucratization where employees rarely participate in the ownership or control of organizations that shape their working lives, worker cooperatives are a vital form of workplace democracy.

Worker cooperatives spring up in a wide variety of business areas, from small retail operations such as restaurants and bookstores to large multimillion dollar manufacturing enterprises. They also take on a variety of cooperative forms. Some are based on each worker owning an equal share of the enterprise; others permit differential ownership among workers, with some limits on the degree of concentration of ownership. Many smaller cooperatives work through direct participation of their workers in all important decisions, whereas larger cooperatives utilize both participative and representative forms of management. No matter how diverse their arrangements, cooperatives share a commitment to democratic ownership and management.

Since colonial times there has been a continuous history of worker cooperatives in the United States. And to a great extent, the ebb and flow of this history is linked to the economic, social, and cultural dislocations of capitalist economic and political life. For example, in the nineteenth century, many worker cooperatives emerged as the result of classical struggles between workers and employers over wages or the conditions of work; other cooperatives were started by artisans who were displaced by the relentless machine processes of industrialization. In the 1930s, the massive unemployment brought on by the Great Depression stimulated the founding of hundreds of worker cooperatives, often with the assistance of state and local governments, expressly for the purpose of creating jobs. Recently a whole new generation of worker cooperatives has been produced from the social, political, and cultural upheavals of the late 1960s and early 1970s, along with our society's current persistent economic problems.

Although some of the essays in this volume treat the history of worker cooperatives, the main focus of this book is on the contemporary scene. In the last few years, there has been a marked resurgence of interest in worker ownership and worker participation among academics, workers, and those involved in public policy (see Frieden 1980; Kaus 1983; Mason 1982; Whyte et al. 1983; Williams 1982; Zwerdling 1978). Clearly, this rekindling of interest in workplace democracy—and the worker cooperative is the paradigmatic example of such democracy—is derived from the deep and pressing problems the American economy faces. What are some of these problems?

THE CRISIS OF THE AMERICAN ECONOMY

For the last several years, the American economy has been in serious trouble. High unemployment, inflation, high interest rates, slow economic growth, stagnant productivity, and job dissatisfaction became commonplace in the late 1970s and early 1980s. At this writing (late-1983), the economy is beginning to pick up, but many economists think that the recovery will be weak and short-lived, in part because the various problems of the economy are so complexly interrelated that by correcting some, others inevitably will be exacerbated.

Unemployment, for example, has remained alarmingly high, approaching 11 percent in 1982. Youth unemployment, at the time, was more than double that rate, and minority youth unemployment was four times as high. The Reagan administration has chosen to accept high unemployment as a cost of controlling the double-digit inflation of the late 1970s and early 1980s. Presently, inflation has indeed declined, down to a new "normal" rate of 4 to 5 percent per year. Unemployment, however, has not declined appreciably and is a politically explosive issue which must be confronted before the 1984 elections. But the traditional remedies of fiscal and monetary policies usually administered to the economy to reduce unemployment will this time almost certainly refuel the inflation (Okun 1981). In fact, inflation may begin to rise for other reasons even before then. For example, as a result of Reaganomics, the huge federal budget deficits are likely to cause interest rates to climb sharply, which is usually seen as a fateful step in the inflationary spiral and one that also portends dire consequences for investment and, in turn, employment.

Past administrations have attacked unemployment by expanding publicly funded jobs and training programs. Training programs, however, do not create jobs for the newly trained, and public employment programs or subsidies to private employers do not create permanent jobs (Palmer 1978). When the subsidies disappear, as they invariably do given the vagaries of our political system, so does the employment, except, of course, where the subsidies support positions that would have existed anyway.

The overall seriousness of unemployment masks the extreme gravity of the issue among certain populations and in certain parts of the country. Not only do young people and minorities have considerably higher unemployment rates than the national average but many urban and rural areas, particularly in the old industrial Northeast, also face unemployment burdens that are double or triple the national rates. This Frostbelt has been particularly hard hit by plant closures and by layoffs; many corporations have relocated their facilities to the Sunbelt to increase profitability by reducing energy costs or to the Third World for the purpose of taking advantage of various governmental subsidies, and lower cost nonunion labor. In other cases, firms have been closed after acquisition by a conglomerate because in some situations, the tax laws make plant shutdowns more profitable than continued operation (Bluestone and Harrison 1982).

In addition to these vexing dilemmas of unemployment, our country now faces a serious productivity crisis. In the 1950s and 1960s, the output produced for each hour of labor increased at an annual rate of about 3 percent per year. By the late 1970s, however, there was no increase in productivity whatsoever. This has serious implications for our competitive position in world trade; the Japanese, Koreans, and other Asians, as well as several European competitors, have increased their labor productivity rapidly while ours has been lagging. Again, there are no clear answers for policymakers on this issue because no one seems to know what are the exact causes for our declining rate of productivity. Virtually all the research on the subject suggests that traditional factors, such as the levels of capital investment or the rate of technological advances, are not the primary reasons for the slowdowns in productivity (Denison 1979).

Finally, even though persistent unemployment causes many people to wish for any job at all, the number of challenging jobs has not kept pace with the education of the population (Rumberger 1981). Education not only increases the technical capabilities of workers but, perhaps more importantly, also heightens their expectations for rewarding work. If one couples this expectation with the prestige accorded by our culture to exciting, glamorous work—especially apparent in television programming and advertising—it is little wonder that a great many workers are plagued by the sharp discrepancy between what they see as valued by our society and their own monotonous daily tasks. Since the early 1970s, the widespread disaffection with available jobs, which has been commented upon extensively and is now thought to be common in the American workplace (see Jackall 1978; Meissner 1971; Sheppard and Herrick 1972; Terkel 1974; U.S. Department of Health, Education, and Welfare 1973), seems directly related to worker turnover, absenteeism, sabotage, wildcat disruption, alcoholism, and other drug abuse. The root of our productivity crisis, in fact, may lie in the underutilization of workers.

In the last decade at least, these problems of unemployment, recurrent inflation, lagging productivity and widespread dissatisfaction with work seem intransigent. Certainly, there are no effective remedies being offered by the major actors in the public arena. The policies of the Reagan administration have produced huge transfers of wealth and income from the poor to the already rich, with no significant increase in economic growth.

In the face of conservative triumphs, the Democrats seem in hopeless disarray, devoid of ideas as well as political nerve. Although the left continues to produce much needed stinging critiques of present policies, it is still debating workable solutions for the dilemmas of the economy (Bowles, Gordon, and Weisskopf 1983; Carnoy, Shearer, and Rumberger 1983). For a time, the country seems caught in a period of intellectual and political sterility. As a consequence, it becomes difficult even to imagine, let alone publicly debate, ways of creatively shaping a future where institutional arrangements reflect a commitment to some sort of fairness and decency, let alone to reason and freedom, the classical post-Enlightenment ideals of the West.

THE POTENTIAL OF WORKER COOPERATIVES

There is, however, intriguing evidence, some of which is presented in this book, that worker cooperatives can contribute to resolving some of our economic problems. Moreover, they can accomplish this in a way that is in keeping with our most deeply held tradition, our democratic heritage.

First, in regard to employment, it is clear that worker cooperatives can provide more jobs, at the same level of capital investment, than traditional capitalist enterprises. In chapter 2, Henry Levin reports striking evidence of this potential. In particular, he discusses a study that found that in large industrial worker cooperatives, the same level of investment created four times as many jobs as in comparable capitalist firms. Other studies (Stern et al. 1979; Whyte et al. 1983) suggest that cooperatives provide employees a convenient structure for assuming the ownership and operation of firms bound for closure. In addition, by vesting both ownership and control in workers, skilled work forces can be kept intact, and jobs saved.

Second, in regard to productivity, there is evidence that worker cooperatives and worker-run firms are at least as productive as their more conventional counterparts, and possibly more productive (Jones and Svejnar 1982). This is discussed by Henry Levin in the upcoming chapter in which he describes the startling performance of a group of cooperatives, in Mondragon, Spain, that had almost a billion dollars in sales in 1981 of semi-conductors, refrigerators, heavy machinery, and other industrial and consumer products. For the same level of capital investment, the cooperatives had far higher labor productivity than comparable capitalist firms. This kind of productivity is also evident in several clusters of American worker cooperatives (see chap. 3 by Derek Jones) and seems to stem from the greater economic incentives cooperatives offer and from their more efficient forms of organization. Since workers own their own enterprises, they share directly in the success as well as the failure of the firm. This not only produces strong personal incentives to be productive, but also considerable peer pressures on colleagues to do their share. Furthermore, it contributes to low rates of worker turnover and absenteeism when compared to capitalist firms.

These incentives also reduce the need for supervisors, thus saving costs, as well as contributing to greater quality control. Edward Greenberg (see chap. 8) found that cooperative plywood manufacturers used only one or two supervisors per shift, while comparable capitalist firms used six or seven. One mill reportedly quadrupled the number of line supervisors and foremen when it converted over from cooperative to capitalist ownership. There are additional organizational reasons for higher productivity among cooperatives. These include the extensive rotation of work roles among members, which maintain worker interest and avoid production bottlenecks; training arrangements that encourage workers to see their training of colleagues as a natural and continuing part of the work process; and the natural incentives inherent in cooperatives which cause workers to maintain equipment properly and to contribute ideas that improve the productive enterprise.

Finally, by increasing workplace democracy, worker cooperatives go a long way toward reducing worker dissatisfaction. The conventional capitalist workplace of today makes the worker only an extension of its system of production, subordinate both to the organization of work and to the technology used in production. Work is broken into little pieces, coordinated by bosses who are coordinated in turn by other bosses. Workers survive and succeed in such a system by tailoring their skills, and indeed themselves, to the external requirements of the system. They have little say in shaping those criteria. In this context, work becomes a way to earn a living, with only a marginal possibility of it becoming a way of life. Admittedly, this is employment, but unfortunately employment that leaves many human needs unfilled and many more talents unemployed.

By contrast, worker cooperatives have found ways of overcoming these forms of alienation, by making the workers the center of the decision process. Cooperative workers decide the appropriate division of labor along with organizational hierarchy, by assessing the effects of their decisions on themselves (on their morale, equity, solidarity, and their actual work tasks) and on the production of goods or services for the marketplace. Therefore, worker cooperatives make it possible for workers to integrate their individual talents and work styles into the overall group work process and structure by directly influencing the nature of that process and structure through democratic participation. In short, cooperatives provide workers with opportunities to shape the public arena in which they spend most of their lives and, in so doing, to control the production of their social identities.

For all of these reasons, worker cooperatives have become subjects of considerable interest in the 1970s and 1980s. They are a response at the local, community, or plant level to problems that seem intransigent at the national level. It would be foolhardy to argue that they provide a total solution to the problems of unemployment, sagging productivity, and job dissatisfaction, especially in a society dominated by large bureaucratic organizations, but they can, at least, give us insight into ways and means of getting at these difficult issues more effectively. In fact, by providing a mechanism for the purchase and operation of firms that would otherwise close, cooperatives offer concrete solutions for our more general economic problems. Finally, in a society that speaks of democracy as its sacred bedrock but, in fact, practices it in a fairly narrow sense, worker cooperatives provide our system a way to engage the active, full participation of men and women in the most fundamental public sphere of all—their work.

DILEMMAS AND CHALLENGES OF
WORKER COOPERATIVES

Clearly, the potential of worker cooperatives is great. The actual record of their accomplishments, however, is much more ambiguous. In fact, the historical landscape is strewn with the records of worker cooperatives that were initiated with the greatest of hope but did not survive. Although some of the plywood cooperatives of the Pacific Northwest have been around for five decades, and although some cooperatives in Europe have been around as long (Jones 1978, 1980*a*), the long-term survival of cooperatives has been punctuated with problems. There are two major reasons for this.

First, worker cooperatives historically have been formed under the most risky sorts of business conditions. Typically, workers have seen cooperatives as a way of saving their jobs, by buying and operating a business that would otherwise close down. Obviously, such a risky undertaking is almost always a last ditch effort to sidestep economic failure and closure. Truly profitable firms are rarely abandoned to their workers. In fact, a firm marked for closure is milked for cash until its economic viability is marginal. Owners or managers allow their markets to deteriorate, the equipment to become obsolete, research and development to be neglected, and credit to be exhausted while they skim whatever liquid assets are available and look for new, more promising investments. These are not auspicious conditions under which to initiate any sort of enterprise. Even the kind of enthusiastic work force that usually comes together to form a worker cooperative cannot resuscitate a moribund business.

In contrast, many new worker cooperatives are formed not as a response to imminent unemployment, but as an expression of deeply felt, personal and political convictions. Usually, these convictions include a commitment to egalitarianism, to nonhierarchical work situations, and to the right of people to make those decisions that directly affect them. Quite often, however, these ideals and ambitions are not matched by the necessary capital or the business skills required for a successful venture. As a result, worker cooperatives get established in the most accessible areas of the economy, where relatively little capital is required. Wherever it is easy to start a new business, however, failure rates tend to be high, because of intense competition and because financial reserves are not adequate for inevitable hard times. A very high proportion of contemporary worker cooperatives get established in the most risky areas of small business in this country—areas such as restaurants, food stores, book stores, print shops, and repair services. Obviously, the small cooperative businesses face the same vicissitudes that jeopardize the chances of their capitalist counterparts.

The second major reason cooperatives experience difficulty achieving long-term survival is a problem not encountered by their capitalist counterparts: they must reconcile their internal requirements for democratic ownership and management with the external requirements of the marketplace and of other institutions on which they depend. One of the main themes of this book is to clarify the various dimensions of this tension between the internal and external demands of worker cooperatives. In fact, this tension is a prism through which one may view the daily lives and problems of men and women in worker cooperatives. The dynamics that are necessary for a capitalist firm to survive and flourish may undermine the democratic imperatives of cooperatives.

This is a point worth underlining. It is a commonplace of social analysis that every society promotes, both explicitly and tacitly, certain forms of productive organization by reinforcing the conditions for growth and survival of some types of enterprise while ignoring or even opposing other possibilities. Specifically, in the United States, the very forms of legal structure, access to capital, entrepreneurship, management, the remuneration of workers, and education all favor and reinforce the establishment and expansion of hierarchical corporate forms of enterprise and simultaneously create barriers to cooperative ones. Worker cooperatives are anomalies to these mainstream trends. Of necessity, they depend on the larger society and its institutional frameworks while, as a matter of choice, they work to achieve different goals and visions of the future. In fact, this anomalous, contradictory character, and the resultant tension it produces, is a permanent feature of cooperatives in a bureaucratic, capitalist society. Only when the internal requirements of a cooperative as a cooperative are reconciled with the external demands on the business as a business can worker cooperatives prosper over the long run.

Resolving the multitude of dilemmas this fundamental tension creates calls for considerable ingenuity and creativity. For example, access to external financial capital often requires a firm to put up its equity as collateral for loans. Since worker cooperatives are owned by their members, or workers, potential ownership cannot be provided to external lenders. Moreover, given the central importance of the principle of worker self-management, lending institutions are not able to place representatives on the boards of cooperatives to oversee operations. Banks, in particular, also feel uncomfortable dealing with managers who can be removed by workers or by boards elected by workers. Therefore, the personal ties so crucial to doing business are not easily formed. As a result, worker cooperatives often have difficulty securing loans from major lending institutions. There are, however, ways of cutting through this kind of complication, and some cooperatives have done so. The Basque cooperatives in Spain (see chap. 2 by Henry Levin; Oakeshott 1978; Thomas and Logan 1982) sponsor a financial agency to provide capital for their movement. In the United States, the Industrial Cooperative Association in Somerville, Massachusetts (see chap. 12 for further discussion) has established a revolving credit fund for initiating new worker cooperatives. In addition, public agencies and private foundations have been sources of capital for many cooperatives. In fact, it is even possible to establish special relationships with private financial institutions.

Another example of the tension between the necessities of maintaining cooperative principles and of meeting marketplace demands is that of personnel utilization during peak or off periods of a business's cycle. Typically, a conventional capitalist firm will hire or release labor as demand for its product rises or falls. Worker cooperatives, however, are committed to supporting the economic needs of their members in bad times as well as good. Therefore, cooperatives are unwilling to lay off or terminate their workers during slow periods. Likewise, cooperatives are also reluctant to hire more workers during boom times for fear of making commitments that cannot be met when the business cycle turns down. Some cooperatives meet this common problem by increasing or decreasing the hours of work for all their members as needed (Berman and Berman 1978). Alternatively, during slack periods, they devote time to long-term maintenance or renovation of the workplace.

Clearly, the tension between the demands of a democratic workplace and the demands of the marketplace is reconcilable. But it is a tension that continuously recurs, and therefore, one that must be consciously and creatively addressed. Otherwise, worker cooperatives might fail as businesses while retaining their democratic principles; or they might fail as worker cooperatives while retaining their economic vitality. This means that in order to survive and flourish, cooperatives have to place a premium on certain kinds of workers—namely, those who can live with the ambiguity of such permanent structural tension, but who can also find creative ways of meeting contradictory demands.

WORKER COOPERATIVES IN AMERICA

By now, our own reasons for studying worker cooperatives should be clear. If these organizations are to achieve their potential to meet real economic and social needs—in our view, a goal worth working for—we must understand more thoroughly the conditions that foster reconciliation between the contradictory demands these organizations face. Moreover, it is precisely because worker cooperatives are anomalous, contradictory organizations that they are worth pondering. They allow social thinkers to look two ways at once—toward the established order which cooperatives implicitly critique and toward an alternative future, the outlines of which they intimate.

There has been a scarcity of research on worker cooperatives in the United States. As a result, this book was designed to lay the groundwork for a thorough examination of the phenomenon. To do this, we formulated a large group of questions about the potential of worker cooperatives, their history, their present characteristics, their operational dilemmas and challenges, and the requirements for their survival and expansion. We used these questions to generate various projects which in turn generated the essays presented in this book. Each section of this book is organized to reflect a particular set of questions asked in the research. When taken together, these essays provide an overall picture of the worker cooperative phenomenon in America.

The first questions that concerned us were fundamental in nature. For example, why study worker cooperatives in the first place? And what real potential do these organizations have to address basic structural issues such as unemployment or declining rates of productivity? In chapter 2, Henry Levin addresses these questions. After a brief description of the Basque cooperatives in Mondragon, Spain, which sold almost a billion dollars of industrial products in 1981, he then compares evidence on employment generation and productivity between these firms and their capitalist counterparts and evaluates the differences in internal organization that appear to explain the higher employment and productivity of the cooperatives.

A second set of questions pertain to the history of worker cooperatives. For example, why historically were particular cooperatives established? In what industries were they established, and what were the typical arrangements for vesting ownership and control in their workers? How were decisions made in those cooperatives, and how well did they perform in comparison with their capitalist counterparts? What were the reasons for their demise, and what was the role of government assistance in the cooperative movement?

Part II of this book attempts to answer these questions. In chapter 3, Derek Jones appraises the historical experience of American worker cooperatives and employee-owned firms. He examines the several hundred documented cases of American worker cooperatives, dating back to 1790, and attempts to discern their patterns of formation and development as well as to gauge their economic performance vis-à-vis one another and against capitalist firms producing similar products. He also looks at the more recent history of employee-owned firms. Finally, he attempts to extract, from a largely ambiguous legacy, lessons for contemporary cooperative developments.

In chapter 4, Derek Jones and Donald Schneider analyze the great upsurge of self-help cooperatives that arose with the assistance of the government during the Great Depression. This is a remarkably interesting and instructive story. Despite the absence of management skills, a shortage of capital, erratic government policies, and a culturally diverse and economically marginal group of participants, the self-help cooperatives provided employment for large numbers of persons who would otherwise have been unemployed. These cooperatives supplied the workers with the economic essentials of life and showed that the participants could create viable enterprises with only subsistence resources.

Given this history, it is important to examine closely the development of contemporary worker cooperatives, to determine how they function and to ascertain what life in cooperatives is like for their workers. Therefore, we must ask, how are cooperatives organized, and how do they differ in their organization from conventional firms? How are the firms governed, and how do individual workers get involved in the decision making? What are the arrangements for ownership and remuneration? What are the major sources of satisfaction and conflict? How is the tension between democratic operation and successful functioning as a business in a capitalist economy resolved? These questions are best answered by studying specific cooperatives.

Part III of this book focuses on the contemporary movement of small worker cooperatives, or collectives, that has blossomed in urban areas since 1970. In chapter 5, Robert Jackall and Joyce Crain delineate the composition and structure of this movement. On the basis of a survey of small cooperatives along with additional sources of information, they estimate that there are between 750 and 1,000 of these organizations throughout the country, clustered mainly in the service sector of the economy. The authors analyze the organizational dilemmas that small cooperatives face, as well as present information on the characteristics of their employees, their products, and services, their remuneration, and other aspects of these collectives.

These factors are developed in greater detail in Robert Jackall's case study of a retail cheese store that is organized as a collective. His essay explores how this successful cooperative attempts to meet the requirements of economic efficiency and cooperative operation. Specifically, he focuses on the productive use of discourse and conflict in shaping social cohesion and in guaranteeing democratic decision making.

Part IV of this book goes on to explore the functioning of contemporary cooperatives by examining the growing popularity of the worker cooperative form of organization for large businesses. In this section, Christopher Gunn presents his analysis of the largest forestry cooperative in the United States, the Hoedads (chap. 7). What is particularly interesting about this cooperative is the way it combines both representative and direct town-meeting-style democracy at the level of the whole cooperative with reliance on consensus decision making at the level of smaller work crews. The economic prowess of the

Hoedads is reflected in its success in competing with the giant lumber corporations for government reforestation contracts. Chapter 8 is an analysis by Edward Greenberg of the governance structure of cooperative plywood firms in the Pacific Northwest. Greenberg evaluates the governance arrangements of these cooperatives in light of democratic theory and examines the attitudes of workers toward their membership and participation in these firms.

All of these essays raise specific questions about the requirements for success of cooperative firms in meeting their internal needs for democracy and the external demands of the capitalist economy. For example, what are the appropriate legal arrangements that best satisfy the reconciliation of these needs? What is the most promising approach for financing worker cooperatives, particularly those where the workers purchase the firm from their former employers to avoid a plant closure? What types of training and experience do cooperative members need to manage their firms and to make democratic decisions? How can cooperatives provide relatively equal pay while obtaining the appropriate combinations of skills which would receive vastly unequal remuneration in the larger economy?

In Part V, these questions are addressed in the course of three essays. In chapter 9, Zelda Gamson and Henry Levin focus on specific internal obstacles to the survival of a democratic workplace. In particular, they examine the absence of a common culture among cooperative members, the lack of democratic norms for decision making, and the scarcity of appropriately trained personnel. The authors not only attempt to describe and analyze these problems, but also suggest some ways of remedying them.

In chapter 10, Henry Levin explores Employee Stock Ownership Plans (ESOPs), which many consider the most promising approach to financing worker cooperatives. Although ESOPs are being used increasingly for employee purchases of conventional businesses, this use has a number of serious flaws. In particular, ESOPs may facilitate the employee purchase of a firm without providing for worker participation in its operation. In the long run, a dichotomy between ownership and control such as this can erode the basis for a self-sustaining cooperative enterprise. In chapter 11, David Ellerman explores this problem and attempts to develop some notions about the ideal legal framework for the establishment and operation of worker cooperatives. In particular, he focuses on the specific nature of property and membership rights in cooperatives, and argues that schemes such as ESOPs, by concentrating on worker ownership, miss the essential point of cooperatives, namely, that they are democratic social institutions based on membership rights. What is needed, Ellerman argues, are appropriate legal structures and mechanisms that reflect and ensure this distinction.

In chapter 12, the editors attempt to assess the future prospects for worker cooperatives in America. This essay brings together the main themes of the history, character, dynamics, potential, and problems of worker cooperatives developed throughout the book. Given the long history of cooperatives in America, there is little question that they will continue to form spontaneously, though perhaps sporadically, in the future. The point of chapter 12, however, is to examine the types of institutional mechanisms that can broaden and solidify the worker cooperative movement and make cooperatives less subject to the vagaries of economic and social shifts. Of course, in an era of profound reaction, such mechanisms must come principally from cooperatives themselves. Today, it becomes particularly important, simply to survive, let alone to make the real social contributions of which they are capable, that cooperatives stress cooperation with one another.

2

Employment and Productivity of Producer Cooperatives

HENRY M. LEVIN

INTRODUCTION

Two of the most serious problems faced by developing countries as well as by advanced industrial societies such as the United States are the high levels of unemployment and the low levels of productivity or slow productivity growth. The purpose of this chapter is to explore some of the evidence on the potential of producer cooperatives to remedy these problems. While specific findings on each of these issues are important, it is even more valuable to understand how cooperatives behave in such a way as to increase employment and productivity. The first part of this chapter focuses on the comparative employment and productivity record of the largest movement of industrial producer cooperatives in the world, the Mondragon cooperatives in northern Spain.[1] The experiences of these cooperatives provide substantial data along with instructive insights for the United States as well as for other nations. The remainder of this chapter attempts to explain the superior employment and productivity performance of these Spanish cooperatives by studying the intrinsic behavior of cooperatives vis-à-vis capitalist firms. These observations will be based not only on the Mondragon cooperatives but also on data available for cooperatives in the United States as well as in other industrialized countries.

The largest producer cooperative movement in the world is situated around the town of Mondragon in the Basque region of northern Spain (Campbell et al. 1977; Gutierrez-Johnson and Whyte 1977; Oakeshott

1978:chap. 10; Thomas and Logan 1982). The Mondragon cooperatives are remarkable for their size, their diversity, the complexity of their product mix, their rapid growth rate, their ability to generate capital and to obtain the technical skills for production and expansion, their success in penetrating both national and international markets, and their establishment of democracy and equality in the workplace.

The Mondragon cooperatives were started in 1956 with a single cooperative firm, expanding by 1981 to some ninety-one industrial firms and four agricultural enterprises. All of these cooperatives operate under the aegis of the same social statutes and share in common a system of social security, clinics, a major financial institution, a research and development center, and a renowned technical school. From about 400 employee-members in 1960, the membership expanded to approximately 8,600 members in 1970. By the end of 1981, nearly 19,000 members were employed in cooperative firms around Mondragon, producing products such as iron and steel, machine tools, winches, lathes, industrial refrigerators, household appliances, and electronic components. The sale of these products amounted to about one billion dollars in 1981, with exports totaling around $200 million.[2] One of these cooperative firms, Fagor, is the largest manufacturer of refrigerators in Spain, while another competes successfully in the world semiconductor market. Cooperative construction firms from Mondragon have been contracted to erect entire factories, production ready, in such countries as Libya, Russia, and Mexico.

To provide sources of financial capital and technical advice, the movement created a banking system which had grown to seventy-six branches by 1977 as well as a research and development center to establish new products and production techniques. The cooperative bank also developed an entrepreneurial division to assist member firms in all aspects of their operations, while service cooperatives were created to provide managerial assistance to a few of the largest of the firms. By 1981, the bank had about three-quarters of a billion dollars in assets and some 271,000 depositors.

A majority of the labor force is trained in Mondragon at the Polytechnical School which is renowned throughout Spain and much of Europe for its exceptional training programs. Students take technical courses to obtain official certification for their careers while at the same time working in cooperative firms within the region. The school, bank, and research and development center are themselves run cooperatively under the same social statutes as the other cooperatives. For instance, each worker must invest to become a member. The value of the investment, however, depends upon the success of the particular cooperative. Loans are also available to prospective members. And all members belong to a general assembly which is responsible for the ultimate control of the cooperatives. The assembly elects the leadership who in turn appoint the management of each cooperative. In addition, there is a social council to represent the interests of the shop floor level on such matters as health, safety, working conditions, payment schemes, and so on.

Every member is assigned a place, or *puesto*, with a value of one to three which depends on the responsibility of and training required for the job. The index determines the level of the job as well as the relative share for each member of any surplus that is distributed. This means that the pay range is about three to one, so that the top executive receives no more than three times the pay of the employee with the lowest training and responsibility.

Income is received in two forms: earnings for labor and the return on each member's capital investment. In addition to their initial investment in the firm, internal capital accounts are accumulated for each member based upon the annual share of the surplus credited to him or her. A rate of interest of 6 percent per year plus the annual rate of inflation on the price level is provided on the capital investment. The investment, however, must be retained with the cooperative until the member leaves, which thus insures the accumulation of capital for sustaining and expanding the movement. For cooperative members at the lower rungs of the occupational ladder, the labor portion of their income tends to be considerably higher than for capitalist workers. Wages, however, are about the same in the middle range, but considerably lower at the upper end of the ladder. Although high-level executives receive less pay than they would in capitalist firms, they do receive large, "psychic" benefits from their solidarity with a dynamic and democratic movement.

COMPARATIVE ASPECTS OF CAPITAL INVESTMENT, EMPLOYMENT, AND PRODUCTIVITY

A comparative analysis of the capital investment, employment, and productivity of the Mondragon cooperatives is instructive. One of the problems in making an analysis such as this is that it is necessary to have an appropriate group of conventional capitalist firms to use as a comparative base. The Mondragon firms tend to be found in the most capital-intensive sectors of manufacturing, such as iron and steel production, consumer durables, refrigeration equipment, capital goods, and so on. While there are no data on specific capitalist firms in these industries, there are aggregate data for the 500 largest Spanish industrial firms as well as statistics for the rest of Spanish industry. Indeed, an examination of the industrial composition of the 500 largest Spanish firms suggests reasonable comparability with that of the Basque co-

TABLE 2.1

COMPARISON OF CAPITAL, LABOR, AND VALUE-ADDED FOR 500 LARGEST CAPITALIST
FIRMS, REST OF CAPITALIST INDUSTRY AND THE MONDRAGON COOPERATIVES, 1972

	500 largest capitalist firms	Rest of capitalist industry	Mondragon cooperatives
Employment	936,500	4,711,000	10,310
Fixed capital*	1,425,000	1,350,000	3,942
Value-added*	381,700	987,000	3,481
Capital per worker	1,520,000	282,000	382,000
Value-added/ fixed capital	.27	.73	.88
Value-added per worker	408,000	207,000	338,000

SOURCE: Caja Laboral Popular, *Analisis de Productividad: Indices Generales* (Mondragon, Spain, 1973), p. 16.

*Millions of pesetas

operatives. If anything, the top 500 capitalist companies show less concentration in heavy manufacturing activities than do the cooperatives.

Table 2.1 provides a summary for 1972 of comparisons of capital, labor, and value-added for the 500 largest capitalist firms, the rest of capitalist industry, and the Mondragon cooperatives. These data are derived from an intensive study of productivity carried out by the Caja Laboral Popular, which is the institution that provides the cooperatives with financial analysis as well as other services. Although the cooperatives had only about 10,000 members in 1972, today they have almost twice as many members. Nonetheless, employment in 1972 for the top 500 capitalist firms and the rest of capitalist industry was substantially greater. Accordingly, the estimates of fixed capital and value-added will also reflect these substantial differences in size. The principal foci of comparison include the amount of capital per worker, the ratio of value-added to fixed capital, and the value-added per employee.

The amount of capital per worker provides a measure of the capital investment required to create each job for each of the categories. Based upon these figures, it appears that the 500 largest Spanish firms utilize about four times as much capital for each job created as do the Mondragon cooperatives. The rest of capitalist industry is even less capital-intensive than the cooperative firms, but it should be noted that this residual category is composed of small capitalist firms that are not producing the heavy industrial products of the 500 largest firms or the Mondragon cooperatives. Obviously, if the differences in amounts of capital per worker derive primarily from differences in the organizational forms taken by the two types of firms being compared—as I argue—then the cooperative approach can have very substantial employment benefits relative to corporate capitalist structure. This possibility is especially important for societies with severe capital shortages and labor surpluses.

The ratio of capital to labor, however, is only a measure of the relative intensiveness of factors of production, and not an indicator of productivity. The efficiency with which capital is being used in production is reflected by the amount of value-added relative to the amount of fixed capital. According to this measure, the cooperatives showed more than three times as large a contribution to value-added per unit of capital than the 500 largest capitalist firms. It is known also, however, that much of the higher product per unit of capital is attributable to the larger labor inputs of the cooperative firms. As a consequence, it is important to evaluate the value-added per worker.

As table 2.1 indicates, in 1972 the 500 largest firms had value-added per worker of about 408,000 pesetas. In comparison, the co-operatives produced about 338,000 pesetas in value-added per worker, while the rest of capitalist industry showed a value-added per worker of about 207,000 pesetas. Thus, as one might expect, the greater capital-intensiveness of the top 500 capitalist firms created greater labor productivity than for either of the other groups of firms. However, once the relative disparities in capital per worker and in value-added per worker are taken into account, rather strong evidence emerges that the cooperative firms have a much higher total factor productivity. Although the top 500 capitalist firms show a capital investment per worker 300 percent greater than that of the cooperatives, the value-added per worker for the 500 largest firms is only about 20 percent greater. This is rather impressive evidence that under a producer cooperative form of organization and worker ownership, basic industrial goods can be produced with considerably greater labor intensiveness while at the same time showing greater total factor productivity than under a capitalist ownership and a corporate form of organization, which the largest of the top 500 firms have.

In summary, the producer cooperatives of Mondragon seem to have a large number of desirable characteristics that would benefit societies with a surplus of labor, a shortage of capital, and low productivity. Cooperatives promise to increase employment substantially by reducing the amount of capital investment required to create each job. Any strategy that will reduce the capital required for the creation of each job to the approximate level suggested by the data gathered from the Mondragon experience, can have a profound impact on economic development where capital is scarce. Obviously, the consequences of improving total factor productivity also seem to be substantial. Furthermore, the cooperative process creates democratic forms of capital ownership as well as a work organization that contributes to the fuller participation of workers in their own enterprise and thus their working lives.

EMPLOYMENT AND PRODUCER COOPERATIVES

In his important book on *Employment, Technology, and Development,* Amartya Sen states:

> The economic decision processes that determine the technology and the level of employment in a given economy depend on the pattern of ownership of the means of production and relations between the different economic classes. (Sen 1975:60)

In terms of employment, I suggest that the organizational behavior of producer cooperatives tends to create more jobs per unit of output and to require less capital for the creation of each job than do the underlying dynamics of capitalist firms. I have already reviewed the rather dramatic evidence of this phenomenon accomplished by the Mondragon cooperatives. In this section, I will propose possible explanations for their achievements in order to provide a framework for further explorations and future research.

On the basis of reviewing the literature and the field studies on several producer cooperatives, including the data gathered from Mondragon, I believe there are three reasons why producer cooperatives have a much greater employment potential than do capitalist firms.[3] I will present each of my reasons in the form of a proposition. No attempt will be made to prove them other than to state the proposition and then to analyze it. As a consequence, my presentation is designed to be provocative while at the same time arguing for further consideration of producer cooperatives.

My first proposition is that, given similar products and levels of output, producer cooperatives will behave in such a way that they will create greater employment and require less capital investment than will capitalist firms. The basis for this claim is contained in three additional propositions relating to the behavior of producer cooperatives: (1) Producer cooperatives in capitalist societies will tend to maximize employment, subject to some boundary level on economic returns. (2) Producer cooperatives will experience relatively higher productivity for the labor input vis-à-vis capital when compared with factor productivities in capitalist firms. And (3) expected values of costs and productivities of labor are subject to less variability or risk for producer cooperatives than for capitalist firms.

MAXIMIZATION OF EMPLOYMENT

This proposition asserts that the objective function of the producer cooperative is to maximize employment, and perhaps employment stability, subject to a boundary constraint on the long-run economic returns. Obviously, there is also a decision that must be made between current returns to labor and capital accumulation, but this particular matter can be treated separately. From the literature that has been explored, the basis for this proposition is that in capitalist societies producer cooperatives seem to have a far greater preoccupation with employment than with the economic returns to their members. In fact, the most successful firms, such as the plywood cooperatives in the United States and the Mondragon cooperatives in Spain, were initiated, in large measure, to provide employment security or to expand the employment base for the local population.[4] In both cases, provisions have been made to reduce the returns to members during recessionary periods, rather than to reduce the membership. In Mondragon, the statutes for the cooperative firms require that job creation be a primary objective, known as the open door policy (Thomas and Logan 1982:43–49).

To a large degree, these efforts toward employment maximization seem to be based on principles of group solidarity, irrespective of whether the solidarity is based upon ideological principles, cultural perspectives, regional values, or just the common experiences of workers having purchased a firm from their previous employer. Under such conditions, the workers seem much more willing to tolerate low economic returns and to permit the economic returns to vary rather than to reduce employment levels.

Most of the theory deduced from self-managed firms argues that such entities tend to maximize the surplus per member or the profit rate on capital rather than to increase employment.[5] However, this theory does not derive from producer cooperatives in capitalist and labor surplus economies, but from self-managed and collective firms in socialist economies, where employment and other social welfare needs are more fully provided by the state. Thus, it is understandable that in capitalist and labor surplus economies, employment is a far more important criterion, for unemployed workers do not have many alternatives in this type of society and have few or no state-provided services. In socialist economies, however, employment and state-provided health, housing, and other services can be largely assumed, so that members of self-managed firms may be concerned primarily with maximizing the economic returns for themselves. In this type of society, the goal to increase employment will come only when self-managed firms see employment expansion as consistent with higher economic returns per member, as, for example, in the case of a firm

experiencing increasing returns to scale. Thus, it is important to recognize that there are crucial differences between self-managed and
collective enterprises in socialist societies and producer cooperatives
in capitalist societies. Obviously, the latter environment will tend to
be far more attentive to employment objectives.

HIGHER LABOR PRODUCTIVITY

This proposition argues that the comparatively higher productivity of
labor vis-à-vis capital, of cooperatives versus capitalist firms, will lead
the cooperatives to hire relatively more labor and to acquire less
capital. As I will argue, there is a strong basis for believing that
producer cooperatives can have higher total factor productivity than
their capitalist counterparts. However, the real effect on employment
will be determined primarily by the relative productivities of the factors
of production. Thus, given a relatively higher labor productivity, more
labor will be hired per unit of capital. The actual mechanisms for
understanding this higher labor productivity will be suggested in the
next section of this chapter.

GREATER STABILITY IN COSTS AND PRODUCTIVITY OF LABOR

This proposition asserts that, given similar outputs and scale, producer
cooperatives will hire relatively more labor than capitalist firms because
of the greater stability of labor productivity and costs under the cooperative form of enterprise. The assumption is made in determining
factor proportions that more than the expected values of the costs and
productivities of the factors of production will be considered. The
stability of the expected values also must be taken into account.
Furthermore, it is assumed that firms tend to avoid risk. My claim is
that producer cooperatives face more predictable cost and productivity
consequences for utilizing labor than do capitalist firms, while the risks
with regard to capital are largely comparable, since capital carries a
rather predictable cost and productivity for both capitalist and cooperative enterprise.

To understand why the risks differ between these two types of firms,
one need only examine the status of labor in each organization. Producer cooperatives are governed by workers and their representatives,
and all their policies must be rationalized in terms of the interests of
the worker-members. In contrast, capitalist firms are organized to
promote the interests and profitability of capital and its accumulation.
Since members of producer cooperatives receive wages as well as any
surplus that is generated, they have strong incentives to avoid dis-
rupting production and adversely affecting costs. Indeed, since the
workers can set the wage structure for any planning period, they can

even reduce wages to meet instabilities created by the market or other external forces. Thus, producer cooperatives are unlikely to face a risk with respect to worker challenges that might result in disruptions, productivity lapses, and wage demands that would affect the cost of labor.

In contrast, capitalist firms must hire workers under wage contracts. This arrangement gives employees few positive incentives to maintain high levels of productivity. If the workers are able to organize effectively, they can confront capital with costly disruptions of production, reduced labor discipline, and higher costs of production. Even in the absence of trade unions, there is always the threat of clandestine challenges to production, such as sabotage. Thus, a capitalist firm takes the risk that the expected value of labor productivity and its costs may be subject to high variability. Furthermore, the factors affecting this phenomenon may depend upon macropolitical and social events beyond the control of the firm. In contrast, the producer cooperative is able to avoid these risks and can depend upon reasonably predictable productivity and cost relations for both labor and capital. Thus, given the aversion to risk by the capitalist firm along with the higher risk associated with the labor input, one would conclude that, even when both firms face similar anticipated costs and factor productivities for the two inputs, capitalist firms will hire less labor than will producer cooperatives.

PRODUCTIVITY AND PRODUCER COOPERATIVES

In addition to the claim that producer cooperatives will tend to utilize less capital and will create greater employment than capitalist firms, producer cooperatives also have the potential for greater productivity. More specifically, for any particular level and combination of factor utilization, they will show higher total factor productivity and a higher marginal productivity of labor vis-à-vis capital than do capitalist firms. The data for the Mondragon cooperatives provide rather impressive support for this contention. In this section, I will suggest the basis for and the sources of these productivity differences. The emphasis of my presentation will be on the differences in organizational incentives present in worker cooperatives versus capitalist firms employing wage labor and their consequences with respect to productivity.

INDIVIDUAL AND COLLECTIVE INCENTIVES

Producer cooperatives have two major characteristics that differentiate them from capitalist firms. And these divergences create differences between the two types of firms in the incentives to contribute to the productive effort as well as in the organization of the productive effort. First, cooperatives are owned by their workers. Thus, it is the workers who will share in the success of the cooperative or who will bear the consequences of its failure. Second, since a cooperative is managed according to democratic principles, the production can be organized to maximize the interests of the workers. In contrast, capitalist firms are owned primarily by outside investors. Workers are paid market wages for their labor time, and profits are allocated to the capitalist owners. Furthermore, the organization of work is determined by managers who maximize their own incomes and status by serving the interests of capital and their managerial control of the work process, rather than by representing the concerns of the workers (P. Walker 1979).

These differences lead to rather different individual and collective incentives for workers in the two types of firms as well as to differing abilities of workers to organize production to maximize their own interests. More specifically, there is a greater incentive for cooperative members to be productive because of the rather direct connection between the success of the cooperative and their own personal gain. Like capitalist firms, cooperatives provide rewards for members according to differences in training, skills, and responsibilities, but the distribution of these rewards tends to be far more egalitarian in the cooperatives.[6]

In addition, there are two major influences that tend to reinforce work effort and productivity in a cooperative. First, if a cooperative does well, all of the workers will be better off. Second, the workers tend to reinforce the productivity and work effort of their members through collegial support and peer pressure. Since the work process is determined democratically, all workers participate to some extent in governing the firm. Further, every worker knows that if difficulties arise in his part of the productive process he will be helped by his fellow workers. There is strong social reinforcement and camaraderie for working together and making a contribution, and likewise there are powerful forms of social sanctioning and disapproval for members who are not putting out a maximum effort.

Although capitalist firms may set out pay structures and procedures for promotion that will reward individual productivity, the system must be administered by procedures and persons external to the work process rather than functioning as an integral part of that process, as happens in cooperative firms. Furthermore, the informational and administrative requirements for identifying and rewarding individual differences in productivity would create unduly high informational and transactional costs for a capitalist firm.[7] Thus, for a capitalist firm the procedures for establishing pay and status differences must be only approximate with respect to productivity differences, and will usually correspond to the nature of the worker's category and experience rather than to direct measures of productivity. Accordingly, for capitalist workers the ties between the incentive structures and productivity tend to be much less direct and more approximate than the rather direct and more accurate connections for cooperative workers.

Moreover, the social reinforcement from worker peers that is integral to a collective organization is antithetical to a capitalist organization, where workers are placed in direct competition with one another for employment, promotions, and pay. In capitalist firms a majority of the work is divided into relatively minute tasks so that the failure of one worker to perform properly is not seen as affecting the pay and status of other workers. In fact, in a world where workers are expected to compete with one another for promotion and employment security, the attempt by one worker to outperform his fellow workers is seen by his colleagues as a threat.[8]

The result is that at both the personal and the collective level, there tend to be greater incentives to be productive in cooperatives than in capitalist firms. The fact is that in a democratic organization these incentives can also influence the shape of the work process itself, which in turn will also have an effect on productivity. Thus, I will identify and conjecture on the sources of individual and organizational behavior that tend to be associated with higher productivity in cooperatives.[9]

PERSONAL BEHAVIOR

Because of the personal and collective incentives in cooperatives for reinforcing productive work, members show lower absenteeism rates, a greater work effort, greater work flexibility, and better maintenance of the plant and equipment than do workers in capitalist organizations. In Mondragon, for example, absentee rates were about half those at comparable capitalist firms in the same region (Thomas and Logan 1982:49–52). In part, the lower absenteeism rates derive from greater loyalty to their work organizations and colleagues and also from the social sanctions of peers against excessive absenteeism. Furthermore, because the work is likely to be more self-actualizing and participative, workers develop a positive desire to engage in the work process. Finally, in cooperatives the fruits of low absentee rates go directly to the workers themselves in the form of larger benefits.

Worker turnover also tends to be lower in cooperatives than in capitalist firms. For example, in 1974, the annual rate of worker turnover in the Mondragon cooperatives was only 2 percent, while in the capitalist manufacturing enterprises in the surrounding provinces it reached about 14 percent.[10] Worker turnover is costly because it entails additional hiring costs, record keeping, and training, and often there are bottlenecks in production because of the lag in time between workers leaving and new ones being hired. Cooperative workers are also less likely to leave for a number of other reasons, including the following: greater employment security, the incentive of payoffs in the future for their present work effort, the collegiality of the work community, a greater involvement in the work process, and the relative nonliquidity of ownership shares, since they can be sold only to new members and not to the general public.

A greater individual work effort is achieved in cooperatives as a result of the reinforcing work environment as well as the expectations of an economic surplus. In a like manner, cooperative workers are motivated to be more flexible and to learn several jobs, so that they will be able to assist other workers at points of bottleneck in the production. There are also incentives to adapt to periods of high work demand as well as periods of slack. Finally, workers in cooperatives have a great incentive to take care of the machinery and the other capital with which they work and thus to reduce breakdowns and increase the productive life of the capital. By contrast, in capitalist firms there is often a disdain for the condition of the equipment and even an incentive to permit it to malfunction and break down to provide temporary respite from the work process.

ORGANIZATIONAL BEHAVIOR

Not only is individual behavior of workers in cooperatives more productive, but the overall organization of production is also able to build upon these cooperative advantages in several ways. For example, the fact that workers have incentives to produce a good product and to be highly productive means that cooperative firms need relatively few supervisors and quality control inspectors.[11] Quality control and a disciplined work effort are internalized into the behavior of workers rather than enforced by external procedures. Thus, the cooperative is able to save the cost of a large cadre of unproductive middle managers which are an integral part of capitalist production where worker discipline and product quality must be ensured by external supervision.

There are also potential cost savings at the lower end of the occupational spectrum, because cooperatives have few, if any, unskilled workers. Given the relatively equal pay scales in cooperatives, unskilled workers will be placed into training programs to obtain skills. Also, to eliminate the need for unskilled workers, cooperative members tend to clean up after themselves rather than relegating these tasks to another class of worker. As I mentioned before, this policy is reinforced by the fact that cooperative members have a large stake in maintaining the condition of their own plant and equipment.

Cooperatives are also able to rotate work roles among members and to train workers for a variety of jobs. As a consequence, this flexibility, vis-à-vis the performing of a routine and repetitive task, enhances the attachment and interest of workers in both the work process and the organization. Likewise, since workers have the opportunity for continuous skill development, members are prepared to perform various different tasks, which reduces the problem brought about by the absenteeism of any particular worker. Furthermore, this flexibility also improves a worker's ability to function with his colleagues, which in turn increases the sense of community among the workers by uniting them in a common set of endeavors rather than separating them into individual task categories, as do the capitalist firms. The arrangement found in cooperatives also eliminates bottlenecks in production because workers are able to shift tasks to assist where help is needed.

In cooperatives, training is also provided more efficiently than in capitalist firms, where competition for status means that workers have disincentives to assist fellow workers in learning new skills. In cooperatives, the need for a reinforcing work community and a flexible work force to maximize productivity means that fellow workers have incentives to assist one another in acquiring new skills. It is also important to point out that in a cooperative training effort, it is the skills and intelligence of those persons who have the most knowledge that will tend to be diffused to the group.[12] The reason for this is that there are group incentives for those who are best equipped to share their knowledge with other members of the group. These incentives are absent in a capitalist firm where a worker's competitive advantage is enhanced by keeping his insights to himself.

In summary, there exist both personal and collective incentives in cooperatives that are likely to lead to higher productivity. The specific consequences of these incentives are that the workers in cooperatives will tend to work harder and in a more flexible manner than those in capitalist firms; they will have a lower turnover rate and absenteeism; and they will take better care of the plant and equipment. In addition, producer cooperatives function with relatively few unskilled workers and middle managers, experience fewer bottlenecks in production, and have more efficient training programs than do capitalist firms.

SUMMARY

This chapter began with the overall contention that producer cooperatives have a greater employment and productivity potential than do comparable capitalist firms. Corroborating data were presented for the largest movement of industrial producer cooperatives in the world,

and an attempt was made to establish the behavioral aspects of producer cooperatives that seem to explain these findings. However, an
important final issue is to ask whether findings on the Mondragon
cooperatives can be generalized to a society such as the United States.

It is important to reflect on the representativeness of the Mondragon
cooperatives as examples of the potential of cooperatives for generating
employment and increasing productivity. These cooperatives are exceptional not only in their size and in their variety of high technology
products but also in their success. To a very large extent they have
been able to resolve the tension between their needs for internal
democracy and equity and the demands of the marketplace and the
external environment. Clearly, a substantial reason for this success is
the ability of the Mondragon group to develop a set of supportive
institutions such as the bank, the research and development center,
the technical assistance services, and the schools, which provide a
basic support system for their survival and expansion.

Yet, as many of the essays in this book emphasize, few cooperatives
have been as successful as those of Mondragon in meeting their needs
for survival and expansion. It is reasonable that a major factor for
their greater success is the common culture and ethnic solidarity created by their Basque origins and affiliations. The Basques have always
been a relatively cooperative culture which historically resisted the
formation of a wage labor proletariat. Their landholdings were very
equitably distributed among families, particularly in contrast to the
hacienda mode of agricultural production in the south of Spain. Moreover, cooperative practices among local families in the various phases
of farming has had a long tradition. For these reasons, it may be that
the Basques had less difficulty in initiating and implementing cooperative industry than groups with a more individualistic tradition.

However, there are two reasons why the observations and lessons
from Mondragon have wider application. First, studies of cooperative
work organizations in the United States and in other countries have
shown structural and behavioral features similar to those of Mondragon, as was suggested throughout. Second, much of the success of the
Mondragon firms seems to be directly tied to the unique institutions
that they have created to support their movement. The bank, the
research and development center, the technical assistance services,
and the schools are uniquely suited to serving the cooperatives, and
it is their creative interplay and integration that seems to explain the
remarkable success of the movement. Thus, to the degree that these
types of institutions can be transplanted elsewhere, one would expect
that much of the success of the Mondragon cooperatives could also
be replicated. For these reasons the Mondragon experience would seem
to have important consequences for raising employment and productivity in the United States.

NOTES

1. Most of the data are drawn from the Mondragon cooperatives. The author conducted interviews and observations in Mondragon in the spring of 1975. Since that time, he has maintained continuous contact through correspondence and reports as well as through the fieldwork of his graduate students who have gone to Mondragon (e.g., Ornelas 1980). Especially important are the annual *Memoria* of the Caja Laboral Popular. In addition, data are drawn from a visit in 1975 to the Meriden Triumph Motorcycle Cooperative and a subsequent analysis (Carnoy and Levin 1976b), and from extensive fieldwork during the summer of 1978 at a major cooperative in the San Francisco Bay Area. Other sources that are heavily used include the information (Jackall and Crain, chap. 5, this volume) derived from the survey of cooperatives by the Center for Economic Studies as well as the studies of Edward Greenberg (chap. 8) for the Northwest plywood cooperatives. In addition, this essay draws heavily on the burgeoning literature on Mondragon and the plywood cooperatives.

2. The dollar figures are based upon the exchange rate at that time.

3. J. Vanek and J. Espinosa (1972) have argued persuasively that labor-managed firms will undertake activities that would not be undertaken by capitalist firms, which are motivated only by very high profit rates. While this point has important consequences for employment generation, I will not address it here.

4. See, for example, Berman 1967, Bernstein 1976b, Bellas 1972, and Greenberg, this volume, chap. 8, on the plywood cooperatives. Also see Carnoy and Levin 1976b for an example of a British cooperative that was inititated to save jobs.

5. For example, see Vanek 1970, 1977c, Dreze 1976, and the surveys by A. Steinherr (1978a, 1978b). A number of authors recognize that membership solidarity may inhibit reduction in the size of a labor-managed firm, even when such reduction would increase the dividends per member. For example, see Bonin 1981 and Meade 1972.

6. A. Steinherr (1978b) discusses the principles of worker remuneration in the labor-managed firm. This relatively high level of wage equality is reflected in virtually all cooperatives. As noted, the maximum differential in returns to labor for the Mondragon cooperatives is 3 to 1. The Meriden Triumph Motorcycle Cooperative was formed on the basis of equal returns (Carnoy and Levin 1976b). For a detailed analysis of pay schemes for a range of cooperatives, see Oakeshott 1978.

7. This view is rather widely accepted in modern labor economics. Recent contributions address how information for a group of workers might be used to make hiring and wage decisions on the basis of market signals. Presumably, such information can be used to establish expected values and probability distributions of productivity for groups of workers, which can be used to inform hiring and wage policies. See Spence 1973 and Hirschleifer and Riley 1979. Indeed, informational and transactional costs are used to justify the modern, hierarchical corporate entity as an efficient approach to production. See Alchian and Demsetz 1972, Stiglitz 1975, Williamson 1975, and the critical discussion by M. Reich and J. Devine (1981).

8. In contrast to the neoclassical position on this subject, it can be argued that the problem of shirking is an intrinsic challenge of the capitalist firm, whereas the cooperative firm has intrinsic incentives and social mechanisms to promote the productive effort of all of its workers. Compare this perspective with the view presented by Stiglitz (1975) which argues that hierarchy and coercion increase the productivity of the firm and the earnings of workers, and thus are in the interests of the workers. Also see the extensive discussion by M. Reich and J. Devine (1981).

9. The following generalizations are derived in large measure from field studies of cooperatives carried out over a seven-year period by the Center for Economic Studies, Palo Alto, California. The earlier project on "The Educational Requirements for Industrial Democracy" was supported by the National Institute of Education from 1973–1977. The later project on "An Economic Analysis of Producer Cooperatives with Respect to Job Creation, Productivity, and Worker Satisfaction" was funded by the National Institute of Mental Health from 1977 to 1980. The earlier work was summarized by Levin (1980), and several of the later studies are reported in this book. The purpose of the following analysis is not to prove as much as to develop an explanatory structure for further inquiry on the comparative differences in productive behavior and their consequences for producer cooperatives. For some evidence that relates the degree of worker participation to productivity in self-managed firms, see Jones and Svejnar 1982, Espinosa and Zimbalist 1978, Cable and Fitzroy 1980, and Jones and Backus 1977.

Employee ownership without democratic management and participation, may not produce changes in absenteeism as reflected in the provocative study by T. Hammer, J. Landau, and R. Stern (1981).

10. Based on internal analysis by the Caja Laboral Popular, provided to the author on his visit in May 1975.

11. This difference is very noticeable in Mondragon, and it was one of the major changes initiated by the Meriden Triumph Motorcycle Cooperative in shifting away from capitalist production, as reported by Carnoy and Levin (1976b). E. Greenberg (chap. 8), also found that while cooperative plywood firms used only one or two supervisors per shift, the comparable capitalist firms used six or seven. A mill that had recently been converted from cooperative to capitalist ownership quadrupled the number of line supervisors and foremen.

12. Educational experiments have confirmed this result. See Slavin and Tanner 1979.

PART II

Historical Perspectives on Worker Cooperatives

The history of worker cooperatives in the United States is rich and varied. Based on scattered historical data, it seems that between 1790 and 1959 there were well over 700 documented cases of worker cooperatives in this country, ranging over several industries. Most were clustered in the craftlike enterprises such as cooperage or barrel making, shoe manufacturing, cigar making, glass making, sheet metal working, foundry work, and shingle weaving, although they were also formed in the less skilled trades of fish canning, coal mining, and agricultural work. The history of their formation can be divided into three long cycles. The first started in 1790 and lasted until the early years of this century, peaking during the 1880s. The second began early in this century and continued until the 1940s, with its peak in the 1930s. A third cycle began in the 1940s and continues today. This last cycle took a great upswing during the 1960s and early 1970s when hundreds more small worker cooperatives, or collectives, arose in several major urban areas around the country.

The immediate reasons for the formation of worker cooperatives are complicated and varied. In the nineteenth century, labor unrest or disputes of one sort or another, often connected either with issues of employment security or changes in the work process, played an important role in the formation of many cooperatives. During the same period, artisans' desires for self-employment in the face of the spreading factory system were also crucial. Massive unemployment in the early twentieth century generated the biggest cluster of cooperatives in our history, namely the self-help groups that tried to create jobs in the midst of the economic wasteland of the Great Depression. Finally, deep social and cultural unrest during the 1960s and 1970s produced a serious questioning of traditional notions of work and careers, giving rise to that era's collective movement. Analytically, then, the key reasons for the generation of worker cooperatives seem to be: issues of employment security (including unemployment); technological change and concomitant rationalization of work; and social unrest which calls traditional notions of work and careers into question. Historically, of course, these factors have often worked in conjunction with one another.

Quite often worker cooperatives fared well when measured against comparable capitalist firms. Despite generally problematic beginnings, scarcity of capital, and the ever-present contradiction endemic to cooperatives between the internal requirements for democratic structure and the external demands of the capitalist marketplace, worker cooperatives have demonstrated the ability to succeed economically, and in a variety of other ways, over a substantial time period (more than a decade). In the nineteenth century, for example, many clusters of cooperatives competed well against capitalist firms in terms of crucial barometers such as productivity and income. In fact, it is worth noting that during this period, the more cooperative a group's internal structure was, the better it seemed to fare in the marketplace. The internal cohesiveness generated by cooperation seemed to produce a great responsiveness to market conditions. While the economic record of some other clusters of cooperatives has not been impressive, they have made important social contributions. The 1930s self-help groups provided employment for thousands of people; and the recent collective movement has given a great many young people opportunities for participation in management unavailable elsewhere. Employee-owned firms, first cousins to worker cooperatives, have saved a great number of jobs for workers who otherwise would have been disemployed (Bradley and Gelb 1983). Recent surveys have suggested that employee-owned firms have higher profitability (Conte and Tannenbaum 1978) and faster employment growth (Employee Ownership 1983) than comparable firms lacking employee ownership.

This section surveys the history of worker cooperatives and employee-owned firms and provides a detailed case study of one cluster of worker cooperatives. In the first essay, Derek Jones pulls together bits of historical data from a wide range of sources to present a portrait of worker cooperatives and employee-owned firms created under various conditions. He analyzes their socioeconomic performance and tries to assess the significance of their complicated and ambiguous history for the present-day worker cooperative movement. In the second essay, Jones and Donald Schneider examine the self-help cooperatives that burgeoned during the Depression. As already noted, these groups constitute the largest single cluster of worker cooperatives on record. Moreover, they are uniquely interesting both because they were supported by state and federal governments and because they were able to address the seemingly intractable problems of unemployment and unemployability with some success.

3

American Producer Cooperatives and Employee-Owned Firms: A Historical Perspective

DEREK C. JONES

The broad American historical experience of producer cooperatives (PCs)* is a surprisingly rich one. By the best estimates available, there were several hundred PCs established between 1790 and 1959. During the 1960s and 1970s, many more PCs were created, though these were typically much smaller concerns and, because of their collectivist na-ture (see the essay by Jackall and Crain, chap. 5, this volume), much different in character than earlier PCs. In addition, in the last decade in the United States, at least fifty failing or failed capitalist firms have been transformed into employee-owned firms (EOFs).* EOFs differ from PCs in many crucial ways; in particular, they do not require employee participation in their management and day-to-day control. Both types of organization, however, represent sharp departures from normal capitalist practice and, in this essay, I consider them together to provide a comprehensive picture of a deep-rooted and persistent alternate tradition in American society. Further, an analysis of the

*Here I define a PC as an autonomous enterprise in which (a) many workers (or members) own stock, (b) ownership is widely distributed among the workers who own much of the voting stock, (c) working-members participate in the enterprise's management and control, and (d) they share in the distribution of the surplus, usually on the basis of work. In an EOF at least one of these conditions is not satisfied. The definition of PC is sufficiently broad to include traditional cooperative enterprises and contemporary collective organizations.

37

extensive and varied historical experiences of PCs and EOFs can illuminate contemporary and, it seems, accelerating developments in this area.

THE HISTORY AND NATURE OF AMERICAN PCs AND EOFs

A STATISTICAL OVERVIEW

There are enormous problems involved in estimating the number of PCs and EOFs in the United States, past and present. The absence both of a federation to provide services for these firms and of either governmental reporting requirements or systematic and regular attempts to survey these firms, inevitably means that estimates culled from scattered published accounts must be treated cautiously. With this caution, it is my own best estimate that 785 PCs were established between 1790 and 1959 (Jones 1980b). However, in this paper I shall focus on those American PCs and EOFs about which we have the most reliable information.

The firms selected for this study can be categorized into twelve clusters. Six of the clusters—cooperatives in foundry, cooperage, shingle, plywood, refuse collection, and reforestation—are distinguished by the nature of the final product or service. A seventh, Knights of Labor (KOL), consists of PCs that were initially financed, at least in part, by local assemblies of the Knights of Labor, and an eighth, self-help (SH), represents a general grouping of PCs established in the 1930s and subjected to close governmental administration. Two of the remaining clusters—early general and late general—include otherwise unclassifiable PCs founded from 1860 to 1889 and from 1896 to 1937, respectively. The last two clusters—employee-owned firms, and collectives—each includes diverse activities and has arisen mainly in the last fifteen years.

In table 3.1, I show for each cluster (excepting collectives) estimates of the number of PCs and EOFs formed by decade since 1840, the period when the most PCs and EOFs were established.[1] Thus the first column reveals that during 1840 to 1899, 47 foundry PCs came into being. The tenth row shows that 270 PCs—more than one-third of the total—were established during the 1930s.

INITIAL ORGANIZATION AND A TYPOLOGY OF PCs

American PCs and EOFs have varied considerably with respect to important aspects of initial organization (see table 3.2). In most cases the dominant practice has been to restrict initial membership to (though

TABLE 3.1

MAIN GROUPS OF PCS AND EOFS IN THE UNITED STATES:
NUMBER FORMED BY DECADE, 1840–1979

	F	C	EG	KOL	LG[a]	S	P	R	SH	T	EOF	Total (by decade)
1840s	4											4
1850s	0											0
1860s	(15)	1	12									(28)
1870s	(10)	3	38									(51)
1880s	(11)	9	55	200								(275)
1890s	(7)	2			1							(10)
1900s		1			1							2
1910s					7	20						27
1920s					11		1	2			3	17
1930s					18		1	(1)	250		1	(271)
1940s							3	(12)			0	(15)
1950s							27				1	28
1960s											0	0
1970s										11	(45)	56
Total (by cluster)	47	16	105	200	38	20	32	(15)	250	11	50	(784)

NOTES: 1. Column abbreviations correspond to eleven clusters distinguished in the text. Thus F = Foundry, C = Cooperage, EG = Early General, 1860–1889, KOL = Knights of Labor, LG = Late General, 1896–1937, S = Shingle, P = Plywood, SH = Self-Help, R = Refuse Collection, T = Reforestation, and EOF = Employee-Owned Firms.
2. Figures in parentheses are less reliable than other entries.
3. For sources of information for different clusters see Jones 1980b.

[a] Entries for this "general" group refer only to respondents to surveys.

not require it of) the current work force. Only with self-help and reforestation PCs, however, did the initial membership comprise only and all workers in the firm. In other cases, membership by groups other than current workers has been permitted. For example, with some foundry PCs, outside (nonworker) capital suppliers constituted a large part of the initial membership. With most EOFs, membership (owners of stock with voting rights) is heavily and unequally concentrated in groups other than the blue collar work force (Conte and Tannenbaum 1978). In some firms, a particular group of workers is excluded from membership: many plywood PCs exclude managers, while cooperage PCs accepted only skilled barrel makers.

In most PCs, ultimate authority has been vested in the membership at the annual general meeting on the basis of one member, one vote.

General meetings to make substantive decisions by a consensus process have occurred most frequently in collective and reforestation PCs, and typically these PCs make the least use of representative democratic processes. By contrast, in the foundry, early general, and KOL PCs, as well as in the EOFs, voting typically has reflected differences in capital ownership, and membership meetings have been held infre- quently. Apparently they have relied on indirect structures to provide their democratic processes. In keeping with these variations, there have been important differences among the clusters with respect to the election or appointment of major officers and managers (see table 3.2).

In plywood, self-help, collective, and reforestation PCs, all of the surplus is distributed to members on the basis of their functional role as workers. To a large extent, this was also the case with cooperage PCs; only extraordinary gains were not distributed on this basis. Refuse PCs have come close to this standard too. By contrast, EOFs and PCs in other clusters have provided profit-sharing systems by which only part of the surplus is distributed to labor; typically in these cases, the basic determinant of claims on the surplus is ownership of capital.

Unlike other PCs and EOFs, plywood PCs usually require a capital stake of more than $1,000. Comparisons of capital stakes required are difficult to make, however, in part because inflation has changed the real value of this capital stake over time. Also, seldom does this entrance fee have to be paid in full by the new members, and there are great differences among PCs concerning assessment rates and as- sessment periods.

For plywood, shingle, and reforestation PCs, a central federation appears to have been an important feature of the economic landscape. Many California SHPCs were also members of federations. In PCs in these groups, as among cooperage PCs, the formal organizational rules and regulations governing PCs are fairly uniform. In each case this appears to reflect the model role played by an early PC in that group. For example, the Cooperative Barrel Company in Minneapolis served as a prototype for cooperage PCs, while in the plywood group that distinction belonged to Olympia Veneer of Olympia, Washington. Among collective PCs, attempts have been made to form informal networks in some regions, though no federation to which substantial numbers belonged has ever been created. Organizing rules character- izing these and PCs in other clusters are diverse.

Bringing these differences among American PCs and EOFs into a sharper focus, it seems that the necessary features for an ideal PC include requirements that: (a) membership be restricted to all of the current active work force; (b) all control and management be vested in the work force on the basis of one member, one vote; and (c) the surplus be distributed to members as workers (rather than as capital suppliers).

It is clear that very few American PCs have begun with this form. However, an ordinal ranking may be developed that reflects how close PCs in different clusters have come to satisfying these three features of an ideal PC. Such a ranking reveals three broad groupings of PCs. On average, the most cooperative clusters in initial organization have been the plywood, cooperage, shingle, SH, reforestation, collectives, and refuse collection PCs. For these groups, the pattern of initial organization seems to show a strong relationship between tendencies for (a) membership to comprise only workers; (b) control to be based on the democratic principle of one member, one vote; and (c) the formula for the distribution of surplus to be based on the work role. On average, the least cooperative clusters have been the foundry and KOL PCs. Here the pattern of initial organization indicates a strong relationship between membership consisting of people other than current workers, rights of control existing on an unequal basis among the membership, and surplus being distributed on the basis of ownership of capital. Among all firms under study, however, EOFs have been the least cooperative. A third, middle group comprises the two general categories where no strong patterns are visible.

ORIGINS OF THE FIRMS AND DISTINGUISHING
CHARACTERISTICS OF THE LABOR FORCE

PCs can be categorized by the nature of their origin. Some began as entities other than PCs (category A in table 3.3). These usually began as capitalist firms, though some were originally other types of cooperatives. These firms may in turn be subdivided into: (i) those that were transformed into PCs at the initiative of the worker-membership, such as some plywood and most SHPCs; and (ii) those that were transformed into PCs at the initiative of groups other than the subsequent worker-membership, as were the Columbia Conserve Company in Indianapolis, International Group Plans in Washington, D.C., and some KOL PCs. Then there are firms that have always been PCs. These are divided into those that began as PCs at the initiative of their workers (category B[i] in table 3.3) and those for whom the initiative for their cooperative nature lay elsewhere (B[ii]).

This typology of PCs by nature of origin can be applied to each group of American PCs (see table 3.3). Though the available data are meager, there is some slight indication that, except for collectives, the more prevalent type of origin in recent clusters seems to be that of workers transforming existing firms into PCs. Most "new wave" PCs (collectives), however, began as new firms and were initiated by the

TABLE 3.2

ASPECTS OF INITIAL FORMAL ORGANIZATION

	Membership			Control and management					Distribution of surplus			Capital stake required[6]		Payt. of officers	Federation
				Voting at AGM		Selection of officers & mgr.		Spec. mtgs.	Basis of cap. ownership[5]	Basis of work	On a combined basis				
	Only and all current workers	Some current workers excluded[1]	Non-worker members[2]	one member one vote	reflect capital ownership[3]	By board[4]	By members	Appeal syst.				< $500	> $500		
F	0		0	0	+		0	—	+		0		0		−
C	0	+		++			++	+		++		++			−
EG	0	+	0	0	+	+	0	—	+	0	0	+	0		−
KOL	0	0	+	0	+	++		—	+	0	+	++	0	−	+
S	0	+	0	++			++	+	++				0		+
LG	0	+	0	++		++		+	+		0	+	0		−
P	0	+	0	++			++	+		++		++	++	+++	+

R	0	+	++	++	++	—	++	++	++	-
SH	++	++	++	++	+	+	--	++	+
T	++	++	++	++	(++)	(++)	--	++	++
CL·	++	++	++	++	++ / ++	++	0	-	0
EOF	++	++	++	++	(--) / (--)	++	+	++	--

NOTES: The code used is as follows: ++ (− −) nearly all PCs in that cluster had (did not have) that characteristic
     + (−) most PCs in that cluster had (did not have) that characteristic
     0 occasionally a PC in that cluster had that characteristic

A blank element means no data are available.

Items enclosed in parentheses are less reliable than other entries.

Abbreviations: payt. = payment; syst. = system; spec. mtgs. = special meetings; mgr. = manager.

[1] Excluded groups were: F & C, unskilled workers; and P, managers.
[2] Nonworker members were: F, philanthropists and local private citizens; KOL and LG, labor unions.
[3] Voting rights conveyed by ownership of capital were limited in the majority of EG and KOL PCs.
[4] Managers of PPCs are appointed by the board which is elected by the general membership. The membership elects other officers.
[5] In CPCs, the surplus is distributed so that ordinary (as a result of trading activities) surplus is divided among worker-members as workers, while extraordinary (as a result of inflation property values, for example) surplus is distributed to members as stockholders.
[6] In many PCs, e.g., C and P, capital stakes could be paid off by assessments drawn on wages. In SHPCs most initial capital was supplied by federal and/or state grants.
· CL = Collective PCs

TABLE 3.3

The Origins of American PCs and EOFs

Transformations(A)	F	C	EG	KOL	LG	S	P	R	SH¹	T	EOF
(i)	2	2	1		1	2	5	0	125		(10)
(ii)		1			2			0	125		(40)
New PCs (B)											
(i)	5	10	8	10	1	2	7	2	0	11	
(ii)			1	3	2	6	6	0	0	0	
Cases for which data are available	7/47	13/16	10/195	13/200	6/38	4/20	18/32	8/15	250/250	11/11	(5)/(50)

NOTE: In A(i) and B(i) forms, the PC was established at the initiative of workers. In A(ii) and B(ii) firms, the initiative arose elsewhere. For this group, however, we do not have case data on from whence came the initiative.

¹ All SHPCs appear to be transformations, usually from barter organizations. Our guess is that about half the time it came from the worker-membership.

original group of worker-members. The practice of workers buying out capitalist ventures has a long history. For all clusters except EOFs, workers have played the initiating role in most cases, though with many SHPCs, others may have fulfilled this catalytic function.

In nearly all clusters, the characteristics of the labor force do not seem to be markedly different from those in comparable noncooperative firms in the same industry. There are, however, some exceptions. Most workers in collective PCs are younger and better educated than workers in comparable capitalist firms. Also, 60 percent of the average work force in collectives is female, a high proportion compared with other firms in the same industries. These features reflect a more marked political orientation than exists in other PCs (see the chapters in Part III of this volume). SHPCs, by contrast, had older and less skilled labor forces than did other firms (see Jones and Schneider, chap. 4, this volume). Both SH and collective PCs suffered much from labor turnover. For SHPCs, new workers entered some cooperatives at the rate of 16 percent of the entire work force each month.

GEOGRAPHICAL AND INDUSTRIAL DISTRIBUTION

Reflecting the industrial base of the economy, earlier clusters of PCs tended to be concentrated in the East. For later clusters there has been a drift to the West. This is apparent even with cooperage PCs, but it is particularly evident with shingle, plywood, refuse collection, and reforestation PCs, all of which have been predominantly located in Pacific Coast states. With SHPCs, too, more than one-third were in California and about 10 percent each in Idaho, Utah, and Washington. While many collective PCs also have been located in the West, substantial concentrations have existed in other urban areas such as Boston, Washington, D.C., New York, and Ann Arbor (Case and Taylor 1979; Jackall and Crain, chap. 5, this volume). EOFs, however, have not been concentrated in the West, but rather in the industrial heartland of the country (Sockell 1978).

As with earlier Eastern PCs, the phenomenon of grouping is often apparent in later clusters. All cooperage PCs were in the Minneapolis area, and more than one plywood PC was established in each of the Northwest cities of Tacoma, Olympia, and Portland. More than half of California's SHPCs were located in the county of Los Angeles, though there were other concentrations in Alameda and Orange counties. Reforestation PCs are geographically close to one another in the Pacific Northwest.

The geographical scope of American PCs has tended to be broad-ranging. This is clear from the distribution of PCs in the late general, KOL, and SH groups. Foundry PCs, too, were found in many states, including California, Kansas, Louisiana, and Missouri; there were no obvious limitations for the national scope of this cluster of PCs.

While most PCs were single-business firms, sometimes within a cluster, a range of activities was represented. KOL PCs, for example, encompassed more than thirty distinct activities, including coal mining, plumbing, and banking. Most SHPCs were engaged in gardening, sewing, canning, baking, and lumbering. Most collective PCs have been established in very competitive areas such as food sales, book selling and printing, and publishing. As a general rule, PCs have tended to emerge in craftlike trades characterized by a high skill content. This was not, however, the case with SHPCs.

THE SOCIOECONOMIC PERFORMANCE OF AMERICAN PCs AND EOFs

It must be stated at the outset that there is an urgent need for more careful empirical studies on the socioeconomic performance of PCs and EOFs. On inspection, much of what passes for hard evidence turns out to be imprecise and impressionistic. Even some of the more recent studies, which employ statistical analyses and hypothesis testing, have important methodological problems.[2] Historical studies necessarily have had to rely on secondary data and have used performance measures that have well-known shortcomings (e.g., accounting ratios and partial productivity indicators). In making evaluations of performance *compared* with other firms (e.g., capitalist firms), sometimes inadequate controls have had to be employed. Moreover, the heterogeneity of the population under examination (in this section) inevitably means that attempts at generalizations will be fraught with difficulty. Bearing these important points in mind, then, I shall review the existing evidence on aspects of socioeconomic performance of American PCs and EOFs.

Elsewhere I have reported the results of a study that employed five indicators to assess the socioeconomic performance of seven clusters of PCs (those excluded from the study were the self-help, refuse collection, reforestation, collectives, and employee-owned firms) (Jones 1979a, 1979b). Despite the fact that PCs and capitalist firms have different goals, some comparisons were drawn with the performance of capitalist firms, and for the sake of discussion, the same indicators were used for both. The measures used were: (a) the ability to survive as a viable enterprise; (b) the ability to grow; (c) efficiency (labor productivity and profitability); (d) the ability to retain democratic structures of government; and (e) the ability to create jobs. The three main results may be summarized as follows.

First, for all indicators there is evidence that PCs in most of these seven clusters can perform well for long periods of time (more than ten years). In some cases, in fact, American PCs have survived for periods substantially longer than twenty years. Moreover, for several clusters the record shows that PCs can grow at least as fast as comparable capitalist firms; and various indicators of efficiency, including profitability and labor productivity, reveal that many PCs have been efficient. In addition, many PCs have been able to retain formally democratic structures and to preserve and to create jobs over long periods of time.

Second, there is substantial variation in socioeconomic performance among PCs in different clusters. In general, and by various measures of socioeconomic performance, it is PCs in the most cooperative groupings—the cooperage, plywood, and shingle clusters—that have performed best. The capacity for longevity, for example, varies considerably, the best performers on average being PCs in plywood and cooperage, and the worst, KOL PCs. With respect to the ability of PCs to retain a formal cooperative structure, PCs in plywood and cooperage have performed the best while the worst have been KOL, foundry, and the two general clusters of PCs.

Third, in all clusters, PCs tend to do much more poorly as they age. While young cooperage PCs in Minneapolis were able to grow so fast that they soon became much larger than the average capitalist firm, this capacity for growth was not sustained; mature cooperage PCs were smaller than the average capitalist firm. In the area of creating and preserving jobs, American PCs have been for some periods at least as good as capitalist firms; by contrast, the absolute performance of mature PCs has been less impressive, though not necessarily inferior to that of aging capitalist firms. Other measures of performance— namely, strike records, the ability to introduce technical change, and the ability to generate money income—generally tend to support these same three conclusions though the available data are limited. This evidence is reported in Jones (1979b).

The ability of some PCs in all clusters to perform well for long periods of time (conclusion 1) takes its evidence from various sources. The strike record for PCs, for instance, suggests that their performance would be difficult to beat. Plywood PCs have been virtually strike free, despite stoppages affecting all other firms in the industry in 1954 and 1963. The ability to innovate successfully is another indicator of good performance. In the early years of foundry PCs, there is evidence of innovative ability. In his survey of PCs in New England, Ford (1913) cites the claim made by cooperators that the Nashua foundry was the only foundry in New England with electric light. For plywood PCs, too, there is ample evidence that many firms, at least during their infancies, were ready innovators.

Turning to money income, the picture is more mixed, thus supporting the second conclusion on the variability in socioeconomic
performance. For instance, comparisons between average wages in
individual foundry PCs in New York, Pennsylvania, and Massachusetts
with comparable county averages in that industry reveal that sometimes PC workers earn more and sometimes they earn less. Evidence
for cooperage PCs reveals a like, uneven record. However, Angus (in
Bemis 1896:611) reports that PCs probably had a distinct edge with
respect to regularity of income. It is also clear that stock in some
cooperage PCs turned out to be a handsome investment. In the plywood PCs, during the twenty-five-year period of 1950–1975, workers
in PCs earned substantially more on average than their capitalist
counterparts—sometimes twice the union rate and nearly always 25
percent more or better on average. Also, in these cooperatives, worker-
members often have reaped enormous capital gains and substantial
yearly bonuses. Further, it is clear that relative pay differentials within
plywood PCs are much lower than in conventional plywood companies
and that income is received on a much steadier basis than by workers
in other firms.

Additional evidence supports the second conclusion on the variability of performance among PCs. When PCs have experienced strikes,
they have tended to occur in firms with large numbers of nonmember
workers, such as the three and one-half month strike against the
Equitable Foundry Company of Rochester, New York, where only
about one-fifth of the workers were members. The available evidence
on money income also suggests that workers in the more cooperative
clusters of PCs (plywood, cooperage, and shingle) fare better in general
than workers in less cooperative clusters.

In an earlier study (Jones 1979b), I concluded that PCs tended to
pass through a life cycle with performance deteriorating as the firm
aged (conclusion 3). There is additional evidence to support this
finding (Jones 1980a). In describing the experiences of older cooperage
PCs, Virtue (1932) notes that PCs were much slower to innovate than
were conventional firms. He notes an eight-year lag between the
introduction of a particular change by a capitalist firm and a similar
development in the cooperative sector. Regarding plywood PCs, Bellas
(1972) argues that many (aging) PCs have recently become reluctant
innovators and that this is increasingly the norm.

Information is also available on aspects of performance for PCs
other than those in the seven clusters discussed so far. For example,
in evaluating the performance of SHPCs during the 1930s (see chap.
4, this volume), Donald Schneider and I found strong evidence that
SHPCs were able to record substantial relief savings and some indication that SHPCs were effective in rehabilitating the unemployed.

SHPCs were usually smaller than capitalist firms and, though able to grow, did so more slowly so that they became progressively undercapitalized. On labor productivity we discovered that: (1) though initially SHPCs were on average grossly inefficient compared with the average capitalist firm, there is evidence that some SHPCs were always as productive in adding value during the productive process; and (2) over time SHPCs were able to raise output per worker substantially, although average figures never approached those for comparable conventional firms. In interpreting these findings on economic performance, the performance of SHPCs is clearly better than at first appears, in view of the difficult conditions under which SHPCs commenced productive activities, the distinctive characteristics of their work force which lowered the quality and effectiveness of the labor input, the low quality and small amount of the capital input, and the nature of SHPC management. The fact that any SHPCs were able to come even remotely close to capitalist averages is no mean achievement.

With refuse collection PCs, too, it could be argued that the familial and ethnic nature of their labor force has rendered them a group apart from other clusters of American PCs. The ability to generalize confidently on the socioeconomic performance of this cluster is further inhibited because studies of refuse collection PCs have focused on a single case, the Sunset Cooperative in the San Francisco Bay Area, and have asked mainly noneconomic questions. Still, the available evidence does reveal a good economic record. Among the six leading refuse collection companies, Sunset recorded, during 1970–1975, the third best average ratio of profits to sales (Perry 1978:161) and did this despite "pay" levels for partners that easily surpassed industry averages (Perry 1978:110). During the 1970s, in terms of sales, Sunset grew at a rate about equal to the industry average, with much recent growth reflecting a policy of diversification, a strategy that has resulted in the acquisition by Sunset of other smaller garbage companies and the formation of subsidiaries for various purposes, including the rental of debris boxes. The firm has proven itself able to introduce technical changes, most recently of a labor-saving variety (Perry 1978:148–149).

While Sunset has been able to provide notable job security for its members, its recent record on job creation for helpers (i.e., nonmembers) has been less impressive. In addition, while Sunset is characterized as being substantially influenced by its rank and file and as being far from a management oligarchy (Russell et al. 1979), the influence of nonmember workers on decision making was probably less than might be expected in a comparable firm with a labor union.

Evaluating the achievements of the three remaining clusters—EOFs, reforestation and collectives—is difficult, not only because the evidence is meager but also because published studies necessarily cover only a few years of experience at most. I begin by reviewing the evidence for EOFs, which is best presented in the general studies by Conte and Tannenbaum (1978), Sockell (1978), U.S. Senate Select Committee on Small Business (1979), and Frieden (1978), the case studies by Zwerdling (1977, 1978, 1979), Hammer and Stern (1980), and Russell (1981), the reports on continuing research by Whyte (1978), Whyte and Blasi (1980), and Blasi and Whyte (1981), and the accounts by Ross (1980) and O'Toole (1979).

In a widely cited study, the first published work to employ a statistical analysis of American EOFs, Conte and Tannenbaum (1978:27) conclude that "the employee owned companies . . . appear to be profitable—perhaps more profitable than comparable, conventionally owned companies; and the ownership variable most closely associated with profitability is the percent of equity owned by the workers themselves." Managers of employee-owned companies were found to believe that employee ownership had a positive effect on productivity.

Data reported by Sockell (1978:11–18) shed some light on the job creating potential of EOFs. For eighteen EOFs whose labor force had changed since the firms became employee-owned (and excluding West Coast plywood firms), ten had reduced their labor forces (by an average of 11%) and eight had increased their labor forces (on average by 56%) since becoming worker-owned.

Other studies of EOFs suggest a similarly uneven picture. Both Whyte (1978) and Frieden (1978) report how, following a changeover to employee ownership, profits rose in a variety of firms such as E. Systems in Dallas, Texas; Jamestown Metals in Jamestown, New York; Library Bureau in Herkimer, New York; Saratoga Knitting Mills in Saratoga, New York; South Bend Lathe in South Bend, Indiana; and Vermont Asbestos in Eden, Vermont. Other EOFs, however, did not improve in this way. Moreover, in cases where profits have risen initially, they have not always been sustained (e.g., the case of Library Bureau in Herkimer, New York). And in certain cases where profits have continued to rise, it is clear that the main reason for the improvement was not the change in the nature of ownership (see, for example, the case of Vermont Asbestos [Johannesen 1979] where continued economic success was due to market forces). Nearly always, however, the available accounts report reduced absenteeism (see Frieden's [1978] account of Tembec Forest Products in Quebec), reduced waste (see Ross's [1980] account of Republic Hose in Youngstown, Ohio), and a deep commitment to job preservation (see the account of Indianapolis Rubber in the *Wall Street Journal* for 22 March 1978).

On the ability of EOFs to retain democratic structure, the evidence suggests a consistently poor record. For instance, Hammer and Stern

(1980) found that in an upstate New York manufacturer of library furniture that was transformed into an EOF after being divested from a conglomerate, employee ownership in itself did not lead to any significant change in patterns of organizational decision making. "Legal ownership . . . was not associated with psychological or self-ownership. Management was still seen as the *de facto* owners of the company to a much larger extent than the workers saw themselves as owners, either individually or collectively" (p. 96). Russell (1981) also reports a pattern of gradual degeneration for an American taxi PC.

If conventional indicators of economic performance are used, studies of new wave PCs (collectives) reveal a poor record. The survey by Jackall and Crain (see chap. 5, this volume) shows collectives to be small, marginal operations, with only about half of the firms making a surplus and these seldom making large surpluses, while paying "wages" much below industry norms. A study of Ann Arbor collectives by Gamson et al. (1978) and the case studies by Case and Taylor (1979) support these findings, and record in depth the high turnover rates for labor in many collectives and the impact these high rates have upon economic performance in small organizations. However, these same studies document impressive social performance. Collectives tend to be highly participative firms and usually are able, though sometimes with considerable effort, to retain democratic priorities and structures.

In summary, the record is neither as overwhelmingly bleak as some critics contend nor as convincingly and consistently positive as some supporters claim. The available evidence indicates a record that is deserving of much more careful and detailed analysis. Particular attention should be paid to determining the reasons for the considerable variation in socioeconomic performance among PCs and EOFs and for the apparent deterioration in performance of older PCs and EOFs. Finding these answers may well require that many firms be studied over a long period of time.

THE USES OF AN AMBIGUOUS LEGACY

No bold generalizations can emerge from these complicated and ambiguous data. There are, however, some important questions that do stand out: What accounts for the considerable variations in performance among PCs and EOFs? Why do many, though clearly not all, PCs have difficulty surviving for more than one generation? Why do some successful producer cooperatives, such as Olympia Plywood in Washington, or successful EOFs, such as Vermont Asbestos in Eden, Vermont, have difficulty maintaining their cooperative or near-cooperative status and transform into capitalist firms? Why is it that many PCs seem to degenerate into noncooperative organizations as they age? There are, in addition, some clues to the answers for these questions, namely the data which point us back to an examination of the internal structures and processes of PCs and EOFs and to the larger social contexts in which they emerge.

ORGANIZATIONAL STRUCTURES AND PROCESSES

It is worth reiterating that, broadly speaking, it is those clusters of PCs with the *most cooperative* features—particularly the plywood and cooperage PCs—that have the longest life, the best economic performance, and the best record of maintaining a cooperative structure over time.[3] As many chapters in this volume point out, cooperatives straddle two worlds. They are committed to internal democracy but must compete in a marketplace that demands efficiency. A great number of cooperatives succumb to the demands for efficiency by progressively negating their cooperative character. The historical record suggests that in the end these firms will end up with neither cooperation nor efficiency. The key to successful, long-lived cooperatives seems to be precisely greater cooperation and a concomitant responsiveness to the economic and labor conditions of the marketplace.

What this means in practice is the systematic cultivation of internal democratic forms, either representative as in the plywood PCs (see chap. 8 by Greenberg, this volume) or participatory as in the reforestation PCs (see chap. 7 by Gunn). Without this sort of participation, cooperatives atrophy over time, lose their reason for being, and either fail altogether or become conventional capitalist firms. Sustained worker participation demands, of course, ongoing educational and training programs for workers; to date, these have been largely lacking in the history of producer cooperatives, and this suggests one clear direction for the future. In order to survive, all organizations must develop the internal mechanisms for self-reproduction. Educational and training programs to shape "participatory consciousness," in Bernstein's (1976b) phrase, are perhaps the most important mechanisms of all for cooperative organizations.[4]

The disappointing historical record of EOFs is directly relevant here. As noted earlier, these firms are the "least cooperative" in the whole historical array of alternative firms presented in this essay. Not only do they typically lack ongoing worker participation in management but their internal financing arrangements also undercut any long-term cooperation. EOFs typically allow outside (i.e., nonworker) investment in the firm. Even when a firm is successful, this arrangement produces two complementary disincentives for a firm to remain cooperative. First, more outside investors will be attracted by a profitable venture, further diluting workers' stake in the enterprise; second, workers themselves, upon retirement, can make much greater personal gains by selling their stock in the company to outside buyers at the market price. Further, as the stock goes higher, younger workers entering the firm will be progressively unable to purchase shares, and the very idea of worker ownership is eroded. The historical lesson of EOFs is that any cooperative firm, in order to remain cooperative while being economically successful, has to structure carefully its internal financing arrangements to protect workers' economic stake in the enterprise and to achieve some kind of equity in the work force, particularly between younger and older workers (see the approach to these issues in Ellerman's essay, chap. 11 in this volume).

CONTEXTUAL ISSUES

Two important contextual issues for the development of PCs and EOFs emerge out of our historical presentation: first, the role of labor unions and, second, that of government.

The American experience illustrates the uneven and ambivalent attitudes of American labor unions toward PCs and EOFs. While earlier clusters of PCs, notably KOL and foundry, received strong support from individual unions and national federations, no such encouragement has been systematically offered by unions in this century. Labor unions such as the Lumber and Sawmill Workers Union in fact have not even championed plywood PCs. Indeed, there have been occasions when that particular union has opposed plywood PCs. The most noticeable instance took place in 1951 after the inception of the Everett Plywood Company in Washington. The union represented the previous work force and charged that the conversion to cooperation had cost some of its members their jobs; the union then demanded that it be recognized as the exclusive bargaining agent for the new work force. A strike resulted and the union lost (Berman 1967:125–126). And Perry (1978:143–144) records how the Sanitary Truck Drivers and Helpers Local 350 filed suit against a refuse collection PC for denying equal opportunity to black and hispanic employees, nearly all of whom remained employees but never became members. With EOFs too, unions usually adopt a low profile, sometimes openly oppose the transformation of a capitalist firm to a worker-owned organization, and seldom agitate for the changeover.[5]

Yet unions are not universally antipathetic toward nor disinterested in EOFs and PCs. The fight to create an EOF at Rath Packing Company in Waterloo, Iowa, was led by union officers who had taken control of the board of directors. Changes in the traditionally hostile or negative attitude of unions toward PCs and EOFs may occur if successful transformations happen. As yet, however, there is no clear conception of what the role of unions should be, either in model PCs or during transformations to EOFs and the creation of other-than-model PCs. Even if the traditional collective bargaining role of unions is abandoned, unions could serve a multiplicity of new functions in PCs and EOFs. They could, for example, become the main vehicle for intercooperative solidarity on social policies (including incomes), or adopt the role of a shelter that would try to insure that PCs use only workable organizational structures. On this issue, there is much to be learned by studying the roles and strategies adopted by labor unions elsewhere, particularly in Spain and in Italy.

Government can play an important role in fostering both PCs and EOFs, although the record to date is very mixed and does not leave a great deal of room for optimism. The laws of any society, of course, encourage some forms of enterprise and discourage others. Matters of tax treatment, liability under the law, eligibility for government subsidies, and social insurance burdens are only a few of the ways in which legal factors can differentially shape business chances. If producer cooperatives are to flourish, at the very least direct legal obstacles to their formation, which still exist in many states, will have to be changed, especially those relating to the collective ownership of property (Ellerman 1975).

The record of federal and state involvement with PCs, especially state government administrations of SHPCs in California (see Jones and Schneider's essay, chap. 4) is also not very encouraging. Much of the uneven performance of SHPCs stemmed from conditions imposed on the cooperatives by the government. The fluctuations in policies of the State Relief Administration meant that long-range planning in SHPCs was particularly difficult and burdened by uncertainties that capitalist firms did not have to face. Neither state nor federal governments ever developed a clear-cut and consistent set of criteria with which to evaluate PCs. Rather than adopting a well-defined evaluative framework responsive to the special aims and purposes of SHPCs, both federal and state governments used a framework marked by a great sensitivity to short-term changes, particularly in economic matters. As such, evaluation was particularly susceptible to the shifting political winds that accompanied changes in administration.

Recent United States public policy on EOFs is also mixed. At least eleven EOFs have received loans or loan guarantees from federal agencies, and these were crucial in the formation of employee ownership (Ross 1980; Zwerdling 1979). There have been some encouraging legislative developments in the last few years. The Small Business Administration Act of 1980 allows the Small Business Administration to make loans to workers who wish to purchase their firms "when they

would otherwise close, relocate, or be purchased by a large business."
Also, the proposal for the Expanded Ownership Act of 1981 (*Congressional Record* 1981) and the creation of a National Center for Employee
Ownership are hopeful signs. Finally, after a period of crisis in the
early 1980s, the National Consumer Cooperative Bank is on firm
footing and is now empowered to loan up to 10 percent of the bank's
total capitalization (about $221 million in late 1983) to producer
cooperatives taken as an industry group.

No systematic and coordinated public policy has yet been developed, however. At most, only one-quarter of existing EOFs have
received loans or loan guarantees from the federal government, and
many requests for aid have been denied. The assistance that has been
provided has come only on an ad hoc basis and from diverse agencies.
And, other legislative proposals, such as the Voluntary Job Preservation and Community Stabilization Act, have not reached fruition
at this writing. More to the point, the legislation developed in this
area and the aid given thus far have not been based on the historical
lessons of the producer cooperative experience. Most important, none
of the new EOFs, even where federal loans were given, have tried to
couple worker ownership with worker control. As stressed above,
worker ownership without substantial worker control is unlikely to be
successful for very long. One must also add that the prevailing (1983)
conservative political climate in the United States is unlikely to provide much encouragement in the near future to enterprises that try
to empower workers.

Still, while the historical legacy of PCs and EOFs in America is
ambiguous, it is also rich and multifaceted. Perhaps the most enduring
lesson that it offers is that workers in an astonishingly diverse range
of industries, crafts, and trades have repeatedly tried to make their
work and their workplaces their own. This historical resiliency is, in
itself, a hope for the future. If institutional contexts more supportive
of cooperatives can be forged, this resiliency could well produce a
much less ambiguous future.

NOTES

1. There are several intractable problems involved in estimating the number of
collectives. Their small size and often brief lives mean that of all the clusters, these
are most likely to escape the reporting net. Attempts at estimation yield widely varying
results. Compare Zwerdling (in Case and Taylor 1979:90), who estimates thousands
of food cooperatives alone, 5,000 to 10,000, with the essay by Jackall and Crain in
this volume (chap. 5), who report a survey that obtained actual information on fewer
than 100 collectives of every sort.

2. For a review of these correlation/regression studies, see Conte (1982). For a review of methodological issues, see Levin (1982). Though Conte and Tannenbaum (1978) state some of the methodological problems and characterize their results as preliminary, some of these points do need emphasizing. In particular, the representativeness of the sample of 30 firms (on which the regression analysis emphasizing the role of worker ownership is based) is questionable. Also, the relationship is unclear between the underlying theory and the particular specification of the model tested.

3. In a broader based study of PCs in several industrialized economies, including the United States, I reach a similar, though preliminary conclusion (Jones 1980a). The most cooperative group of PCs, the famous Mondragon PCs in Spain, are judged to be the most successful.

4. See also Vanek 1975a:intro. In a pioneering account of the conditions necessary for sustaining viable PCs, great stress is laid on education and the protective and supportive roles to be played by a shelter organization. For empirical evaluations of the Vanek and Bernstein models, see Jones 1980a and Jones 1979b, respectively.

5. In a survey of the attitudes of union officers and staff toward worker ownership, Stern and O'Brien (1977:12) concluded that "there is a good deal of skepticism about employee unionism, particularly with respect to current collective bargaining practices."

ACKNOWLEDGMENTS

Earlier versions of this paper were presented at seminars held at Dartington Hall, Devon, England in September 1980, and at Albany, New York, in October 1981. The essay has benefited enormously from Robert Jackall's comments on earlier drafts as well as from his editorial assistance.

4

Self-Help Production Cooperatives: Government-Administered Cooperatives During the Depression

DEREK C. JONES
AND
DONALD J. SCHNEIDER

INTRODUCTION

Self-help production cooperatives (SHPCs) formed during the 1930s comprise the largest sector of producer cooperatives (PCs) in United States history. Between 1931 and 1938, over half a million families were affiliated with 600 self-help organizations in thirty-seven states; about 250 of these were productive associations.[1] Between 1934 and 1938 these production cooperatives received more than $4,730,000 in state and federal funds to support their productive activities. SHPCs represent the only major historical attempt by the U.S. legislature to incorporate workers' participation in management into government programs. Not only were state and federal funds provided to support self-help programs but also an array of rules were made to govern self-help activities. Despite the recent reawakening of interest in PCs, this particular cooperative experience rarely has been examined.

Given the current interest by many western industrialized econ-omies in worker ownership and alternative means of preserving em-ployment,[2] this is a particularly appropriate time to reexamine the SHPCs. Throughout this study we will attempt to illuminate the difficulties, both avoidable and unavoidable, that arise when the gov-ernment becomes involved in the administration of a cooperative program. Also, we will look at the socioeconomic performance of SHPCs and at the nature of relevant evaluative criteria. A review and assessment of the methods used to aid and to evaluate SHPCs may contribute to the development of sharp and more appropriate guidelines for formulating future public policy regarding PCs.

To clarify the special context in which SHPCs developed and the features that differentiate SHPCs from other American PCs, this essay will describe briefly both the history of the self-help movement and the nature of SHPCs. Since SHPCs evolved in a unique economic and social environment, some may question the contemporary relevance of analyzing this experience. Nevertheless, we argue that an analysis of SHPCs points to several issues that need to be carefully considered when contemplating future government programs involving self-management and worker ownership. Above all, we argue that an explicit and coherent definition of the nature and purpose of the self-managed sector and a consistent policy toward this sector are needed to ensure that a program can function over time.

HISTORICAL CONTEXT AND DEVELOPMENT

During the Great Depression, mass unemployment existed at the same time crops rotted, unpicked, in the fields. Lacking an adequate government program to cushion the impact of unemployment, in 1931 and 1932 people spontaneously began to unite surplus labor and surplus produce in primitive forms of self-help organizations. Unemployed workers harvested the fields to feed their families in return for providing labor to the farmers.[3] Workers formed cooperatives to trade produce among themselves in order to obtain a wider variety of goods. Associations were formed to foster trade between cooperatives. Although cooperatives existed across the United States, they were concentrated in California where access to produce was easy. This study will deal primarily with California cooperatives for two reasons: the self-help sector became more highly developed in California than in any other state, and a significant data base exists for California covering the years 1934 through 1938.

As the cooperative organizations grew, some began to undertake the production of new goods, rather than being solely concerned with bartering. Soon the cooperatives exerted political pressure for food and cash subsidies from local governments (Taylor 1939). In August 1933 the Wagner-Lewis Relief Act provided for federal grants to self-help organizations. While early grants under this act were to be used primarily for the relief of unemployment and as working capital, later grants and loans could be used to buy fixed assets. Soon the bulk of existing and newly formed cooperatives were engaged in production and were receiving grants (see tables 4.1 and 4.2).[4] In California the State Relief Administration (SRA) established the Division of Self-Help Cooperative Service to administer the federal grants. The early productive activities of cooperatives receiving grants included gardening, baking, and canning, though SHPCs were involved in a broad range of activities including lumbering and soap making.

Rules governing the disbursement of federal grants and loans greatly affected the cooperatives.[5] Initially, no federal funds could be used to buy fixed assets or land. An SHPC had to pay its members at least 30¢ per hour in scrip, making sure not to reduce the wage of labor in the community. Each SHPC had to use a uniform accounting system. Perhaps the most significant rule stated that no SHPC goods could find their way into the open market. In effect, a self-help economy was created which functioned separately from the open market economy. These rules reflected the government's desire to allow the cooperative sector to operate as long as the free market was not disturbed.

A switch from federal to state funding and changes in rules regarding administration of the funding shaped the growth of SHPCs in several distinct stages. Federal funds were available until October 1935; thereafter in some areas, state government stepped in to fill the void. The first state to do so was Utah in March 1935, followed shortly thereafter by California in August 1935. Until the end of 1938, California provided grants to SHPCs (see table 4.3).

Throughout the entire subsidy period, the Division of Self-Help of the State of California disbursed all funds, and its policies greatly affected the activities of the cooperatives. Those policies fluctuated greatly. Clark Kerr (1939:387) calls 1934 through early 1936 the period of "autonomous cooperatives." During this time the division exercised no control over the administration of individual grant units, and grant money was easily available. However, the subsidies soon dropped drastically.

In late 1937 the subsidies once again became readily available, but the pattern of self-help production in California was changed by a new philosophy toward SHPCs and a new set of regulations. The goal of rehabilitating members through self-directed cooperatives was abandoned. Instead, the aim was to save relief money through strict government control of individual units (Kerr 1939:507). Kerr and Harris (1939:10) call 1937 through 1938 the period of "controlled cooperatives." The division set production quotas, supervised unit management, established membership requirements, and took control of purchasing, selling, and intercooperative distribution. Also, the division decided to value goods at competitive wholesale prices; thus, the self-help economy was no longer insulated from the external open economy.

TABLE 4.1

NUMBER OF SELF-HELP ORGANIZATIONS AND MEMBERSHIP IN THE UNITED STATES, 1931–1938

| Year | Numbers of Units | | | Worker-Members ('000s)[b] | | | Average number of worker-members[b] per unit |
	Nongrant units[a]	Grant units	Total	Nongrant units[a]	Grant units	Total	
1931	93	0	93	12.2	0	12.2	131
1933	411	0	411	71.9	0.0	71.9	175
1935	112	225	337	6.6	12.2	18.8	56
1936	57	190	247	1.2	7.3	8.5	34
1937	34	159	193	0.9	4.8	5.7	30
1938	32	122	154	1.7	4.2	5.9	37

SOURCE: Data taken from Kerr 1939:14, 16, and from *Monthly Labor Review* 1939c:133.

[a] Nongrant units operated without federal or state aid for production. In fact, most of the nongrant units were barter organizations and as such were ineligible for federal assistance under the provisions of the Wagner-Lewis Relief Act.
[b] "Worker-member" figures indicate the number of members who actually worked during the month (usually June) when data were collected.

TABLE 4.2

Distribution of Self-Help Organizations and Membership 1933–1938 for Selected States

State[a]	1933 Units #	1933 Units % Total	1933 Members #	1933 Members % Total	1935 Units #	1935 Units % Total	1935 Members #	1935 Members % Total	1938 Units #	1938 Units % Total	1938 Members #	1938 Members % Total
Alabama	4	1.0	500	0.7	5	1.5	571	3.0	1	0.6	40	0.7
California	176	42.8	30,035	41.8	167	49.4	8,745	46.5	75	47.5	2,240	38.3
Colorado	10	2.4	450	0.6	12	3.6	271	1.4	1	0.6	15	0.3
D.C.	na	na	na	na	15	4.5	1,060	5.6	1	0.6	297	5.1
Idaho	8	2.0	200	0.3	27	8.0	1,296	6.9	9	5.7	100	1.7
Michigan	9	2.2	2,396	3.3	7	2.1	565	3.0	2	1.3	220	3.8
Missouri	8	2.0	2,000	2.8	8	2.4	448	2.4	6	3.8	200	3.4
TVA	—	—	—	—	10	2.9	500	2.7	8	5.1	400	6.8
Utah	5	1.2	1,500	2.1	29	8.8	629	3.5	19	12.1	263	4.5
Washington	40	9.7	2,000	2.6	24	7.1	481	2.6	20	12.7	380	6.5
Other	151	36.7	32,789	45.6	28	8.4	4,246	22.5	16	10.1	1,703	29.1
Total[b]	411	100.0	71,860	99.8	332	98.7	18,812	100.1	158	100.1	5,858	100.2

Source: Data taken from Kerr (1939:chap. 1), various tables.

[a] Data reported for those states with the most SHPCs in 1935, the year when the productive period began.
[b] Numbers may not sum to 100% because of rounding.

TABLE 4.3

NUMBER OF SELF-HELP COOPERATIVES AND MEMBERSHIP IN CALIFORNIA, 1932–1938

	Date	Number of Units			Worker-Members ('000s')[b]			Average number of worker-members[b] per unit
		Nongrant unit[a]	Grant unit	Total	Nongrant unit[a]	Grant unit	Total	
1932	June	35	0	35	6,900	0	6,900	197
	Dec	142	0	142	30,355	0	30,355	214
1933	June	176	0	173	30,025	0	30,025	171
	Dec	153	4	157	14,000	940	14,940	95
1934	June	112	48	160	7,790	3,836	11,625	73
	Dec	90	86	176	3,780	5,960	9,740	56
1935	June	89	78	167	3,850	4,895	8,745	52
	Dec	67	74	140	2,050	3,665	5,715	51
1936	June	55	71	126	1,130	2,490	3,620	29
	Dec	42	62	104	1,000	1,980	2,980	29
1937	June	33	61	94	820	1,295	2,115	23
	Dec	25	49	74	670	715	1,385	19
1938	June	30	45	75	1,570	670	2,240	30
	Dec	29	41	70	1,710	580	2,290	33

SOURCE: Data taken from Kerr (1939:tables 6, 7).

[a] Nongrant units operated without federal or state aid for production.
[b] "Worker members" figures indicates the number of members who actually worked during the month when data were collected.

On January 1, 1938, the director of the division proposed the cessation of all aid.[6] The cooperatives, which had been under strict government control since 1937, had become dependent on this aid. Most California SHPCs appear to have disappeared before the end of the Second World War.

In other states, particularly Idaho, Missouri, Utah, and Washington, attempts were made to establish SHPCs as permanent self-supporting units, in part by the use of more liberal grants and also by allowing SHPCs to sell on the open market.[7] Little published information is available on these firms; apparently they, too, soon succumbed.

Hence, even this brief historical overview shows that there were marked differences between SHPCs and other American PCs. Whereas most American PCs began as new ventures or as transformations from traditional firms, most SHPCs represent transformations from another cooperative form, namely, the barter organization. SHPCs arose in a context of generalized unemployment vastly different from the conditions facing most other emergent U.S. PCs. The development of SHPCs, unlike that of other American PCs, was heavily influenced by specific government policies and their administration.

THE NATURE OF SELF-HELP PRODUCTION COOPERATIVES

DEFINITION AND PURPOSE

Self-help production cooperatives may be defined as democratic associations of the unemployed or underemployed who organize to obtain the necessities of life through their own production of goods (Kerr and Harris 1939:10). Obtaining the necessities of life was surely the aim of the first self-help pioneers, but as the original organizations evolved and as the government began to exert influence, other aims and purposes were proposed. Soon after the onset of government involvement, government officials stated that SHPCs gave form to the idea that relief clients should be put to work on productive and rehabilitative projects. Thus, apart from providing the material necessities of life, SHPCs served the social and psychological needs of the unemployed. Production in SHPCs was considered a desirable alternative to relief or transfer payments by government officials because of the rehabilitative functions performed.

Finally, with the widespread use of government money to help cooperatives, another purpose for SHPCs was popularized. The government began to describe SHPCs as vehicles to save relief costs. The usefulness of SHPCs was measured by the government and by some public sectors purely in terms of dollars and cents. The reports of the California State Relief Administration clearly reflect the government's preoccupation with the monetary aspects of SHPCs. In California, attitudes within the self-help sector varied both among cooperatives and over time. Kerr states, "Three unconventional self-help organizations in Northern California differed from the customary California pattern and from each other. They were the experimental U.X.A. (Unemployed Exchange Association), the business styled B.U.A. (Berkeley Unemployed Association), and the 'revolutionary' P.C.L. (Pacific Cooperative League)" (1939:659). The U.X.A. desperately attempted to "combine active democracy and business efficiency, with education as the amalgam." The B.U.A. focused on economic benefits and sacrificed democracy for efficiency. In contrast, the P.C.L. had a definite concept of the future society it desired, and the driving forces behind its operation were social rather than economic (ibid.:654–660).

All the cooperatives were affected not only by the philosophies of their members but by the philosophy of the government unit that oversaw their operation. For instance, in California the philosophy of the State Relief Administration changed radically in 1936. Until this time the rehabilitative aspects of SHPCs were stressed, and attempts were made to establish the program on a permanent basis (Kerr 1939:479). In July 1936 a new director of the S.R.A. was named, and the goal of rehabilitation was abandoned. The autonomy of individual cooperative units was sacrificed to save relief money through strict government control. Cooperatives were forced to conform to the new policies in order to receive grant money, and their governance and operation changed drastically in many cases.

Thus, although the self-help movement grew out of the simple desire to obtain the necessities of life, the specific aims of individual cooperatives became more diverse over time. The marked heterogeneity of purpose of SHPCs clearly distinguished them from other bygone clusters of American PCs (see Jones 1979b). To the extent that this heterogeneity of purpose was further complicated by the changing, and rarely explicit, policies and attitudes of the bureaucracy that disbursed federal and state grants, SHPCs stand alone among American PCs.

GOVERNANCE AND ORGANIZATION

The types of relationships between members within specific cooperatives and between different cooperatives were several and varied over time. Many of these variations can be traced to the changes in aims and purpose previously discussed.

The first California self-help cooperatives were relatively small, and their activity involved exchanging labor for excess produce. These units were governed by town meeting democracies based on equality of vote. Participation was direct, and most issues were voted upon. As cooperatives began to receive grant money to produce their own goods, the internal organizations of the units usually changed. In most cases the town meeting democracy was considered no longer feasible as the cooperatives became more concerned with productive efficiency. To assist the cooperatives, the State Division of Self-Help Cooperative Service, which provided limited technical assistance, published a model constitution for self-help organizations. By 1935 one-third of the grant units (SHPCs) in California had adopted this constitution (Kerr 1939:412). The model calls for a city manager type of government. Directors were elected from and by the membership of each cooperative in elections staggered over a three-year period. The directors appointed the managers, and the managers appointed their subordinates. A survey of self-help organizations in 1936, by which time most had evolved into SHPCs, showed that most cooperatives held frequent meetings which were well attended. Several SHPCs had 100 percent attendance at general meetings.[8] In these respects SHPCs belong in the most highly democratic group of American PCs.[9]

However, in 1936 when the new California State Division director began to stress efficiency at the expense of autonomy, the SHPCs became less cooperative. Ostensibly, the units still governed themselves democratically, but the managers became more dependent on the approval of the division than on that of their fellow members. Selection of managers itself was subject to approval by the division (Kerr 1939:518). In general, the state government exerted increasing control over all aspects of SHPC operations. The tendency for cooperatives to become less democratic over time has been observed for other American PCs (Jones 1979b). In other cases, however, the decline in democracy usually resulted from an organizational structure adopted voluntarily by the cooperative rather than from control imposed by an external agent. The imposition of direct government control over SHPC organization relates back to the differing aims and purposes of SHPCs as perceived by the workers and the government. By ignoring the social functions of the cooperatives, the government necessarily was led to conclude that the units were economically inefficient and needed direct "help." Thus, the root cause of this intervention was the government's narrow conception of the purposes of SHPCs.

In California the external organizations to which cooperatives belonged greatly affected the nature of the individual cooperatives. Most SHPCs were members of federations of one type or another. In northern California the cooperatives were wide distances apart, and inter-cooperative trade was difficult. Therefore, the cooperatives did not interact to any significant degree. They tended to be large and to undertake several different projects in order to supply their members with a variety of goods. Out of necessity these northern SHPCs tried to develop self-sufficient self-help economies.

In contrast, the cooperatives of southern California were densely concentrated, especially in the Los Angeles area. Because of their close proximity, intercooperative trade was easily accomplished. A single cooperative could specialize in production because it could obtain a variety of goods from trade with others nearby. This group of southern cooperatives can be characterized as an integrated self-help economy. The degree of integration achieved by this large group of self-help units is unique in the history of PCs in the United States.

FINANCE, EARNINGS, AND DISTRIBUTION OF SURPLUS

In nearly all SHPCs, initial productive assets were financed by government grants rather than by the individual members' supply of either loan or equity capital. Initially, the cooperators believed that they owned all assets purchased with grant money. During the policy change in late 1936, however, it was announced that the state would retain ownership of all grant-financed assets. This confused and changing notion of the members' property rights again sets SHPCs apart from most other American PCs.

In most SHPCs all workers were paid the same wage rate, and surplus was distributed according to the number of hours worked. Exceptions to this general rule were "key workers" who received wages from the Works Progress Administration (California State Relief Administration 1938:7). The W.P.A. paid these workers directly because they were considered essential to the operation of the cooperatives. In theory the W.P.A payments were to be given only to accountants and managers, but in practice these payments were disbursed as favors.

MEMBERSHIP AND THE NATURE OF THE WORK FORCE

Focusing now on the individual worker-members of the self-help units, all workers received a share in the surplus of the SHPC. The surplus was defined as the difference between the operating advances of money made to the unit and the value of the goods delivered to the cooperative warehouse. In 1938 the average member received between $20 and $30 worth of goods per month, though there was wide variation around this figure.

Several aspects of the SHPCs' work force distinguish these firms from other American PCs or conventional firms. The average California SHPC member was nearly fifty years old (Kerr 1939:380–383), though the initial SHPC work force had a high percentage of young people between the ages of 20 and 24 (table 4.4). These young workers quickly left, and Panunzio (1939:102) has speculated that the youth were the first to find private employment when business improved. Stripped of their youthful members, SHPCs comprised mainly pensioners and other older workers who wished to supplement their relief payments with additional income. Once unemployed, these older workers saw little chance to regain their lost jobs in the foreseeable future, if at all; self-help was their only method of obtaining necessary income.

The normal occupations of most self-help members had been in manufacturing and mechanical industries. Although the occupational makeup varied considerably among units, an overabundance of manual workers and a dearth of clerical or white collar workers were common problems. Whatever the occupational makeup of the work force, a great deal of occupational displacement occurred in all cooperatives. Retraining was necessary on a large scale. Unlike work forces in other American PCs, that of the SHPC did not consist mainly of workers experienced in a particular trade or activity. Retraining was a major aspect of the rehabilitative function of SHPCs because it widened the range of workers' skills and thus made them more employable.

Turnover was a constant problem in cooperatives. In 1934 and 1935 it was estimated that while one-half of SHPC membership was stable, the other half was constantly changing. Accession rates of 16 percent per month were recorded (Kerr 1939:386). Unfortunately for the cooperatives, the older members were most stable, and the more efficient younger workers were most quicky drawn back to private employment.

The attitudes of the self-help participants toward the self-help method varied as greatly as did their own personal characteristics. Interviews with members in 1935 revealed the following.[10] Almost 90 percent of those surveyed favored self-help production over relief payments. Their reasons ranged from the pragmatic "it relieves the taxpayer" and "they have saved the country thousands of dollars" to the hopeful "it gives us something to build to and look forward to" to the utopian "they are the vanguard of the new social order." Obviously, SHPCs were different things to different people.

Cooperators nevertheless did agree almost universally on several points. Government aid and supervision was seen as essential to continued operation. Members cited the leadership and expertise of the Self-Help Division. A large majority of the cooperators expected to regain cash employment in the future; they did not wish to remain with the cooperatives once outside jobs opened up. Finally, while most

TABLE 4.4

DISTRIBUTION OF GRANT UNIT MEMBERS IN CALIFORNIA BY AGE, 1935–1937

Age	December 1934	December 1935	December 1936	December 1937	Employed population of California (1930)
Under 20	1.2	0.9	1.8	5.3	4.7
20–24	41.8	3.0	5.1	5.5	12.6
25–34	13.1	10.0	10.1	14.2	25.3
35–44	22.0	21.7	22.6	20.0	24.1
45–54	25.5	23.2	22.8	24.2	18.2
55–64	19.4	21.2	19.4	19.1	9.9
65–74	10.6	16.2	14.2	9.3	3.8
75 and over	1.8	3.8	4.0	2.4	0.6
Unspecified	1.6	0.0	0.0	0.0	0.2
Total	100.0	100.0	100.0	100.0	100.0

SOURCE: Kerr 1939:383.

cooperators saw self-help as a valuable way of retaining their self-respect and of earning their food, many saw little incentive to increase efficiency. Each worker received equal pay regardless of his productivity, and advancement was frequently on the basis of popularity. This lack of incentive seems related to the prevalent desire to return to cash employment.

One subset of the total self-help membership was perhaps the most important force in the perpetuation of the cooperatives: the leaders of the cooperative movement, who were also the managers and officials of individual units. Kerr (1939:420) describes the common element among these leaders as "an almost religious belief in the validity of self-help." Like the other members, the managers rarely had prior experience in their positions, but leadership ability, rather than technical skill and business acumen, was most important. Lacking the authority to hire, to fire, or to adjust pay, the managers used leadership rather than material incentives to manage the cooperative. Of course, management difficulties were compounded because some members were not committed to cooperative methods. Personal conflict over managers' "bossiness" was sometimes cited, but many workers reported working harder in cooperatives because "there ain't no foreman over you" and "the manager is one of us" (ibid.: 417). Overall, the opinions and attitudes of SHPC members cited above point to a fact that cannot be overemphasized: members themselves held widely divergent views of the aims and purposes of self-help cooperatives. Thus, many members did not function comfortably within the cooperative framework because they had no clear or consistent conception of its purpose.

Before evaluating the performance of SHPCs, it is useful to review the unique characteristics of the self-help work force. The cooperators were predominantly old, they relied on self-help to supplement relief or other forms of income, they came from diverse occupations, they needed extensive retraining, they frequently remained cooperative members for only short periods, and they held a wide variety of attitudes toward self-help. Membership rights were derived from supplying labor and not capital, and because of the vague way in which property rights were defined, worker-members in SHPCs, unlike worker-members in most American PCs, had no claims to the firm's assets. Whereas other American PCs had limited and closely regulated memberships, SHPCs tended to pursue open membership policies.

These characteristics set SHPCs apart from all other groups of PCs and conventional firms. In terms of economic efficiency, the work forces in SHPCs were of poor quality, and the institutional framework clearly did not produce large incentives. These factors, along with the heterogeneity of purpose and the unique economic context in which SHPCs developed, must be remembered when appraising the economic performance of SHPCs.

PERFORMANCE

THE MEANING AND IMPORTANCE OF PERFORMANCE

Identifying the appropriate criteria with which to evaluate the performance of PCs is always difficult,[11] but with SHPCs the problems are multiplied. While criteria for evaluation may be inferred from the ideology and behavior of other PCs, SHPCs varied so greatly in these respects that a single criterion or set of criteria for evaluation surely would be inadequate. Therefore, in the following section we will evaluate the performance of SHPCs as units of production, as organizations to save relief costs, and as means to rehabilitate the unemployed. While it is impossible to quantify completely the performance of the heterogeneous sector of SHPCs, the data presented highlight important trends and characteristics. When combined with the record of observations of actual cooperative behavior, these data do allow one to reach certain conclusions.

The multifaceted evaluative framework is radically different from the dollars-and-cents criteria overwhelmingly evident in government reports. Examination of the California State reports dealing with the period 1934–1936 reveals that when it came to assessing performance, the emphasis was almost exclusively on economic productivity. The economic benefits of relief savings were also mentioned, but the less tangible social and rehabilitative aspects of performance were usually ignored.[12] In later reports, although the focus shifted from productivity to relief savings, the economic dimensions of SHPCs continued to be stressed (California State Relief Administration 1938:14–26).

The government's focus on purely economic criteria reflects an extremely restrictive approach toward evaluating performance of PCs in general and SHPCs in particular. The importance of this restrictive approach lies in its consequences for the self-help sector; much government policy, particularly decisions to cut off state financial aid to most SHPCs in the late 1930s, was heavily influenced by the pessimistic conclusions of official reports.[13]

In the following sections we reevaluate the SHPCs' economic performance and review the assessments made in government reports. Improved estimates of productive efficiency are offered as part of a less restrictive approach to the evaluation of SHPC performance.

EFFICIENCY AS PRODUCTIVE UNITS

In the public reports dealing with SHPCs, much emphasis was placed on the criterion of efficiency. Measures used in California State reports between 1934 and 1936 to shed light on productive efficiency included total value of production, value added per man-hour, and average real income per man-month. Official estimates of productive efficiency were made only for two years.[14] We submit that there were several important weaknesses in the methodology used in these reports which undermine the value of the official conclusions on productive efficiency.

First, a two-year time span is too short. Improvements in productive efficiency could be attributed to initial shock effects. It is more useful to know whether improvements continued thereafter. Second, the analytical value of examining productive efficiency for SHPCs alone is questionable. More significant is a comparison with conventional firms. Third, the particular measures of productive efficiency employed are also debatable. Fourth, official reports frequently failed to stress the major problems involved in using the available data on SHPCs. We note two specific problems. The reliability of the basic building block upon which the data base was built, namely, the monthly report submitted by individual SHPCs, is problematical. Respondents were seldom trained accountants, and they voiced their distress at the unique accounting system developed for SHPCs. Also, since this accounting system included a system of internal markets in which output prices were established, figures on the value of output are uncertain.

In the remainder of this section we provide improved estimates of the productive efficiency of SHPCs for a longer period of time using a broader range of measures. Also, comparisons are drawn with conventional firms in similar industries using a variety of methods. Often SHPCs are compared with a sector of conventional twin firms. Because many cooperatives, especially those that received federal and/or state grants, engaged in similar types of major projects, it is possible to isolate a set of five activities that represent SHPC production as a whole. These activities are baking, canning, lumbering, sewing, and soap making. In 1937 cooperatives whose major projects were in these categories produced 71.7 percent of all grant unit output; in 1938 the figure was 70.9 percent. Canning produced the highest percentage of total output, 53.6 percent in 1937 and 47.8 percent in 1938 (Kerr 1939:74).

Once the set of five projects is assumed to be representative of SHPC production as a whole, a conventional twin sector may be assembled. From the *Census of Manufactures of 1939* for the state of California (U.S. Bureau of the Census 1942*a*), data on the following products are chosen for comparison: canned and dried fruits and vegetables, bread and other bakery products, lumber and timber basic products, work clothing, and soap.

Sometimes data specific to California are not available for the time period under study. In these cases United States data are used to allow for comparisons over the entire production period for which cooperative data are available. Like the California data, these United States data are collected in conventional twin output categories.[15]

SIZE, INVESTMENT, AND GROWTH

The size of SHPCs, in terms of average number of workers per unit and average value of output per unit, is examined in the charts below. These statistics furnish an idea of the scale of operations of SHPCs relative to comparable conventional firms.

The worker-member data for SHPCs in 1935 and 1936 reported in table 4.5 are deceptive. During these early years SHPCs were still adjusting to production. The average worker-members worked only about 72 hours a month in 1935—about 40 percent of the figure for a full-time counterpart in a conventional firm.[16] The drastic drop in average membership may be attributed to the shedding of nonproductive members and to a raising of the average hours worked each month by a worker in a SHPC to 136 in 1938—about 77 percent of

TABLE 4.5

COMPARATIVE OUTPUT AND LABOR FOR SELF-HELP PRODUCTION COOPERATIVES
AND CONVENTIONAL FIRMS IN CALIFORNIA, 1935–1939

	Labor (# workers)		Output per month ($)	
Year	Conventional	SHPC	Conventional	SHPC
1935	28.4	61.0	11,603	822
1936		41.5		710
1937	31.3	23.2	13,408	1,012
1938		14.5		1,391
1939	58.4		28,587	

SOURCES: Conventional data taken from U.S. Bureau of the Census (1942a) and U.S. Bureau of the Census (1942b). Data for SHPCs computed from Kerr 1939:71, 73, and 737.

NOTE: Data for SHPCs refer only to grant units.[17]

the figure for a comparable full-time worker in a conventional firm. Figures for 1937 and 1938 more accurately represent the size of the SHPC productive unit. This unit employs fewer workers than its conventional twin.

We also see that SHPCs never approached the average output levels of the conventional twin. Especially in California where the large canneries drove up the output figures, the conventional firms dwarfed the SHPCs in average output. However, since SHPC output figures are valued using wholesale prices whereas data on capitalist figures include retail prices, the SHPC data are comparatively underestimated. Note also that SHPCs were able to expand output per month greatly between 1935 and 1939 in spite of the precipitous drop in average membership per unit.

One area in which data on individual project categories are available concerns average output per month. The State Relief Administration provides data for 1936 for four main activities. In table 4.6, we compare these data with figures for conventional firms.

It is evident that of the four types of SHPC projects, baking comes closest to approaching the scale of output of conventional firms. The data cited earlier on the distribution of bakeries by size suggest that the few large SHPC bakeries pull up their average output figures. Half of the bakeries in the United States produced output very close in volume to the output of SHPC bakeries. Nevertheless, the output figures for SHPCs are again dwarfed by those of conventional firms.[18]

Regarding investment, the following data provide some idea of the situation of SHPCs relative to conventional firms in the extent to

TABLE 4.6

COMPARATIVE OUTPUT OF SELF-HELP PRODUCTION CO-OPS IN CALIFORNIA AND
CONVENTIONAL FIRMS IN FOUR ACTIVITIES, 1935–1939

	Baking		Canning		Sewing		Lumbering	
Year	Conv.	SHPC	Conv.	SHPC	Conv.	SHPC	Conv.	SHPC
1935	5,398		19,729				6,899	
1936		438		382		56		85
1937	6,912		23,717		24,986		8,422	
1938								
1939	5,457		39,392		9,983		30,793	

SOURCES: Conventional data taken from U.S. Bureau of the Census 1942a and 1942b. SHPC
data taken from California Emergency Relief Administration 1935:55 and 1937:11.

NOTE: All entries are in current price dollars.

which a firm replaces or adds to capital stock in relation to the amount
of output it produces.[19] These data show that SHPC investment was
extremely low in relation to investment in conventional firms. Between 1935 and 1938 annual investment in SHPCs per $100.00 of
output fell from $1.85 to $0.09. For conventional firms in 1939, the
corresponding rate was $3.31. Also, as SHPC output increased in later
years (see tables 4.5 and 4.6), investment failed to keep pace.

Overall, the size data clearly indicate the small scale of SHPC
production. SHPC output increased over time, but it never approached
the scale of conventional twin productions. Although comparisons on
growth are difficult to make, for some indicators at least, namely output
and capital, the evidence shows that SHPCs were able to grow. Still
it appears that SHPCs accumulated capital more slowly than did capitalist firms. Consequently, SHPCs probably became progressively undercapitalized compared with conventional firms.

PRODUCTIVITY

A great deal of qualitative data bear on the question of productivity,
particularly labor productivity, in SHPCs. Survey data reported by
Kerr (1939:418) show that in 1936 a majority of SHPC managers
believed their workers to be more efficient than workers in capitalist
firms. Kerr (1939:751) argues too that "there was a general trend
toward greater efficiency in the use of non-administrative hours from
1936–38," in part because of a tendency to shed nonproductive members and also because of learning effects associated with the increased
hours worked by those members that remained. Also, Panunzio

(1939:107) reports that SHPCs were "definite improvements" over the preproductive phase cooperatives.

By patching together data scattered through Kerr's dissertation and the State Reports, it is possible to get a more precise picture of what was happening to labor productivity during 1935 to 1938 in selected individual SHPCs.[20] For all firms for which this could be done, output per worker improved, sometimes dramatically. For example, in the Bell No. 6 SHPC, output per man-hour grew from $0.24 in 1935 to $1.49 in 1937 and $2.02 in 1938. In the Highland Park Cooperative, the comparable figures are 12¢, 32¢, and 50¢.

Because of a lack of suitable data on capital in conventional twin firms, the only measures of productivity that can be computed are output per worker and value added as a percentage of the value of production. Output per worker data are presented in table 4.7.

From the SHPC data it is clear that as membership dropped between 1935 and 1938, output per worker increased. This supports the assertion that the drop in SHPC membership was due to a shedding of nonproductive members. Between 1935 and 1937 output per worker nearly tripled. The increase of nearly 35 percent between 1937 and 1938 took place even though state and federal grants expended during 1938 were only two-thirds the amount expended in 1937. Thus even as aid dropped in the period of controlled cooperatives, the SHPCs increased output per worker.

Table 4.8 presents value added as a percentage of total output for manufacturing firms. This chart suggests how effective each project was in adding value to the raw materials in the production process.

In sewing and soap making, SHPC projects were approximately as effective as their conventional twins in adding value during the production process. Since these two activities required little capital, and since lumbering which presumably required more capital was least effective in adding value, the hypothesis that undercapitalization hindered SHPC worker productivity is supported to some extent.

EFFICIENCY AS RELIEF ORGANIZATIONS

Self-help cooperatives provided relief to the unemployed in several ways. In addition to providing them with small amounts of food and wages, SHPCs offered the unemployed chances to learn new skills, to participate in the management of a productive enterprise, to remain active, and to avoid the psychological strain fostered by long periods of idleness. Unfortunately, it is not easy to quantify the additions to human capital or the psychic income that workers derived from SHPCs. Earlier we reported members' personal accounts of the psychic benefits

TABLE 4.7

OUTPUT PER WORKER IN CALIFORNIA
SELF-HELP CO-OPS AND CONVENTIONAL FIRMS

Year	Conventional	SHPCs[a]
1935	408.3	34.0
1936		35.8
1937	461.5	94.1
1938		126.2
1939	470.4	

SOURCES: Conventional data are taken from U.S. Bureau of the Census 1942*a*;121, 171, 418, 517, 788. SHPC data are calculated from Kerr 1939:713–719, 737.

NOTE: All entries are in current price dollars.

[a] SHPC data have been adjusted to reflect the fact that members worked fewer hours than employees of capitalist firms.

of cooperative membership, but in this section the efficiency of SHPCs in providing relief will be considered in purely monetary terms. Implicit in the following discussion is the understanding that the real benefits of SHPCs are greater than the nominal benefits, for the reasons just mentioned.

The efficiency of SHPCs in providing relief to the unemployed assumed increasing prominence in the later official state reports in California. Indeed, it was the central criterion used to assess performance in the state report for 1938 (California State Relief Administration 1938:14). Savings in relief costs owing to self-help cooperation arose because families who were eligible for relief did not apply for it; instead, they relied on their cooperative income. In addition, some families continued to accept relief and supplement their income with cooperative goods. There are, however, important measurement problems involved in estimating these savings. Kerr (1939:839) puts it this way: "It necessitated a knowledge of the members in a local organization who would have been on relief and how much this relief would have cost; and how much more relief the members would have received except for their self-help income." In 1935, it was estimated that 3,000 families eligible for relief worked in SHPCs and chose not to apply for relief. For six months the relief costs to these families would have been $900,000; the public aid given to cooperatives was $520,000. In addition, at the end of the period, $290,000 in plant, equipment, and materials remained in the hands of the cooperatives. Thus, through

TABLE 4.8

VALUE-ADDED AS A PERCENTAGE OF TOTAL OUTPUT FOR
SELF-HELP CO-OPS AND CONVENTIONAL FIRMS IN FIVE
MANUFACTURING ACTIVITIES, 1930–1939

Activity	SHPCs (1937–38)	Conventional 1939	Conventional 1930
Baking	38	51	19
Canning	30	37	26
Lumbering	18	63	67
Sewing	42	40	47
Soap making	42	45	42

SOURCES: Data for conventional firms for 1939 are from U.S. Bureau of the Census 1942a, 1942b; and for 1930 from Kerr 1939:746. SHPC data are taken from Kerr 1939:746.

SHPCs the government supported 2,000 families using only $230,000, a savings of $670,000 in six months (California State Relief Administration 1938:11).

In part because of the measurement problems inherent in this method, Kerr (1939:829–885) prefers a different method to compute relief savings. Using reliable information for individual organizations, relief savings per hour are estimated as the difference between compensation received by SHPC workers and the amount of public funds expended. Hence in 1936, hourly compensation to California SHPC workers averaged 26.5¢ per hour and the cost to public funds was 4.7¢ per hour. Thus, less than 5¢ of public money yielded over 26¢ of value to SHPC workers; the government saved 75 percent of relief costs to SHPC members by supporting cooperatives. In addition, the figures Kerr uses are conservative estimates of relief compensation. These figures only represent the goods, services, and cash that was formally distributed and reported. Meals furnished to workers and perishable food that was distributed to prevent spoilage are not included in compensation statistics. However, there are less optimistic estimates on the relief-saving value of SHPCs in California. In one report it is argued that "the net cost of the Federal and State Governments was . . . about one-half the value of the compensation of the self-help workers" (M.L.R. 1939c:1341). Even this report, however, indicates considerable relief savings.

Overall it seems clear that the state and federal relief funds used by SHPCs were well spent. For several years SHPCs were a cost-effective way of providing relief for the unemployed.

REHABILITATION OF THE UNEMPLOYED

The social and psychological functions of self-help cooperatives were never the subject of careful investigation by officials charged with monitoring the performance of SHPCs. Consequently, precious few data are available with which to empirically evaluate these dimensions of performance. Although the opinion surveys cited in the section on membership give statistical backing to claims of the favorable attitudes of the cooperators toward self-help, few other data of this kind are available. Two surveys reflect favorable attitudes toward self-help in the community at large. Eighty percent of the Californians surveyed in 1934–35 were in favor of self-help. A national survey conducted in 1938 by the American Institute of Public Opinion reported that 85 percent of those surveyed would like to see the unemployed produce goods for their own use (Kerr and Harris 1939:24).

Survey data reveal that the cooperatives generally were thought to be useful by and for everyone involved; for more specific information, records of direct observation are needed. Kerr and Harris rate the SHPCs as being "fairly successful" in maintaining the morale of members. In addition, cooperatives provided occupational training opportunities. Cooperatives focused members' thinking toward production when otherwise it would have been toward gaining greater relief payments (Kerr and Harris 1939:23).

Panunzio (1939:111) stressed the psychological aspect of self-help. He maintains that SHPCs helped people avoid "the psychological distress and the character breakdown suffered by the unemployed who have been compelled to eat the bitter bread of charity." Many others attest to the value of SHPCs in relieving the mental and physical distress consequent on unemployment. Members were able to regain the self-respect that was perhaps lost when they were forced to rely on relief.

Overall, self-help cooperatives were vehicles by which individuals and groups were able to avoid the personal and social disintegration often brought on with mass unemployment. The severe economic hardship of the Depression strained individuals as well as relationships between individuals; SHPCs allowed the unemployed to work together in a community to bear the strain more easily.

SUMMARY AND CONCLUSION

In sum we find that there is strong evidence that SHPCs were able to record substantial relief savings and some indication that SHPCs were effective in rehabilitating the unemployed. SHPCs were usually smaller than capitalist firms and, though able to grow, did so slowly, thus becoming progressively undercapitalized. Regarding labor productivity we find that: (1) although initially SHPCs were, on average, grossly inefficient compared with the average conventional firm, there is evidence that some SHPCs were as effective in adding value during the productive process; and (2) over time SHPCs were able to raise output per worker substantially, although average figures never approached those for conventional twin firms.

These findings on economic performance must be considered with reference to the peculiar conditions under which SHPCs commenced productive activities, the distinctive characteristics of their work force which lowered the quality and effectiveness of the labor input, the low quality and small amount of the capital input, and the nature of SHPC management. The performance of SHPCs is clearly better than at first appears. The fact that any SHPCs were able to come even remotely close to conventional averages is no mean achievement.[21]

EFFECTS OF GOVERNMENT POLICIES AND PRESCRIPTIONS FOR FUTURE POLITICS

At various points in this chapter we have indicated the importance of government policies for SHPCs. In this section we address this issue specifically. It is apparent that much of the uneven performance of SHPCs stemmed from conditions imposed on the cooperatives by the government, both state and federal. The fluctuations in policies of the California State Relief Administration meant that long-range planning in SHPCs was particularly difficult and burdened by uncertainties that conventional firms did not face. In light of the varying attitudes toward self-help held by the members themselves, the fluctuation in government policies and attitudes was especially disruptive. The government added to the uncertainty of the SHPC environment by its changing politics. The temptation to adjust policy to "correct" problems that arise in a new public program are great, but the adjustments made in the self-help program seem to have caused more disruption than correction.

Of special importance was the change introduced in 1937 whereby the new director declared that the state retained ownership of all equipment purchased. This new, forced separation of the workers from the ownership of the means of production was probably especially disruptive in those cooperatives most committed to the cooperative method on ideological grounds. Surely this declaration reduced the members' feeling that the cooperative was their own personal organization. During the same period, the autonomy of SHPCs tended to be reduced on issues such as the appointment of the manager and the establishment of production quotas. In addition, the accounting system imposed on SHPCs meant that cooperatives had to devote much of their administrative resources—certainly more than in comparable conventional firms—to bookkeeping. Without adequate cash markets, SHPCs experienced constant cash flow problems. The need to requisition supplies through government agencies also hindered effective performance. Of critical importance too in many states, such as California in 1939, was the decision to cease state financial aid to SHPCs. It can be argued that had the criterion and methods used by the government for evaluating performance been different, the conclusions and recommendations might have also been different. In turn, this suggests that different public policy decisions might have been taken and that the life of SHPCs perhaps might have been somewhat longer than was the case.

To gauge the effects of government policies more precisely, Kerr constructs a monthly index of production and divides the period of SHPC production into sections according to his evaluation of government policy. He identifies eight distinct periods of specific government policy. After comparing the time sequence of government policies with the fluctuations in the index of production, he concludes:

> The cooperatives were able to produce when given the opportunity. Government policy was the decisive factor influencing the volume of their production. When it was favorable, the monthly index of production was as high as 265; and when it restricted the cooperatives, the index fell as low as 47. (Kerr 1939:108)

Another way to examine the problem is by employing simple regression analysis. Using data on seventy California cooperatives, a study of the effects of government grants may be made. The amount of grant funds expended by individual cooperatives is regressed on total SHPC output. Table 4.9 shows simple regressions for the group as a whole and then for the subsets of large and small cooperatives.

The regression points to an unambiguous correlation between government grants and output which in all cases is statistically significant at the .005 level. Although the model does not control for other factors affecting SHPC performance, the results offer support for the view that in certain situations government financial support was critical for the success of capital-starved PCs.

In understanding why government policy was so erratic and often unhelpful, the following factors seem to be important. It is clear that neither state nor federal governments ever developed a clear-cut and consistent set of criteria with which to evaluate PCs. Rather than adopt a well-defined evaluative framework responsive to the special

TABLE 4.9

THE RELATIONSHIP BETWEEN FEDERAL GRANTS
AND OUTPUT IN 1935

Type	Correlation coefficient	t-value
All	.80709	9.206
Large	.71762	5.494
Small	.40333	4.062

NOTE: All coefficients are significant at the 0.005 level.

aims and purposes of SHPCs, a framework was used that was flexible and sensitive to short-term changes. In its strict emphasis on economic matters, this framework betrayed the influence of existing evaluative processes which were developed for other organizational forms. As such, evaluation was particularly susceptible to shifting political winds and changes in administration.

It has been observed that many California SHPCs were closed down when operating at their highest level of efficiency (Kerr 1939:chap. 31). Coinciding with improved performance in surviving SHPCs, however, were applications by many to be established as permanent productive organizations rather than remain as temporary relief units. These applications appear to have strengthened resistance in influential quarters, especially in the business community, against the SHPC form.[22] It is as if all along PCs were seen by government officials as a temporary expedient. They believed that it made sense to provide financial assistance while unemployment was widespread; but once the economy began to show signs of marked improvement, further support would serve only to slow down the recovery. Because they were not conventional organizational forms, it was believed that SHPCs necessarily caused the economy to perform suboptimally.

The experiences of SHPCs suggest lessons of lasting relevance for government policies in the general area of PCs. Various considerations point to the need for a specialized resource center to be established on a permanent basis to advise and assist with the particular problems of PCs of all kinds. Functions of this body would include assistance in devising suitable organizational structures, membership policies, and income policies. Technical assistance on a large variety of matters— for example, legal and financial—could be provided by this organization. The internal organization of the resource center would have to be designed to accommodate the varying needs of PCs transforming from capitalist divestitures, PCs representing new enterprises, and PCs transforming from other cooperative forms.

The special aims and purposes of PCs suggest that a separate accounting framework would have to be developed to monitor and evaluate performance. It should be designed to capture social benefits and, in order to reflect the special nature and problems of PCs, record information on aspects of membership, such as age, and aspects of governance, such as attendance at meetings and competition for elected offices.[23] Finally, cognizant of the scattered and often chaotic nature of official records on SHPCs, future official records on PCs should be kept in a centralized location.

The larger question is whether or not the government shelter organization would be able to effectively discharge its duties.[24] Specifically, would it be able to insulate itself sufficiently from shifting political winds in order to patiently develop long-term policies, rather than responding to the pressures to show quickly that the program is working? The experience of SHPCs leaves this question open to debate. The experience of SHPCs also suggests that such an institution is likely to have a much tougher job once the aim is delineated as the intention to establish permanent (rather than temporary relief) organizations. Again, the way in which the official government reports evaluated SHPC performance, particularly their focus on short-term dollars-and-cents criteria and their concomitant tendency generally to ignore social benefits, is instructive. This approach is strikingly reminiscent of the techniques used by the British House of Commons Public Accounts Committee when condemning government support of new worker cooperatives and by the Department of Industry when advising the Minister for Industry against this same policy (U.K. Committee on Public Accounts 1976). It is questionable whether studies will proceed much differently in the United States.

In addition to illuminating the needs for a shelter organization and specialized accounting procedures, the SHPC experience showed that PCs could provide employment, for a few years at least, for those who because of age or industrial change could not get a job. The use of self-management to relieve unemployment merits further examination. In particular, the experience of SHPCs suggests that the use of PCs as vehicles to employ either existing pockets of the unemployed or socioeconomic groups who experience above-average incidence of unemployment should be studied further.[25]

Finally, by examining variation in the ability of SHPCs to survive, we gain insights into which kinds of PCs (and in which contexts) are most likely to succeed and thus, are most deserving of public support. Three specific factors seem important. First, there appears to be an inverse relationship between the ability of a grant unit to survive and the size of the populated area within which it functions. Most successful were those in localities with fewer than 10,000 people. Community support apparently was most forthcoming in smaller communities. Second, the need for capital is reflected in the different survival rates of those SHPCs that did and did not receive state/federal support. More than half that did receive aid survived from 1933 to 1938; fewer than one-fifth that did not receive aid were able to persevere during that period. Thus, when financial resources are scarce, enterprises with low capital output ratios should be preferred; in cases where capital needs are greater, consideration should be given to workers who themselves partially bear the capital-supply function. Third, the nature of the project is important. Kerr (1939:457) argues that projects needing little technical skill, little capital, and with established technical processes, markets, and a high ratio of labor costs per unit of output are likely to perform best. Calculations based on data reported by Kerr for SHPCs in southern California from 1933 to 1938 support these arguments. The best survival rates were recorded by sewing (9/11) and canning (8/10) SHPCs, while only 14 of 36 gardening SHPCs, with insecure markets, survived more than three years.

CONCLUSION

The problems of self-help production cooperatives were manifold. Little capital, unstable and heterogeneous labor, untrained management, ideological confusion, and shifting government policies plagued the cooperatives. Despite these factors, they employed a large number of previously unemployed and seemingly unemployable people, supplied the basic necessities of life to many families, saved the government relief costs, and eased the psychological and sociological problems of many unemployed. The record shows that self-help cooperatives performed a valuable service. In short, the use of self-management to relieve unemployment merits further experimentation.

The history of SHPCs points to two essential elements of future government programs regarding PCs of all kinds. First, the nature, aims, and purposes of the self-managed sector must be clearly thought out and stated. A clear mission statement is an important precondition for success and allows for a meaningful evaluation of performance. Second, a consistent long-term policy commitment to the sector must be made. This commitment will allow the cooperatives to operate in a relatively stable environment.

Sectors of the labor force that seem unemployable to conventional firms and cyclical periods of massive unemployment are two problems to which governmental use of self-management obviously may be applied. More than anything else, the experience of self-help cooperatives should prompt the exploration of the potential that self-management holds for dealing with economic and social problems.

NOTES

1. The remaining 350 associations were primarily barter organizations. They collectively bartered surplus labor for surplus products but did not themselves engage in the production of new goods. See Kerr and Harris 1939:1–17.

2. For discussions of recent legislative proposals regarding the PCs in the United States, see U.S. Senate Select Committee on Small Business 1979:22–26.

3. For an interesting account of the origins of some California barter cooperatives, see Burgess 1933.

4. Most nongrant units were barter (and not productive) organizations. Accordingly, the subject of this paper is the grant (productive) units. The maximum number existing at any one time was 225 in 1935 (table 4.1). However, owing to the establishment of (or conversion to productive status of former barter organizations) new SHPCs after 1935, we estimate that about 250 different productive organizations existed during the 1930s.

5. See United States Department of Labor, Bureau of Labor Statistics, *Monthly Labor Review* (Oct. 1933):808, for an expanded account. Hereafter, this publication is referred to simply as *M.L.R.*

6. Kerr 1939:564. In 1938 a new federal law again allowed grants to be made by the government to SHPCs. No grants ever appear to have been made under this program.

7. See *M.L.R.* (1939a, 1939c). Note also that legislative activity at the state level continued into the 1940s. In 1941 in Utah, an act was passed that created a new body to direct the activities of SHPCs. See *M.L.R.* (1941).

8. This survey is reported in *M.L.R.* (1938).

9. See Jones 1979a, 1979b, and the historical essay by Jones (chapter 3 in this volume) for discussions of this point.

10. Survey results taken from Kerr 1939:390–395.

11. For a more complete discussion of performance for SHPCs see Schneider 1979.

12. For example, see California State Relief Administration 1936. In that, while most of a section of the report (part IV) records estimates of economic productivity, only three pages (pp. 57–59) cover relief savings, and there is no discussion of other benefits of SHPCs.

13. Harry Black, the acting assistant director and author of California State Relief Administration 1938 noted, "The conclusion is inevitable that the units go deeper and deeper into debt to the State month by month" (p. 22). Note also that the report was "prepared at the request of the members of the Citizens Relief Committee on the State Relief Administration." (cover page).

14. Note, however, that even during this brief period there is some evidence that productive efficiency improved. For example, see California State Relief Administration 1937, where it is noted that "the average production per man-hour was about 17 cents for the first half of 1935, and about 24 cents for the same period of 1936. This increase in the productivity of the cooperative labor was also noted in the semi-annual report, December 1935, page 43, where it was stated that during 1935 the average value per man-hour had increased from 16.6 cents for the first half to 23.1 cents for the second half of the year" (p. 8).

15. Because most of the SHPC data are aggregate for the entire SHPC sector in California, the data for conventional firms are aggregated in a capitalist twin sector. Each output category has been weighted to approximate the composition of the SHPC sector. The weights for canning, baking, sewing, lumbering, and soap making are 6,

1, 1, and 1, respectively. Data in monetary terms has been deflated according to the wholesale price index into 1935 dollars. The wholesale price index is used because the Division of Self-Help valued goods in the controlled period according to competitive wholesale prices.

16. Estimates of hours worked in SHPCs are given in Kerr 1939:756. Estimates for capitalist firms are interpolated from the chart in U.S. Department of Commerce 1973:41.

17. Labor force calculations were made by adding the total membership in grant units for June and December of the given year together with the December figure for the previous year (Kerr 1939:73) and then dividing by the comparable entries for number of grant units (ibid.:71). This averaging technique is used because both membership and number of units varied so much over the year. Output calculations were made in a similar way using the data in the last column of Kerr 1939:table 46.

18. Kerr (1939:738–740) argues that the output of SHPCs compared with that of many capitalist firms was much less than these figures imply. Comparing 1937 figures on SHPCs with 1930 census data for all firms, he concludes that "approximately one-third of the private business establishments in the United States . . . were in the same general (size) class (as SHPCs)."

19. Capitalist data are taken from U.S. Bureau of the Census, 1939 (1942a):121, 171, 418, 517, 780. SHPC data are calculated from Kerr 1939:713–719, 737.

20. The basic sources are Kerr 1939:tables 35–37, and California State Relief Administration (1938), appendix.

21. By making the following fairly reasonable assumptions, it can be concluded that SHPCs on average were more efficient than comparable capitalist forms. Assume that during a typical month: (i) SHPC labor on average worked only 40 percent of the hours worked by capitalist workers; (ii) SHPCs were considerably undercapitalized, perhaps on average having less than one-third of the capital of an average capitalist firm; (iii) because of the use of wholesale (rather than retail) prices, SHPC output was undervalued by about 20 percent; (iv) constant returns to scale prevail, and similar technologies exist in the average SHPC and the average capitalist firm. Then even if other things (such as the quality of labor) were equal, we would expect output per worker in the SHPC to be only (0.4 × 0.33 × 0.80) or 0.11 of that for a capitalist firm. The gap between average SHPC productivity and average capitalist firm labor productivity was not this great.

22. See also the resistance engendered in Idaho when some SHPCs sought to become fully self-supporting (Idaho Cooperative Loan Association 1939).

23. We have in mind a form based on the bilan cooperative, which was once used by French PCs. See Antoni 1970:107–127.

24. The further question concerns the likelihood of a U.S. administration establishing such an institution. It must be admitted that the chances of such a development are slim in a country without a strong labor movement, and probably nil during the term of the present Reagan administration. Yet, in a different political context it is not an impossibility. Few would have foretold the establishment of a cooperative bank in the United States a decade ago.

25. Elsewhere PCs have been used as a strategy for aiding particular disadvantaged groups in the labor force with great success. The Polish experience with cooperatives for the disabled is especially noteworthy. See Trampcznski 1973.

PART III

The Contemporary
Small Cooperative Movement

One of the striking results of the tumultuous social upheavals of the 1960s and early 1970s was the development of the small worker cooperative or collective movement. In urban areas all across the country, but particularly in the San Francisco Bay Area, the Boston/ Cambridge area, the Washington, D.C. area, Minneapolis, Austin, Ann Arbor, Seattle, and Eugene, hundreds of small democratically organized businesses grew up, mostly in the service sector of the economy. In the early days of the movement, many of the young men and women who staffed collectives were self-termed "refugees" from the 1960s movements. Even those who had not been deeply involved were aware that their lives had been significantly touched by one or another of the great issues from that period. On the one hand, the growth of the collective movement represented a weary retreat from the turmoil of massive protest into countercultural familial havens; on the other hand, it crystallized much of the most searching criticism made of American society during the 1960s while refocusing attention on what may be the most fundamental social issue of all, namely, the nature and structure of work and of ownership in our society. Of course, as the years have progressed many of the original members of the collective movement have moved on to other work; still the movement retains the countercultural quality they imparted to it. However, the central thrust of the movement—to develop decentralized, nonhierarchical, and humane workplaces—remains unchanged.

This section examines the broad outlines of the small worker cooperative movement and provides a detailed case study of one collective. In chapter 5, Robert Jackall and Joyce Crain describe the general composition, shape, and contours of the movement and explore, in a thematic way, some of the recurring dilemmas of collective work. The authors focus, in particular, on the anomalous and paradoxical character of cooperative institutions in a capitalist society. They suggest that the best hope for small cooperatives lies in their recognition of their anomalous character and in their concomitant willingness to unite in a creative way seemingly irreconcilable principles. In chapter 6, Robert Jackall extends and deepens this analysis of the paradoxes of collective work in his study of the Cheeseboard in Berkeley, California. Based on the experiences of the collectivists themselves, he explores how open conflict is a central feature of cooperative work, because of the freedom that collectives grant to workers, in contrast to bureaucratic work where conflict, though savage, is usually suppressed. At the Cheeseboard such open conflict is actually the key to its cohesion. By exploring these ambiguities, the essay provides a richly textured picture of the daily work life in a successful and long-lived collective.

5

The Shape of the Small Worker
Cooperative Movement

ROBERT JACKALL
AND
JOYCE CRAIN

Small worker cooperatives, or collectives, are a vital form of work organization found on the economic fringe of our capitalist society.[1] Democratically owned and operated by their workers, these cooperative enterprises are generally small urban businesses clustering in the service sector of the economy—in distribution, food production and service, retailing, repair and maintenance, and a variety of social services. We estimate that in the United States in 1980 there were at least 750 to 1,000 of these organizations producing goods or tangible services, which is a great increase from 1970 when very few existed.

This chapter is divided into three main parts. The first section is a brief presentation of descriptive statistical data on the collective movement derived from a set of surveys done between 1977 and 1980, as well as a discussion of some of the difficulties encountered collecting those data. The second section is an interpretation of those data, focusing on three issues: (1) the key characteristics of cooperative workers; (2) the typical career paths taken by individuals and groups in the collective movement; and (3) an analysis of some of the organizational dilemmas that small cooperatives face. In our view, these organizational dilemmas are important for understanding the peculiarities and potentials of the cooperative form of business. The data that underpin our discussion are extensive and varied; still, our examination is not meant to be an exhaustive or definitive statement, but rather a broad thematic overview of a complicated, sprawling social phenomenon. Finally, the concluding section will explore the significance of the anomalous character of cooperatives in a capitalist society.

AN OVERVIEW OF THE SMALL WORKER COOPERATIVE MOVEMENT

RESEARCHING THE MOVEMENT

Our research on small worker cooperatives was carried out under the aegis of the Center for Economic Studies in Palo Alto, California. In 1977, the Center received a grant from the Center for Studies of Metropolitan Problems of the National Institute of Mental Health to examine the ability of worker cooperatives to address unemployment, worker alienation, and other problems of the modern workplace.[2] Part of the task of the Center was to examine the then-burgeoning collective movement.

Small worker cooperatives are somewhat difficult to research for a variety of reasons. First, they are generally small, tight-knit, homogeneous groupings which operate by consensus rather than by majority rule; strong opposition even from one group member can undercut requests for research access, as often happened in our case. Understandably, internal group ties are more important than communication with outsiders. Second, this type of opposition, when it occurs, has structural rather than idiosyncratic roots. Small cooperatives are marginal economic organizations in our society; their workers are overworked and underpaid, and they see themselves as such. This economic marginality is compounded and in many respects shaped by the incongruity between the internal requirements of maintaining a democratic workplace and the external exigencies of the capitalist marketplace. The tensions generated by this incongruity make many members of collectives feel beleaguered, a feeling that can be quickly converted to a suspicion of those perceived to be representatives of the established order, particularly those thought to be merely observing rather than trying to change society. Third, even when access is gained, one must often settle for an interview with one person designated by the cooperative; usually the reason given for this is time constraint but, in our case, it often seemed to be a way of resolving disagreements in the cooperative about our requests for access. In any event, this was obviously an unsatisfactory and problematic way of getting information but sometimes the only one available. Fourth, small worker cooperatives seem to develop and flourish in geographical clusters where the social and cultural climate is favorable. In the

United States their largest concentrations are in the San Francisco Bay Area; in the Boston/Cambridge area; in Washington, D.C.; in Austin, Texas; in the Pacific Northwest, particularly near Eugene, Oregon; and in Minneapolis, Minnesota, and Ann Arbor, Michigan. On one hand, this clustering facilitates research; on the other, the constraints of time and money limited our own personal fieldwork to the first two areas listed above, although through an associate we covered Washington, D.C. as well. In addition, this volume contains as essay describing the largest collective in the Pacific Northwest, the Hoedads Co-op (see Christopher Gunn's essay in Part IV). Fifth, once access is gained, fieldwork in a cooperative organization, while demanding the peculiar skills of fieldwork anywhere—such as chameleonic adaptability—also, and more importantly, requires constant leaps of imagination to understand the potential significance of marginal, and very likely, transitory social structures.

Despite these problems, our research followed a fairly standard sequence. (1) Beginning in the summer of 1977, we first undertook preliminary fieldwork to identify the principal issues facing small cooperatives. We visited eighteen cooperative groups in the San Francisco Bay Area, interviewing more than two dozen cooperative workers as well as several long-time observers of the movement. (2) We extended and deepened this knowledge through a series of literature reviews, focusing in particular on the publications from the cooperative movement itself.[3] (3) We made intensive case studies of several cooperative groups. These included analyses of a book distribution firm, of a cooperative press which later failed, and of a retail cheese store. The last study constitutes the next chapter of this volume (Robert Jackall on the Cheeseboard) and suggests some of the ethnographic richness of the collective phenomenon. (4) Working with all of these sources of information, we fashioned a questionnaire for a nationwide mail survey. We should note that there are particular difficulties in mail survey research with marginal groups like small worker cooperatives. Generally, cooperative workers (for the most part sons and daughters of the bureaucratic new middle class) have an antibureaucratic mentality that regards most paperwork as a symbol of a destructive rational/technical social order. In this view, surveys are seen as deindividualizing exercises meaningless to internal group life. Our own mail survey to 521 groups (see appendix I for the final questionnaire and appendix II for a list of the organizations contacted to glean names of potential worker cooperatives) produced disappointing results (70 responses, only 22 of which were actually worker cooperatives). This spurred us to other efforts to obtain broader statistical data. (5) These efforts took the form of in-person surveys through the New School for Democratic Management which employed business biographies to get profiles of its client groups as well as on-site interviewing in the Boston/Cambridge and Washington, D.C. areas by a colleague and in the New York area by a local organization sympathetic to our research.[4]

A STATISTICAL LOOK AT THE MOVEMENT

These various efforts enabled us to compile a total statistical sample of ninety-five small worker cooperatives. This is a small sample, and its representativeness is problematic. Still, the data (tables 5.1, 5.2, 5.3) are interesting and, it should be noted, agree closely with the observations and reports of several other researchers who have also examined the small cooperative movement.[5] Moreover, in our own field research in two different areas of the country, the same patterns emerged.

We classified our results into six broad products/services categories (see table 5.1) which convey an accurate picture of the range of activities small worker cooperatives are engaged in. These categories and the percentage of each category to the total sample are: bookstores (7%); printing and publishing (18%); social services, mainly health related (10%); food distribution, including warehouses and distributors of products primarily to the cooperative movement (13%); nonfood sales and production, encompassing such products as energy systems, bicycles, films, and records (20%); and food sales and production typified by bakeries and restaurants (32%). One should note that almost half of our sample is engaged in a food-related business, and this is the general pattern of the movement. Utilizing the products/services categories, table 5.1 provides data on the length of time cooperatives have been in business, average net worth, and average sales. It also indicates the variety of legal forms cooperatives assume, since the laws in most states do not provide a unique form of incorporation for worker cooperatives. The patterns of initial funding sources for the different categories of cooperatives are also provided in table 5.1. Table 5.2 contains data on the average number of workers in each category, as well as their demographic and educational characteristics. Finally, available data on the remuneration of these workers is supplied in table 5.3.

Using these statistical data as a framework, we want to draw on our other knowledge of the small cooperative movement—our fieldwork, both preliminary and intensive; our extensive literature surveys; and our informal association with the movement over a number of years—to provide an interpretive analysis of some of the central characteristics and themes of the movement.

TABLE 5.1
Business Dimensions

Category	Sample size	Time in business med. (in yrs.)	avg.	Avg. net worth (000)	Avg. sales (000)	Legal Form (in %) Tax-able corp.	Co-op	Tax exempt	Part-ner ship	Initial Funding Source (in %) Loans: emp. & friends	Worker invst.	Grants/ govt. funds	Loans/grants fr. other co-ops
Bookstore	6	6.3	6.5	17.8	70.9		50		50	100			
Printing and publishing	17	6.0	8.4	NA	135.0	100				56	11	33	
Social services	10	5.0	5.7	13.1	63.2			100		14		86	
Food distribution	12	4.5	4.6	41.0	563.0	57	29		14	67	17		17
Nonfood sales and production	19	4.0	5.2	30.4	63.8	58	12	12	6	62	19	13	6
Food sales and production	31	4.0	5.0	13.6	210.0	83	9		13	65	12	6	18
All categories combined	95	5.8	5.0	23.3[a]	200.9[a]	66	14	12	9	57	13	22	9

[a] Since there is a wide variance in the net worth and sales of these organizations, a more representative statistic is the median. The median net worth for all groups was $18,500 and the median annual sales were $80,000.

TABLE 5.2

CHARACTERISTICS OF WORK FORCE

Category	Sample size	Avg. no. of empl.	Sex (in %) M	Sex (in %) F	Avg. Age	% White	Education (in %) High School	Education (in %) Some College	Education (in %) College Grad.	Education (in %) Graduate School
Bookstore	6	4	35	65	29.5	88	13	13	47	27
Printing and publishing	17	8	39	61	29.4	87	3	19	52	26
Social services	10	8	21	79	29.6	96	5	36	38	21
Food distribution	12	12	37	62	27.8	93	19	48	24	9
Nonfood sales and production	19	13	54	46	28.1	98	30	45	74	26
Food sales and production	31	10	34	66	25.8	90	19	39	36	6
All categories combined	95	10[a]	39	61	27.7	93	15	34	38	13

[a] Since there is a wide variance in the size of these organizations and the number of employees, a more representative statistic is the median. The median number of employees is 6.5.

TABLE 5.3

REMUNERATION OF RESPONDENTS

Category	Average hourly earnings of worker cooperatives	Average hourly earnings by industry[a]
Bookstore	$3.58	$4.28
Printing and publishing	3.78	7.09
Social services	5.13	5.69
Food distribution	4.17	6.66
Nonfood sales and production	3.78	Not available
Food sales and production	2.73	5.87
Average—all categories	3.63	

[a] SOURCE: *Employment and Earnings, February 1980*, U.S. Department of Labor, BLS, 27, no. 2:94–100.

AN INTERPRETIVE ANALYSIS OF THE SMALL COOPERATIVE MOVEMENT

CHARACTERISTICS AND CAREERS OF COOPERATIVE WORKERS

The first thing that strikes an observer of the cooperative movement is that its participants are young (average age 27.7 years), educated (51% have college degrees, and an additional 34% have some college), and white (93%) (see table 5.2). In short, the movement is a distinctly white middle-class phenomenon; the low salaries and erratic uncertain career paths exclude, by self-selection, most minorities and all but a handful of those from working-class origins. This movement is one of the direct successors of the social upheavals of the late 1960s which were largely middle-class based—specifically, the antiwar, university reform, and countercultural movements. Its psychological basis, as with most of those movements of the 1960s, is the progressive institutionalization in the middle class of what Kenneth Keniston (1971) has called the "stage of youth"—an extension of adolescence and sanctioned ambivalence marked by experimental tentative probing without the felt necessity for lasting commitments to other people, to careers, or to institutions. Unlike earlier movements, however, the collective movement is not focused around a single overriding issue, such as Vietnam, which sooner or later *had* to be resolved; nor is it the result of a whirlwindlike, but short-lived, cultural explosion, such as the emergence of the counterculture movement in the late 1960s. Rather, the collective movement is focused on, by way of rejection, the most central institutions in American society: the big bureaucratic organization, the very lifeblood of the new middle class; hierarchically arranged and professionalized work, hallmarks of these same bureaucracies; organized competition, the mode of status allotment within bureaucracy; and orderly, stable careers, the enduring promise of the big organization. In place of these, men and women in cooperatives advocate small, decentralized participative workplaces where one's present well-being is not mortgaged for future security. With such values, collectivists are best seen as another cycle in the long history of youthful revolt in this century against the cultural and social consequences of the triumph of industrial capitalism.[6]

It is interesting to note that a slight majority (61%) of the workers in small cooperatives are women. The movement seems to appeal to women because of both traditional female socialization and new feminist attitudes. Traditional female socialization, of course, propels many women toward occupations in food-related and social service work, and these abound in the collective movement. Moreover, feminism has placed a premium on group cooperation and camaraderie among women, and on doing work with political implications; both of these experiences are widely available in the cooperative movement. Also, the cooperative movement is still one of the few areas in our social structure where women can not only earn pay equal to men's for equal work, but also where they can choose to work in occupations that are normally male preserves—such as trucking, warehousing, and carpentry. Still, in all likelihood the numerical dominance of women in the cooperative movement is the result of the same alienation from bureaucratization that fuels the collective movement as a whole. Women may simply be somewhat more attuned than men to the advantages of collective work because the collective movement stresses the same virtues of self-reliance and initiative extolled by contemporary feminism.

Individual Careers and Crises.   Cooperative workers go through patterned career cycles similar to those that all occupational groups experience. The differences are that career cycles of cooperative workers are more informal, more intense, and more disjunctive. Friendship networks are the key selective mechanism for cooperatives. It is virtually impossible to become a member of most cooperatives without personally knowing at least one already established member. Such informal selection insures homogeneity, perhaps a prerequisite for social groups that operate by consensus. We shall comment later on the organizational risks of institutionalized homogeneity. The important point here is that the affective ties which are the basis for selection into collectives bind workers to one another and to their groups in very personal and intense ways. On one hand, such ties provide collectives with a resiliency that is necessary to cope with their marginality; on the other, they personalize and thus intensify even routine disputes, often producing tangled emotional situations that are very difficult to reconcile. Many collectives founder on the very intensity that is their hallmark.

The key experiences, good and bad, of collective work are marked by a similar intensity. Initially, workers find the control of the workplace that collectives afford them a profoundly liberating experience, particularly those who have had traditional work experience. This is usually coupled with a real pride in their work, which stems from their control of the workplace and from their co-ownership of a business. Therefore, they are able to be the craftsmen, the honest tradesmen, the dispensers of wholesome foods, or the nonbureaucratic social workers they want to be. Because they control their daily work and their work-related self-images, they have a strong feeling of shaping their social identities in positive ways (Jackall 1976). Moreover, these experiences are shared and, as a consequence, camaraderie in collectives runs deep. We want to stress the profound motivating quality of these experiences. Despite the many problems of worker cooperatives, they offer a unique place in our society for many young people to taste actual self-determination, ownership of productive capital, and the singular joy of seeing one's self and one's deepest values expressed in one's work.

The euphoria that accompanies such experiences is difficult to sustain, however, principally because of the economic marginality of cooperatives. The median net worth of all the organizations in our survey is only $18,500, and the median annual sales figure is only $80,000. Since the median number of employees in the sample organizations is 6.5, these are very small figures indeed (see tables 5.1 and 5.2 for a complete breakdown). Start-up money comes principally from loans from family, friends, or other co-ops, or from investments from the workers themselves (see table 5.1). Access to normal capital markets is severely limited, either because banks or funding agencies will not lend to worker cooperatives or because they wish to impose controls unacceptable to cooperative groups. As a result, most small worker cooperatives are permanently undercapitalized and must rely on labor intensity to produce their surplus. Wages, however, are low (see table 5.3) and fall below prevailing rates for their occupations. Only the social service category comes close to the average hourly rate paid in capitalist enterprises.[7] And, except in rare cases, benefits are limited, with only modest health or vacation payments available. Such marginality in the marketplace constantly throws workers back upon themselves and their groups and, over a period of time, can turn the intensity that marks the cooperative experience into a burden.

The principal career crises of cooperative workers are directly related to the external economic marginality of cooperative ventures. The possibility of economic collapse is an ever-present danger to most worker cooperatives and obviously constitutes the most extreme sort of career crisis for a group of employees. We do not know with any accuracy how long cooperative businesses last. Although our survey showed that the median time in business for the groups surveyed was 5.8 years (see table 5.1) one must bear in mind that most of these organizations were born in the 1970s as part of a social movement. Therefore, their potential longevity is still undetermined. We were also unable to ascertain with any accuracy what the failure rate is for worker cooperatives. It is doubtful, however, that the failure rate is any greater than the very high failure rate of small businesses in general.

There is rarely a clear-cut denouement for cooperative groups; rather, a group begins having economic troubles, limps along gallantly by extracting more and more work from its members, until finally when many members in the group or at least the key individuals become burned out and withdraw, it quietly closes up shop or continues to exist but not as a cooperative. Burnout, mentioned repeatedly in the literature on collectives, may be seen as one psychological response to resolve long, enervating declines or to withdraw from a stable but very marginal status quo.

A different sort of career crisis is generated by the flat career paths typical of small worker cooperatives. To some extent, the lack of expansive opportunities in these groups is a matter of conscious choice resting on a democratic ideology that recoils from placing one individual above another. More immediately, however, this lack of opportunities results from the scarcity of resources available to cooperatives. The upshot is that young, middle-class men and women, schooled from their infancies in the virtues of upward mobility, enter groups that offer no opportunity to achieve a higher position and little opportunity to explore, at least through one's work, new areas of one's self and thus grow. In part this is because the labor-intensive demands of cooperatives are so high and time-consuming. The result is that, except in a few unusual organizations that have achieved a balance between the requirements of the group and the personal needs of its members, most men and women in the movement expect to and, in fact, do move on after a stint at cooperative work. While moving on is the only rational choice for individuals to make in order to honor their own potentials, such institutionalized transience has clear and detrimental consequences for cooperative groups. In small organizations, the crises of individuals play a large role in determining organizational fates.

ORGANIZATIONAL DILEMMAS

Just as the careers and crises of individuals in the movement are shaped largely by external forces, so the organizational dilemmas of small worker cooperatives tend to develop from their anomalous status in a capitalist, bureaucratic society. In a market society that is increasingly bureaucratic—fragmented, standardized, and above all, hierarchical— and where there are limited opportunities for spontaneity or self-direction at work, worker cooperatives, small and large, are important arenas where men and women can try to establish whole new forms of management, authority, and relationships with their co-workers. Worker cooperatives are decentralized where centralization is the norm; they encourage spontaneity where standardization is dominant; and they provide people with great freedom where social uniformity is often imposed. We want to examine a few of the internal organizational dilemmas such incongruency with the larger social structure generates.

Deprofessionalization Versus the Need for Expertise.   One of the crucial characteristics of the small worker cooperative movement since the early 1970s has been a reaction against the monopolization of knowledge so central to professionalism. American society is increasingly dominated by experts—formally trained, self-governing, certified guardians and practitioners of knowledge. Many small cooperatives, in keeping with their general antibureaucratic stance, set as one of their principal goals the democratization of knowledge and, in particular, the goal of making technology accessible to people. This is undoubtedly a very worthwhile aim since extreme specialization of knowledge is at the root not only of many social ills but also of many moral ills in our society. However, the ideology of deprofessionalization, still widely extant in cooperative groups, is fraught with three dangers which create troubling organizational problems. First, this ideology often becomes tinged with a more general antirationalism, indeed anti-intellectualism, which is sterile at its core and which promotes the search for simple answers to complex problems. Some collectives have atrophied as much from a lack of critical thinking and imagination as anything else.

Second, the ideology of deprofessionalization understandably slows the proliferation of cooperatives with a professional orientation. For instance, many young men and women came out of the movements of the 1960s and went into the professions, formed radical caucuses there, and were ripe for alternative work arrangements. They found, however, that in the small worker cooperative movement their hard-earned skills were not valued and were often resented. With the notable exceptions of some law cooperatives and family health clinics, which have democratized knowledge while reserving certain judgments—and legal liability—to the lawyers and doctors in their groups, cooperatives have been unable to work out arrangements where professional knowledge and skill are respected and utilized without being made into a fetish. Third, and perhaps most important, the ideology of deprofessionalization leads some cooperatives to forgo expertise even in their business practices, often with disastrous consequences. There are numerous stories in the cooperative movement about groups running into severe economic problems without giving thought either to developing their own business expertise or to consulting an outside business expert.

Business today requires more expertise than ever before. Markets are more segmented and complicated; competition is more intense; and the need for long-term rational planning is a necessity even for small businesses. Cooperatives have to find better ways to integrate experts or at least expert knowledge into their social structure and ideology. The presently inactive New School for Democratic Management was the first organization to address this need in an institutional way. More recently, the emergence of several groups, both national and regional, geared toward providing technical expertise to the cooperative movement (e.g., the Industrial Cooperative Association in Somerville, Massachusetts, and the Philadelphia Association for Cooperative Enterprise) suggests that some cooperatives are beginning to recognize that the goal of deprofessionalization may depend on a judicious reliance on professionals.

Freedom Versus Cohesion.   Small cooperative workplaces provide great freedom to workers in contrast to the conformity and subordination demanded in big corporations. They allow workers room to make everyday work decisions, to participate in shaping overall policy, and essentially to live their lives as they please. Whenever a group of individuals, even those with common goals, have such freedom, the result is an ongoing state of conflict—a struggle of personal wills. The problem, of course, is that any group of people must develop some degree of cohesion in order to function at all, particularly small groups that are hard pressed economically. This dilemma, in one form or another, runs through all the literature on small worker cooperatives. How do cooperatives achieve cohesion while honoring the freedom they promise?

Most cooperatives try to avoid this dilemma through their homogeneous selection, a phenomenon discussed earlier from the perspective of the individual. There is evidence that in this regard cooperatives may not be too different from other businesses. It seems that a great number of jobs in our economy are allocated through some type of informal mechanism. It is our impression, however, that cooperatives place a higher premium than other organizations on affective attributes. From an organizational standpoint, a friendship network is certainly an effective mechanism for ensuring similarities in members' backgrounds, world views, work habits, and aspirations, which in turn reduces the diversity of an organization's membership as well as some of the potential grounds of conflict. The dilemma is that this may also be the root of long-run atrophy. Organizations cannot expect to maintain their vitality without constant infusion of new ideas, whatever the costs in social cohesion.

Some cooperatives end up trimming their members' freedom by demanding adherence to some ideology. A portion of the cooperative movement in the San Francisco Bay Area, for example, is quite ideological, and one can find there varieties of anarchist, marxist, and democratic centralist groups that require doctrinaire stances of their members. Other groups do not demand adherence to an ideological line, but rather to points of unity which serve as a common conceptual ground. The problem with demands for ideological conformity of any sort is the risk of factionalism and, in fact, the cooperative movement, particularly in San Francisco and Minneapolis, was riven in the late 1970s by serious ideological disputes. These occurred not only between organizations but also within organizations and led to episodes such as the seizure of property, lockouts, verbal abuse of others, and the dissolution of scores of individual cooperatives and the collapse of whole federations.[8] The surest way to lay the basis for conflict among cooperative workers is to prescribe a certain set of beliefs: the contradiction between freedom in the workplace and ideological rigidity will sooner or later cause extreme tensions.

Increased conflict itself, however, as several essays in this volume point out, is an inevitable consequence of increased freedom in the workplace. Paradoxically, cooperative work has a greater level of open conflict than traditional work situations because it does not suppress the tension, competition, and disagreement among people that any work produces. But such conflict need not be divisive. As the case of the Cheeseboard of Berkeley, California, clearly illustrates (see chap. 6), conflict can, in fact, be cohesive and, indeed, constructive (see also chap. 9 by Gamson and Levin). What is required is a commitment to the ongoing negotiation of conflict and indeed of social reality itself. In the Cheeseboard, cooperation emerges through the embrace of conflict. In such a way, groups can create and recreate themselves while giving their members room to act as they wish.

Spontaneity Versus the Need for Permanence.   One of the keys to maintaining a democratic work situation is to foster an organizational spontaneity—that is, a responsiveness to new ideas, a willingness to break up routines when they become problematic, or indeed to change whole organizational arrangements to fit workers' needs and aspirations. These characteristics are especially necessary in collectives since, as we have indicated, most often collective workers are young, highly mobile, and in transition in their own lives. This means that turnover in collectives is high (though certainly not as high as in the highly routinized secondary labor market where rates of between 20% and 33% a year are typical) and that without organizational responsiveness to newcomers, workplace democracy becomes meaningless. Spontaneous organizations, however, are inherently unstable and lack the permanence that big bureaucracies exhibit. To the extent that they are perceived as impermanent, they become problematic to the very workers who constitute them. No one likes to pour his or her energy into an organization that is known to be here today and gone tomorrow: men and women in our society, even young people in transition, are very oriented to building their lives around institutional pillars. When these pillars are known to be shaky, it makes sustained effort extremely difficult. Further, if cooperatives are known to be impermanent, what possible social impact can they be seen to have in a society dominated by "eternal" multinationals?

Cooperatives face, therefore, the problem of being both spontaneous and institutionally solid. What this probably requires is an acceptance of certain bureaucratic features—for example, more careful record keeping, codification of procedures, orientation programs to provide newcomers with a thorough sense of the history and lore of a cooperative, and so on. Despite its dangers, such standardization can bring several benefits, among them the elimination of inevitably repeating past mistakes. Moreover, one can mitigate the dangers of standardization by standardizing spontaneity, that is, by combining rational planning techniques, procedures, and mechanisms with a commitment to suppleness and flexibility in applying them. Many cooperatives are now moving in this direction. For instance, a common pattern is to establish a regular mechanism (such as a weekly operational meeting) specifically devoted to discussing which business procedures are working, what their implications are for the business itself and for the social structure of the group, and what changes, if any, should be made. In these small ways, the institutional frameworks for a long-term organizational future can be pieced together, while maintaining the characteristic vitality of the organizational form.

CONCLUSION: THE SIGNIFICANCE OF ANOMALY

Men and women in cooperatives and social theorists alike often see cooperatives as socialist islands in a capitalist sea. The imagery here is of small outposts, bastions of socialist virtue and practice, in a hostile environment. To some extent, this view is an accurate one because, as we have argued in this essay, the internal structure of worker cooperatives directly contradicts basic institutions of our market society, which is not sympathetic to worker-owned and -managed businesses of any sort. Moreover, cooperatives are trying to shape new institutional arrangements and relationships between people; that is their great strength and, in our view, the reason why every effort should be made to create the social conditions that will enable them to flourish. Our examination of some of the dilemmas worker cooperatives face, however, suggests that this oppositional imagery may oversimplify the actual relationships between cooperatives and capitalist institutions of the larger society and may indeed obscure solutions to those dilemmas. Cooperatives are organizational anomalies which by nature are paradoxical. Those that survive and flourish do so not by celebrating their oppositional character to the larger system—in a sense, that is a given—but by finding organizational frameworks where seemingly irreconcilable principles are merged, such as working toward the demonopolization of knowledge through some reliance on professionals, or developing genuine cooperation by embracing conflict, or standardizing spontaneity.

What this demands of men and women in cooperatives is a personal and organizational flexibility—essentially a willingness to adapt without being transformed, to innovate without abandoning principles, and to borrow from the larger social structure those tools needed to survive. It is curious, indeed paradoxical in itself, that several small worker cooperatives have to date lacked this kind of flexibility, especially given the experimental character of the organizational form. The results have been, needlessly in our view, the career paths that we have outlined: great enthusiasm and hard work at the founding of a cooperative; incipient financial and personal problems; growing factionalism and disillusionment with the organization; the burning out and/or moving on of key members; and finally, organizational disintegration or continued existence in a noncooperative form—in short, what men and women in cooperatives call histories of noble failures. Clearly, however, as the Cheeseboard, the Hoedads, and other cases of small and large, long-lived, successful cooperatives demonstrate, it is possible to retain the nobility without having to endure the failure. To accomplish this requires an acceptance of the paradoxical nature of worker cooperatives as well as a commitment to the suppleness needed to resolve the dilemmas cooperatives pose.

For social theorists, the paradoxical nature of cooperatives has a more abstract but no less important significance. The anomaly of these organizations makes them not only a fruitful place to expand the dimensions of organizational taxonomy and theory (Rothschild-Whitt

1979), but also, because of the incongruity of cooperatives with the larger society, an excellent place to develop a grounded critique of some of the central institutions of our society. Moreover, insofar as cooperatives successfully develop the suppleness to merge seemingly opposing principles and create new workable organizational forms, they can lead to an understanding of both the theory and practice of creative social change.

NOTES

1. We will generally use the technical term *small worker cooperative* throughout this essay to denote small worker-owned and -managed businesses. The word *collective*, widely used in the cooperative movement, is derived from the leftist political tradition, particularly from the anarchist wing of pre-1939 Republican Spain. An influential book conveying this tradition, and its terminology, to American worker cooperatives was Sam Dolgoff (1974). The experience of Maoist China, often highly romanticized, was perhaps an even more important source for ideas about collectives. The word is currently used, however, not only as self-description by leftist groups of every political shading but also by other groups who have no specific political affiliations or ambitions at all—such as dance, theater, or mime groups and even capitalist businesses aimed at youth. The word seems to be selected now more for its countercultural ring rather than for its denotative attributes.

2. The title of the grant (MH29607), which extended from June 1977 to July 1980, was "Producer Cooperatives: Urban Work and Mental Health."

3. Some of the key sources of information about the collective movement are: *Cascade: Journal of the Northwest*, Box 1492, Eugene, Oregon 97401; *Communities: Journal of Cooperative Living*, Twin Oaks Community, Rt. 4, Louisa, Virginia 23903; *Cooperative Times: Journal of the Lane County Federation of Worker Controlled Businesses*, Eugene, Oregon; *Co-ops and Social Change Newsletter and Directory*, P.O. Box 4595, Austin, Texas 78765; *D.C. Democratic Economics*, Strongforce, 2121 Decatur Place, N.W., Washington, D.C. 20008; *Food Cooperative Directory*, 106 Girard Street, Room 110, Albuquerque, New Mexico 87106; *Elements*, Public Resource Center, 1747 Connecticut Avenue, N.W., Washington, D.C. 20009; *Jam Today: California Journal of Cooperation*, P.O. Box 195, Davis, California 95616; *The New Harbinger: A Journal of the Cooperative Movement*, North American Student Cooperative Organization, Box 1301, Ann Arbor, Michigan 48106; *Rain: Journal of Appropriate Technology*, 2270 N.W. Irving, Portland, Oregon 97210; *SCOOP: Cooperation in the Northcountry*, Scoop, Powerhorn Station, Box 7271, Minneapolis, Minnesota 55407; *Self-Reliance*, Institute for Self-Reliance, 1717 18th Street, N.W., Washington, D.C. 20009; and *Working Papers for a New Society*, 123 Mount Auburn Street, Cambridge, Massachusetts 02138.

4. Robert Margolis (1978 and 1980) undertook on-site interviewing for us in the Boston/Cambridge and Washington, D.C. areas in the summer of 1978. His reports and paper present data on the nineteen collectively run businesses and service or-

ganizations that he visited and also contain some trenchant observations on the problems collectivists face. Project Work assisted us in the Greater New York area and in Rockland County by contacting several groups and administering our questionnaire to those that were worker cooperatives.

5. See, for example, Gamson et al. 1978 and Gamson 1979; Case and Taylor 1979; and Rothschild-Whitt 1976.

6. The origins of this revolt may be found in the extraordinarily vital collection of men and women—anarchists, communists, free love advocates, labor organizers, literary figures, artists, agitators, and free spirits of every sort—who came together in Greenwich Village in the first part of this century. Together they claimed and won a personal freedom of expression which lay the basis for all the other cultural revolts of the young in this century. In comparing this period with the 1960s, William O'Neill, a student of both periods, calls the early Greenwich Village period "an earlier and better revolution." See O'Neill 1978:xvi.

7. Higher salaries among workers in the social services category were in part due to the now defunct CETA program and to support from other grants.

8. For a description of the factional battles in the San Francisco Bay Area, see People's Cooperating Communities Trucking Collective (1976). For a view of the breakup of the Minneapolis cooperative federation, see Rishkojski 1977 and Olsen and Olson, 1980. Finally, for an interesting description of the collapse of a federation of cooperatives in Austin, Texas, see the collection of articles in *Communities: Journal of Cooperative Living* (1977).

APPENDIX I

Mail Questionnaire of Producer Cooperatives

Name of organization _____ Date established _____

Address _____ Phone _____

Name of person(s) completing form _____

1. Brief description of product(s) made or service(s) performed _____

   _____

2. Is your organization incorporated? _____ Non-profit? _____ Other (please specify legal form) _____

3. If your organization charges for its products or services, what was your gross
   revenue from sales, fees or other income during 1975? _____
   1976? _____ Estimated 1977? _____

4. If your organization provides free goods or services, how many people or households did you reach in 1976? _____ Expect to reach in
   1977? _____

5. Please fill in the following financial information:

Assets	Fiscal 1975	Fiscal 1976
Cash		
Accounts receivable		
Inventory		
Fixed assets (net or deprec.)		
Other (specify)		
Total assets		
Liabilities		
Accounts payable		
Loans outstanding		
Other (specify)		

Total liabilities _____   _____
Net worth (total assets
less total liabilities) _____   _____

6. Have you ever been refused a government or commercial loan? _____

   If so, why? _____

7. Please supply the following information on worker members of your organization.

	Paid	Volunteer
Number of males		
Number of females		
Approximate age of most worker members		
Education:		
High school only		
Some college		
College graduate		
Graduate school		
Average number of hours worked per week		
Wage/salary scale:		
Highest		
Lowest		
Average		

8. Did your organization generate a surplus beyond wages in 1976? _____ If so,

   how was it distributed? _____

   _____

9. Circle the statement which best describes how work is structured in your organization.
   (a) Each person performs a specific task for a long period of time.
   (b) Everybody shares all the tasks almost all the time.
   (c) A few people have specialized jobs and all the rest are shared.
   (d) Other (please specify) _____

   _____

10. Who makes the everyday decisions in your organization? _____

    _____

    Who makes the major policy decisions and how is this done? _____

    _____

11. What do you consider your organization's most significant problems and most important successes?

APPENDIX II

Organizations Contacted for Names of Worker Cooperatives

All Cooperating Assembly, Minneapolis, Minnesota
Arizona/New Mexico Federation of Co-ops
Associated Cooperatives, Richmond, California
Center for Community Economic Development, Cambridge, Massachusetts
Confederation of Appatlantic Co-ops, Roanoke, Virginia
Co-op West, Los Angeles, California
Co-ops and Social Change Network, Austin, Texas
Cooperative League of the U.S.A., Washington, D.C.
Cornucopia, Chicago, Illinois
Delaware Valley Coalition for Cooperation, Philadelphia, Pennsylvania
Distributing Alliance of the North Country Cooperatives, Minneapolis, Minnesota
Earthwork, San Francisco, California
Eastern Massachusetts Federation of Cooperatives, Cambridge, Massachusetts
Federation of Southern Cooperatives, Atlanta, Georgia
Greater Illinois People's Co-op, Chicago, Illinois
Institute for Self-Reliance, Washington, D.C.
Maine Federation of Cooperatives, Hallowell, Maine
Michigan Federation of Food Co-ops, Ann Arbor, Michigan
Milwaukee Area Co-op Services, Milwaukee, Wisconsin
Minnesota Association of Co-ops, Saint Paul, Minnesota

New England Cooperative Training Institute (NECTI), New Haven, Connecticut

New England Food Cooperative Organization, Allston, Massachusetts

Philadelphia Federation of Food Co-ops, Philadelphia, Pennsylvania

Southern California Cooperating Community, Los Angeles, California

Southside Community Enterprises, Minneapolis, Minnesota

Strongforce, Washington, D.C.

Western Massachusetts Federation of Cooperatives, Orange, Massachusetts

6

Paradoxes of Collective Work: A Study of the Cheeseboard, Berkeley, California

ROBERT JACKALL

INTRODUCTION

For a variety of reasons the small worker cooperatives or collectives that are flourishing in urban areas across America have unmistakable sociological significance. In contrast to bureaucratized work, for example, these cooperative work organizations create distinctly different experiences for workers (see Jackall 1976), though all the dimensions of these differences are still not clearly understood. Collective organizations are subject to the same tendencies toward bureaucratization (Weber 1958) and oligarchy (Michels 1915) as any other kind of organization and represent, therefore, fruitful and manageable sites for the study of such tendencies. At the same time, members of collective organizations generally fight against, on principle, bureaucratizing and centralizing tendencies (though not always successfully); as a result, these groups are ideal sites for studying people's moral and affective, as opposed to instrumental, commitments to organizations (see Kanter 1972).

This essay focuses on one of the most successful and long-lived of these collectives—the Cheeseboard in Berkeley, California, a retail store specializing in fine domestic and imported cheeses. The essay is an ethnographic account of the structures of the Cheeseboard collective and of the experiences of its members.* In particular, it focuses

*This essay was written in 1978. See the research note and afterword for some more recent (late 1983) details.

109

on the relationships of collective members to the organization and on the dilemmas and paradoxes that collective work creates for both the organization and its workers. The central paradox in the Cheeseboard, which affects all other aspects of the collective, emerges from the democratic structure of the store which allows workers great freedom of individual action and expression. The product of such freedom, even among people with somewhat similar backgrounds and experiences, is an ongoing state of open conflict and often tension. Clearly, workers in traditional bureaucratic workplaces also experience conflict, but the structural root of this conflict is not freedom but rather a competitive constriction. Further, bureaucratic structures repress and contain conflict rather than allow it free expression. The collective, however, even while it generates conflict, depends for its success on cooperation and negotiation. As a consequence there is a disparity between the structural genesis of conflict in the collective and its functional imperative for cooperation. This essay explores in depth how Cheeseboard workers as a group resolve or at least come to live with such contradictions. Only through a detailed analysis of individual cases can we extend our knowledge of phenomena such as the collective movement or understand why certain collectives such as the Cheeseboard flourish while others bloom, but fade rapidly.

THE SHAPING OF A COLLECTIVE

The Cheeseboard is the leading cheese store in the San Francisco Bay Area, marketing hundreds of quality cheeses from all over the world. A visitor to the store is beseiged everywhere by the sight and pungent aroma of milk which, in Clifton Fadiman's phrase, has successfully made the leap to immortality. Huge 300-pound wheels of Swiss cheese dominate the wide front window of the store. The 40-foot long refrigerated display case is filled with blocks, slabs, and slices of cheese of every description. On one side of the case, customers roam back and forth selecting their favorite cheeses; behind the case is a work area, with long hardwood slicing counters, scales, and a cash register. Several 5- to 6-pound wheels of brie ripen on the counter near the register. Cheese and tomato sandwiches on freshly baked bread, made by the morning work crew for lunchtime sale to local workers, are stacked near the scales. On the wall above the workers is a huge blackboard, listing the most popular cheeses and their current prices. To the right as one faces the display case stands a beverage cooler filled with juices and premium foreign beers. Behind the cooler is the kitchen area where workers do all the food preparation and most of the slicing and wrapping of cheese for display. In the early mornings the smell of bread baking from the huge commercial ovens in the kitchen permeates the entire store and mingles with the enduring earthy smell of cheese. Behind the kitchen is the home-built walk-in refrigerator where workers keep extra stock of their commodity.

The Cheeseboard was started in 1967 as a privately owned business by a married couple in their middle thirties. Both husband and wife had excellent business acumen, and they quickly developed a thriving enterprise in what was an unexploited specialty field in the area. As the business grew, the owners hired a few workers, mostly part-time, paid them well, and provided good benefits. Even more important, the owners established an extended familial atmosphere in the store, and this, together with the sheer force of their personalities, generated intense feelings of loyalty among the workers. Both of the owners were, and remain today, charismatic figures of a sort—the woman gracious, warm, loving, and generous; the man magnetic, vastly experienced and traveled, and imbued with a deeply felt, though eclectic, political vision of a new society. It was, in fact, the husband's perception of a sharp contradiction between his political ideals and the private ownership of the Cheeseboard that prompted him to suggest, in 1971, that the six wage-workers of the store, together with the two owners, buy the business and make it into a collective. The idea was well received, and the following mechanism was used to make the transfer from private to collective ownership. All the workers, including the two owners, deducted $.50 an hour from their wages and pooled their money until a total of $10,000 was reached, which took the better part of two years.[1] The owners accepted this amount for the store, and the Cheeseboard became a genuinely worker-owned and -managed enterprise, though nominally it assumed corporate form.

The business has continued to grow and, with its economic growth, the collective membership has also expanded. By 1975, the volume of business was more than $5,000 a week, a 67 percent increase over 1971, and the tiny converted alleyway that housed the store could no longer contain the throngs of customers it attracted. So in July 1975, the Cheeseboard moved to the more spacious quarters a half block away that I have already described; the larger space in turn has generated still more business. The present volume (August 1978) averages $8,400 a week, with allowances for seasonal variations.[2] At the moment, the collective has twenty-two members, thirteen men and nine women. Only fourteen of these—six men and eight women—work regularly, that is between fifteen and thirty-eight hours a week. The other members substitute when requested.

SELECTION OF MEMBERS AND COMPOSITION OF THE COLLECTIVE

A friendship network is the principal means of selecting new collective members when they are needed and, because this process illustrates some central aspects of the Cheeseboard, it will be useful to consider it now. No one is even considered for the collective unless he or she is known, and known fairly well, by an established member. When a nominee is proposed, he or she must be accepted by the entire collective for a trial period. There is no fixed rule for the length of the trial; it rarely exceeds a week, and it often lasts only a day. The important thing is that the nominee works with everyone in the collective, so that all collective members have the opportunity to gauge the quality of his or her work and social compatibility. If, at the end of the trial, there is a positive consensus about the nominee, he or she is admitted to the group. There is also no fixed rule about how a new member establishes a claim to or equity in the store. Sometimes a nominee works the trial period for reduced wages or no wages at all and, if accepted into the group, contributes that time to the store. In other cases, full wages are paid from the start and the newly accepted member buys, for one dollar, his or her share in the store. In effect, the Cheeseboard has worked out a system of token equity. The important point, however, is that everybody, old and new member alike, is thought to have an equal claim to the store, which in itself is the meaning of collective ownership.

There are very few cases where a prospective member is rejected outright by the collective. Rather, the rejection process is generally one of mutual recognition that the collective is not the right situation for the person, and as a consequence he or she withdraws voluntarily. This mutual recognition is at least partially shaped by a less formal selective process than that described here and is one that is quite complicated. I suggested earlier that the original owners of the store retain a measure of charismatic authority within the collective. Basically, they have been models for the organization: of hard work and dedication to the group; of loving generosity; and of political commitment to the idea of the collective. Their values have become thoroughly institutionalized in the collective and are an intrinsic part of the structure of the Cheeseboard. Moreover, the group has aged together over the last several years, and the original owners' roles have been transformed from mother and father roles to those of coworker and friend. While their charisma has been routinized and diffused throughout the group, they remain the embodiment of the ideals of the group and, as such, the most important members. They are, in effect, symbols of the group and of its ideals, although they deny this vehemently because it violates the egalitarianism which is the sole dogma of the collective. The candidate who does not respond positively to the ideals of the group, or to the charisma of the original owners who symbolize those ideals, has little chance of group acceptance or indeed of feeling comfortable in the group. Affective and moral, rather than instrumental, ties to the organization are thus emphasized from the earliest days of a new member's association with the Cheeseboard. Even after many years in the store, these ties remain the most important bonds between individuals and the group. There is, however, considerable disagreement among members about the relative strength of their commitments. This topic is examined later in the essay.

Despite marked personality differences among collective members, Cheeseboard workers share in common many aspects of background and experience. The median age is thirty-six years, with the youngest member being twenty-nine and the oldest forty-eight. Their ages make them somewhat anomalous in the collective movement, which is dominated by youths in their early twenties. The majority of Cheeseboard workers have had at least some college education, and many are college graduates. They are all white. Almost all are of middle-class origin, and many are the sons and daughters of professionals or managers. In general, however, their lives have not followed typical, orderly middle-class patterns. Rather, their occupational careers have been episodic, where they have abandoned, for one reason or another, straight careers such as editing or engineering, or have drifted in and out of jobs in the secondary labor market such as typist, secretary, store clerk, waitress, and so on. In addition, their personal lives, though generally far more stable than those of most youths engaged in collectives, have often been marked with periods of sharp emotional turmoil occasioned by experiences such as an unhappy love affair, divorce, or abortion, which rend personal relationships and call one's self-identification into serious question. While neither their occupational nor personal experiences are very exceptional, given the social standards of the San Francisco Bay Area, the fact is that for them the Cheeseboard offers a secure familistic structure where both personal drift and emotional turmoil can be partially resolved; this is one important source of the attractiveness of the collective to its members.

THE STRUCTURE AND EXPERIENCE OF COLLECTIVE WORK

Every type of work has its routines and problems, and the Cheeseboard is no exception. The demands of retail business create a regularized and often tedious set of tasks for the workers; in addition, serving the public and working closely with other people often leads to clashes of will and personality. In a great many work situations, exactly these conditions lead to worker alienation from their jobs (U.S. Senate 1972; Langer 1970*a*, 1970*b*). The collective structure of the Cheeseboard, however, provides a social framework where workers not only are able to tolerate the inevitable ambiguities of any job but can also fashion long-term commitments to one another, to the store, and to the idea of collective work. Exactly how this happens requires some detailed explanation.

COLLECTIVE ROUTINES

At the Cheeseboard, work is done either out front or in back. Work out front consists of dealing with the public and selling cheese and sandwiches; work in back means preparing food, cutting cheese, doing administrative tasks, and cleaning up. The morning crew of four workers begins the day at 8 A.M. in the rear part of the store, which is relatively shielded from the commercial area. These workers bake two kinds of bread; cut onions, cheese, and tomatoes for sandwiches; make mock *boursin*, an inexpensive version of the French spread; stock the large cheese display case in the front of the store; estimate how much cheese will be needed that day and cut it, wrap it, and set it aside in the walk-in refrigerator; check the cheese stock and place orders for those that are low in supply, make up and box any special "food conspiracy"[3] orders to be picked up that day; and, finally, do any necessary cleaning before the 10 A.M. opening. Despite the great amount of work compressed into this two-hour period, early crew workers value the shift highly as a family time when they can discuss their own personal problems and exchange information and viewpoints about different happenings and disputes in the collective. During this early morning period there is a sense of peacefulness and of personal warmth and intimacy in the store.

When the store opens, its rhythm and tempo change. The pace of work essentially becomes set by the flow of customers into the store, and new workers come on to handle the essential business of the collective—selling cheese. The Cheeseboard is located in the northside of Berkeley and is one of a cluster of specialty shops in the area, the others being a *charcuterie*, a butchery, a chocolate shop, a vegetable market, a fish store, a plant store, as well as coffee houses, excellent restaurants, and cafés. Taken together, these shops attract a steady circulating clientele, a large portion of whom are students and professionals from the nearby university. In addition, the Cheeseboard's own reputation for the best variety and quality of cheeses around draws customers from all over the Bay Area. The prices at the Cheeseboard are low because the collective has an across-the-board markup of only 50 percent compared with the usual 80 to 100 percent in other local cheese stores.[4] The store also has a generous discount policy, allowing 5 percent off for anybody who requests it because of need, and much greater discounts—up to 25 percent—for older people. Moreover, collective structure appeals to the characteristically liberal political sensibilities in Berkeley. On any given day, at least 300 customers pour into the Cheeseboard; on weekends and before holidays, the numbers are much greater.

As in any retail operation, workers' experiences at the front counter vary considerably, depending on the quality of their interaction with customers. There are some negative aspects to this interaction. Many customers are in a hurry and push that hurry onto workers. Again, the middle-class and collective socialization of Cheeseboard workers has not prepared them for the social subordination that many customers try to impose on retail clerks; conversely, other customers expect workers to be experts about every variety of cheese and essentially to decide what they should buy. Finally, workers sometimes feel animosity toward customers, especially those of the upper middle-class, because this clientele is able to buy what workers consider a luxury item in a society marked by sharp social inequality. On the whole, however, Cheeseboard workers get along fairly well with customers, bantering with them, exchanging gossip, and flirting with them. Workers counteract the cheese expert role by insisting that customers taste a cheese before buying it, an expensive practice but one that facilitates worker-customer interaction and eliminates any complaints about quality.[5]

For their part, Cheeseboard customers appreciate not only the low prices but the evident camaraderie among the workers, although not all customers understand the meaning of the large sign on the main wall of the store pointing out the collective ownership and operation of the enterprise. Despite the generally affable quality of worker-customer interaction, work out front is more demanding and exhausting than work in back, principally because there is no way of controlling the pace of work. Disputes among workers often grow from this discrepancy, as when, for instance, a worker will continue to work in back despite a press of customers out front because he or she does not want to face the hassles accompanying a heavy flow of customers.

Work out front continues all day, interspersed with various necessary chores in back. More cheeses must be ordered, others grated, still others packaged and priced. Dishes from the morning food preparation have to be washed, and the cheese case has to be refilled periodically. An entirely new work crew comes on duty between 1 and 2 P.M. to carry on. There is always a flurry of selling in the late afternoon as people buy food on the way home from work. Finally, the store closes at 6 P.M., and the final money tallies, clean-up, and preparation for the next day begins and lasts about an hour.

All of these routines in the Cheeseboard are structured around the demands of the work itself and, in general, the responsibility for the work is shared equally by collective members. There are only a few specialized jobs in the store. One of these is bookkeeping, which is subdivided into three tasks with each task done by one person for a year at a time. Less formally, the ordering of certain cheeses also becomes specialized as individual workers become familiar with one or another cheese distributor, but such patterns are always a matter of convenience rather than principle.

There are, however, some tasks in the store that are considered choice ones, and the way in which these are allocated provides important clues for understanding the dynamics of the collective. Baking bread, for instance, is thought by most workers to be an inherently satisfying and highly valued job. Again, doing the money tally at the end of the day is seen as a peaceful respite during an always hectic cleanup time. To get such tasks, or similarly to obtain choice work hours, a worker must fight for them—that is, assert a claim of priority, but one based on the recognition by the collective of one's contribution to the store. One worker explains how this works:

> No, there's not really any specialization. Anybody can fight for what they want to do. What do I mean by fight? It's not complicated, but it's not easy either. But if you give to the store and everybody sees it, you can get the job you want and the hours you want. You've got to *fight** though. For instance, R. couldn't stand working with somebody who was slow— nothing personal about it—so he took over [the bread baking on that shift] saying: "I only make bread once a week and I want to do it this day." Nobody could say: "Hey, R., what are you doing?" because he fights all the time, but he really gives to the store.

Collective routines are, then, intermeshed with the status structure of the collective, which in turn determines the measure of power a person has. Status is allocated principally according to others' perceptions of one's hard work and generosity toward the collective. Freedom to bend work routines to one's own liking is negotiable and depends above all upon performing those routines well.

The way in which choice tasks are allotted in the Cheeseboard suggests that conflict is a central feature of life in the collective. As I have already pointed out, this is true in virtually any work organization, as the literature on traditional work settings amply demonstrates.[6] Even many small cooperatives are shattered by personal animosities or ideological disputes. The Cheeseboard is more successful than most organizations, however, in resolving or at least in containing conflict among its members. The reason for this is not only that

---

*All emphases within quotes belong to the speaker and were so recorded during fieldwork.

Cheeseboard workers are selected carefully and are bound by affective and symbolic ties but also that they have fashioned several integrating perspectives and have developed specific integrating mechanisms which unite them even in the midst of conflict.

CONFLICT AND INTEGRATION

To understand the balance that Cheeseboard workers achieve, it will be helpful first to examine in greater detail the conflicts endemic to the group. Perhaps the most pervasive conflict is the tension among workers generated by different time commitments to the store and especially by different styles of working. As noted earlier, workers' hours at the store vary considerably, from fifteen to thirty-eight hours a week, depending on financial needs, outside interests, and the needs of the business. The amount of time spent at work connects people to the store in different ways and with varying degrees of intensity. As a general rule, the more hours people work in the store, the greater understanding they have not only of the ebb and flow of business but also of the complex social relationships that constitute the collective. Moreover, those with longer work hours are more likely to be perceived by others as committed to the store and as having its best interests at heart; consequently, they are more likely to become influential in the group.

Conversely the less people work, the less connected they feel to the store and the more likely they are to be perceived, at least by some, as exploiters—people using the store simply to facilitate the pursuit of private goals. The more widespread such a perception is, the less influence these workers have in the store. People who work more thus become resentful about those working less; they feel that others are benefiting from their hard work. Those working less become fearful that workers putting in more time at the store will accrue unwarranted influence. Cutting across this issue is the question of work style. Everyone works differently, and stylistic variations are an issue in many workplaces. In a collective, however, the boundaries that limit the expression of individual differences are much wider than in hierarchical, more standardized situations. Cheeseboard workers see themselves as their own bosses and have no formal external rules to follow in shaping work practices. One worker points out what happens:

> People get bugged at work. It comes with the feeling of controlling your own situation. Nobody is telling you how to do it, and you want everybody to do it your way.

As a result, some workers who work more slowly than others, but who consider themselves careful, are appraised by faster workers as simply inefficient. Others, for whom the social relationships of the collective are crucial, see themselves as people-oriented and spend time talking to other workers and customers, only to encounter the ire of their more task-oriented fellows. Some deplore what they consider the irresponsibility of other collective members and wish that those members would notice when aprons need cleaning or would stop leaving pieces of cheese in the case too small for sale. The freedom that collective work gives people makes even the accomplishment of routine tasks an arena for the struggle of personal wills. While bureaucratic settings tend to suppress conflict, collective settings make it more manifest.

Such struggles among workers often become so generalized that they are thought of as personality conflicts. One worker relates:

> What happens is that there are really basic personality conflicts. Real differences in character traits. People feel very strongly about doing something a certain way. It's a matter of *style*. Then sometimes an individual issue comes up and we get into an argument about it and, sooner or later, the whole thing gets carried over into the style and personality thing. And everyone holds grudges.

At any given time, there are several pairs of Cheeseboard workers who are arguing constantly with each other over work styles or, at another level, over store policies, such as how much workers should pay for the food and drink they take on the job. Workers in constant disputes are, as one would expect, usually tense around one another, and this is evident to the rest of the collective. Indeed, sometimes two workers reach such an impasse in their personal interaction that they stop talking with each other. This is particularly true when unresolved sexual tension or, worse, sexual rivalry complicates, or indeed creates, work difficulties. Personality conflicts may thus be viewed as crystallizations in a fairly constant and extreme form of the ongoing quarrels and tensions that make up daily work life at the Cheeseboard.

All of this conflict occurs, however, within a social context where workers have constructed common integrating perspectives about their organizational experiences. The most important of these is workers' image of the collective as an extended family, which emerges principally from the friendship structure of the group. As one would expect in an organization where recruitment occurs through a friendship network, all collective members interviewed claim good friends within the group even though most also look outside the collective for their closest relationships. In addition, workers feel that they can confide in virtually any other person in the group, even those with whom they have conflicts, and that the confidence will be respected. Further, workers rely on one another for personal favors. For instance, several members care for each other's children, often for extended periods of time; again, workers cover work hours for one another in times of private emergencies or even just to satisfy personal whims. These and other dimensions of friendship eliminate some potential conflicts and soften other conflicts when they do occur. It also makes some conflict more painful and difficult because discord with friends is more diffuse and disruptive to one's life than conflict with people who are only work colleagues in a conventional sense. However, somewhat paradoxically, workers feel that the emotional pain of conflict with friends is in itself an integrating factor; it creates a bond of deeply felt experience and heightens feelings of familial intimacy. Workers constantly compare the collective with a family. For some, the group is seen as an actual family, a substitute for long-lost relationships with parents and siblings. For instance, one worker states:

> The collective provides one with a sense of family. I always wanted to identify with a group and now I *do*. . . . It's a surrogate family.

For most, however, the familial emphasis is more muted and symbolic, though nonetheless pervasive. Even when workers do not get along well with one another, they feel committed to each other, just as blood family members feel they share the same fate. This feeling deepens the longer workers stay with the store, and workers come to see their personal biographies intertwined with the organization. For example, one long-term worker pinpoints the key reason she stays at the Cheeseboard:

> I'm so deeply involved there. Since I've been there, it's become so woven into my life. All the changes that I've been through in my life are tied up with the store.

The result of such emotional involvement is a basic commitment among most Cheeseboard workers to the idea of the collective, and this commitment means working out, rather than retreating from, whatever difficulties emerge in the group. Another worker:

> In general, I would say that there's a commitment to the *framework* of the store, although I'm not exactly sure what that is. There's a commitment by most, although not all, to work things out. People value things about the store and value them so much that they have to work things out.

The genuinely libertarian perspective of the collective—particularly its nonideological character—is also an important integrating factor in the group. One of the banes of the collective movement has been

its political factionalism, often of an extreme sort. Within the movement, there are several varieties of social democrats, democratic cen-
tralists, anarchists, and so on. Historically, of course, this fragmentation
has always been a problem for the political left because the left, unlike
the right, cannot in principle coalesce around private property. In the
San Francisco Bay Area, many collective groups spend a great deal of
time and energy battling one another, frequently over obscure disputes.
Such external struggles have decisive internal structural repercussions,
and many collectives become doctrinaire, demanding adherence by
their members to a group line. But doctrinaire ideologies are inherently
contradictory to the general freedom that workers have in decentralized work situations and, in time, disputes within collectives spring
up, usually expressed in ideological terms and usually marked by the
same ferocity evident in outside disputes. In fact, even personal quarrels often become politicized, and whatever unity the collective had
becomes fragmented and dissipated.[7] Cheeseboard workers, by contrast, see themselves and their work as political, but not within any
worked-out ideological framework. For these workers, working and
owning collectively in a society dominated by wage labor and private
property are political statements in themselves. In addition, by general
agreement, the store has always given 3 percent of its profits back to
the community, most often to collectives that need financial aid, and
this is seen as a political action. But, with some important individual
exceptions, the group as a whole feels no need to proselytize others
to the virtues of collective work. Further, except for these images of
collective work as political and except for general taken-for-granted
Berkeley radical liberalism—for example, support for farmworkers,
opposition to military spending, support for environmental controls,
and so on—there is no larger ideological consensus in the group and,
by informal agreement, no attempt is made to reach one. The general
rule is: Anyone may engage in whatever political activities he or she
wishes; however, the Cheeseboard as a collective will not take an
ideological stand that requires political conformity of its members.
While this approach creates some problems for those collective members who are very active politically and who would like more institutional involvement by the Cheeseboard in their concerns, it gives
the organization a flexibility and consequent stability that many other
collectives have been unable to achieve. These are important aids in
weathering conflict.

    In addition to these general integrating perspectives, the collective
also employs more specific mechanisms to resolve conflict. The most
important of these, practiced at least by most members of the collective, is direct discussion between quarreling parties. People simply talk
out their tensions with one another, often during the quiet morning

shifts or outside of work over coffee or drinks. Sometimes, when antagonisms build to the point that direct discussion is not possible, other collective members intervene. They talk privately to the individuals involved, try to divert the conflict, defuse it, or make it humorous. By acting at all, they assert implicitly the value of group unity and put moral pressure on their fellows to settle differences. In extreme cases, meetings are held, and the group as a whole tries to mediate differences, but this has happened only rarely and without much success. I should note that neither the group nor individual members intervene in disputes where sexual tension or rivalry is acknowledged to be the key issue. There is a general feeling that these are private matters and, despite their destructive potential, that outside parties have no mandate to intervene. Other tensions between people that have escalated to the level of personality conflicts also seem unresolvable to the collective, and ways are sought simply to contain the conflict. In such cases, disputing individuals take different shifts, avoid situations where disputes will erupt and, in general, back off from their quarrels, establishing what are basically armed truces with each other. The group facilitates such patterns of accommodation by rearranging schedules and so on, and acts as a silent patrol to enforce the truces. In these situations, workers' commitment to the basic framework of the collective is crucial; it enables people to live with interpersonal friction that they might otherwise find intolerable.

CONSENSUS AND FREEDOM

The paradox in all of this material is evident. On one hand, as I have already stressed, the decentralized, nonhierarchical structure of collective work shapes attitudes of great freedom among workers and lays the groundwork for a struggle of personal wills. On the other hand, the collective forces individuals to take others' viewpoints seriously and puts a premium on workers' full appreciation of the negotiated character of social reality. The simultaneous tension and merger between workers' autonomy and the expectations of the collective for consent to the group is particularly evident in the decision-making process at the Cheeseboard.

There are three levels or spheres of decision making in the group. At the most basic level, each worker decides what has to be done with regard to his or her individual job. Although the work itself and the sometimes conflicting definitions of others impose a certain standardization on work tasks, workers' scope of autonomy in their everyday activities is great. When a decision affects the collective as a whole, the group must be consulted, although the mode of consultation varies with the importance of the decision. In minor matters, such as small equipment purchases or changes in order or delivery schedules, a simple majority vote suffices, and this is taken either in writing through a notice on the staff's bulletin board or, with great dispatch, at the monthly group meetings. Despite the need for group consultation, this intermediate level of decision making is as routine as the first. At one meeting I attended, the collective disposed of nineteen items of business in fifteen minutes, including passing motions for the expenditure of several hundred dollars. However, when major matters are at issue, such as the long-term disposal of the growing surplus funds, or proposals to rationalize accounting and ordering procedures to gain greater control of cash flow, decision making is done only by consensus at the monthly meetings.

Achieving consensus, even in a well-knit group such as the Cheeseboard, is a very complicated and time-consuming process. The essential rule is that no group action is taken against the strong opposition of even one collective member. This means a commitment to extended discussions at meetings to reach decisions. When an important issue is raised, the group typically engages in a preliminary discussion to see what the support or opposition for the motion is; often a straw vote is taken to clarify people's positions. If there is unanimity of opinion in favor of the motion in either the preliminary discussion or the straw vote, the decision is considered made, and it is the responsibility of the proposer to see that the decision is implemented. If opinions are split on an issue, the group returns to the discussion and continues it until there is unanimity for or against the proposal. Quite often, this means tabling the proposal and continuing the discussion at a later meeting. A recent decision by the collective to post a sign publicly announcing the collective character of the Cheeseboard took one and a half years to make because of disagreements about the possible ideological implications. Once this sort of decision is made, it is generally felt to be a lasting one, because extended discussion generates firm group support. One worker says:

> This type of discussion is the only way to set *solid* decisions. Otherwise people feel that they're being railroaded into something. When you discuss it like we do, then you know what you've done, and you can clearly *stand behind it*. Then the decision becomes permanent because it's really personal to me.

There is, however, no spontaneous group implementation of a decision, even after lengthy discussions. This remains the responsibility of the person who proposed the idea and of those who most strongly supported it. Unless these people put their time and energy into realizing a proposal, it will not be carried out.

Personal leadership and style are critical components of reaching a consensus in the Cheeseboard. Although some workers single out the two original owners as being the most generally influential figures in the collective, most agree that decision-making influence is diffused and situational. Workers who have good ideas—that is, good for the collective as well as fresh and innovative—and a convincing mode of presenting them at meetings influence the collective the most; this shifts from issue to issue depending on people's concerns. To be heard at all, of course, one must have the respect of the group which, as noted earlier, depends upon group perceptions of one's contribution to the store.

Apart from one's everyday activity, then, individual freedom of action in a collective is contingent upon one's ability to formulate and express creative ideas that find resonance with unexpressed needs of the group, while one accepts the group's rules for earning respect. One worker brings these ideas together:

> When people come into the store—for some, the freedom I'm talking about is given right away, and it's theirs right away. It's when a person gives to the store and claims the freedom. If they are respected by others, other people will give it to them. But it has to be fought for, to be claimed. You have to be smart enough to know that what you want is good for the whole group. . . . You must claim the respect of others, and it has to be for the good of the store, and it has to be felt as such.

Consensus decision making is a way of structuring workers' ongoing negotiation of social reality in a way that gives everybody an equal chance for participating, at least by veto, in the decisions that affect them. Such structuring does not lead, as it often does in other work situations, to a stifling of individuality nor to the practice of "group think." On the contrary, achieving consensus at the Cheeseboard is an arena for the exercise of disciplined individual freedom. In fact, the very vitality of the store depends upon the ideas and actions of individuals. The process of reaching consensus does help to channel individuality into group solidarity, and this gives real substance to the idea of working collectively. In fact, the knowledge that consensus is needed for any major change in the collective underpins workers' definitions of the key advantages of collective work.

THE ADVANTAGES OF COLLECTIVE WORK

Cheeseboard workers see great advantages to belonging to and working in a collective. The first of these is a sense of control over everyday work processes and over one's larger scope of action in the store; this sense grounds the freedom that the store affords workers. One worker describes the importance of control:

> The thing that I like best is that I get to control how things are done; I have impact. I actually control something I care about. Like, if I feel that not enough information is around about something—by temperament I like to organize things—it's wonderful to be able to set up some system where there's a flow of information. In another job, I wouldn't be able to do this.

Workers often contrast this feeling of control with previous negative experiences; control is the critical variable in transforming their experiences of work. Another worker states:

> What I like best is the fact that the store is a collective. That's the difference. It's the structure that appeals to me the most. I like working with cheese . . . but even if it were a paper bag factory, the fact that I can control my situation there—that's what's important. Why. . .? I've worked for a lot of people since I was 17. . . . I've never had any pride in any work I've done [before now].

The essence of collective work is each worker's control over his or her immediate work situation. Such control generalizes managerial skills and, over a period of time, shapes in individuals not only a practical know-how but also a general feeling of capability which is the core of pride in one's work. Another worker says:

> Every year I become a little more confident of myself as someone who counts.

Another states:

> In general, the Cheeseboard has changed my life a lot. It's given me more confidence in myself—being given responsibility; having to be responsible. . . . It's very expanding.

Many workers suggest that as a result of their experiences in the store, they feel fully able to begin their own business should they ever choose to do so. Such self-confidence is crucial for their self-image. Another worker says:

> I think it's affected me profoundly. I believe now in my capability of being something. I've always felt impotent before about getting things done in the world. I believe I could start a business of my own if I wanted to. I've

gotten practical knowledge and a sense of self as well that I couldn't conceive of before.

In presenting themselves to outsiders, workers stress their co-management of the store and how this has shaped their sense of self. As workers in other collective situations have also experienced (Jackall 1976), control of the workplace helps workers gain control over their appraisals and subsequently their presentations of themselves—in short, over their social identities. I should note that such experiences have profound effects on workers' perceptions of their futures. Without exception, these men and women argue that after the Cheeseboard experience, they could never again work in situations that they do not control. One worker expresses this:

> Yes, working there [Cheeseboard] has certainly influenced me in relationship to any other jobs. I don't know if I would ever work for somebody again unless the job were very special. In the future, I would have to have control over what I do; what you have—in my life—I've realized more and more control over my life—emotionally, economically, in many ways. . . . Self-determination increases responsibility. It's a self-altering experience.

Control over one's work is the social groundwork for a transforming emotional and cognitive independence.

The control that workers experience at the Cheeseboard has other ramifications. Perhaps the most significant effect is their sense that they can create an honest business operation—a value they all consider important—and, in fact, they feel that they have accomplished this. They set fair prices for their cheeses; they supervise the quality of their cheeses with great care and refuse to sell cheeses that are not up to their standards; they steer customers toward the best buys in the store, even though this often means reducing store profits. In short, they see themselves providing a basic service for people in an honest way, and they constantly reiterate the importance of this. For instance, one worker discusses what she likes best about being in the collective:

> I guess most of all I can sell customers a product I know to be the best. This is really important because the whole selling thing in America is such a shuck. But in this job, you can be totally honest.

Another worker states:

> It's [working in the Cheeseboard] not a *con*. It's an honest business, and that's as important as anything else. More important than anything. It

doesn't contradict my morals. It satisfies my ethics. I don't want to rip anybody off. And we don't rip people off. We don't exploit our customers, or our workers, or other businesses, or the people we buy from. There's a *justness* there.

Workers' control at the Cheeseboard affords collective members a way of uniting their private ethics and their public roles and of fashioning a way of working and surviving decently.

Workers also feel that working in a collective has taught them the value of cooperation with others; they see this as an important transforming experience after growing up in a society that stresses individual competitiveness. At the most rudimentary level, cooperation means the stretching of self required to work in relative harmony with a diverse group of others. More specifically, it means learning always to take into account others' perspectives about issues—to be ready to negotiate even the taken-for-granted frameworks of daily life. Such willingness to negotiate leads, over a period of time, to a sense of unity with others which undercuts the separation between people intrinsic to a capitalistic social order. One worker comments:

> For me, it's an assertion of humanity, of commonness among people. I wouldn't want to do without the interaction which the collective allows and fosters. . . . It's a chance to get rid of the tradition of separateness in our society; to obliterate the distinction between *mine* and *yours*.

Despite the many conflicts that persist in the collective, and probably because those conflicts are *manifest* rather than suppressed, cooperation is a key dimension of workers' experiences and, in their view, of their growth and development in the store.

Finally, collective work provides workers with feelings of great security. At one level this means emotional security. The Cheeseboard is a very stable organization. It is financially sound and has an extremely low turnover of personnel; only a few people have left the group in its eight years of existence as a collective. By contrast, one of its leading rivals among cheese stores in the Bay Area has a 50 percent turnover each year, with a worker's average stay being one year.[8] The average turnover in clerical jobs in the area's large organizations is about 33 percent. Such organizational stability, coupled with the friendship network and familistic imagery discussed earlier, provides a well-set anchor for many workers. At a more basic level, there is a great job security for Cheeseboard workers. The understanding in the collective is that once a person is admitted to the group, he or she is a co-owner of the store and will always have a job as long as the store survives. Consensus decision making continually reaffirms and guarantees this understanding, as it does workers' sense of control and cooperation, by making full participation in the direction of the store a matter of principle. A person may even leave the collective for an extended period and be assured of a job upon returning, provided there are work hours that need staffing. This understanding assures workers of a solid, reasonable income, particularly for part-time work. The wages and benefits at the store are good, certainly when compared with almost all other collective groups[9] and even when compared with a great many mainstream occupations.[10] All Cheeseboard workers earn $6.00 an hour from the start and have half their health insurance paid for by the store through Kaiser Health Plan of California. There is also a special sick leave program which compensates at full wages workers who miss up to ten days of work through illness; further compensation must be voted by the collective. The collective also loans money to workers for short periods at no interest and at low interest for major purchases such as houses or, in one case, a truck; it also has provided funds for special schooling for one collective member's child. There is the general sense that this kind of support is available to all. Such security directly underpins the freedom discussed earlier. One worker puts it well:

> Freedom and security are indivisible. That's where the collective is important. The person gets the sense that they can take care of themselves through the collective. And there's a real transformation—from wondering how you will survive to, in the collective, your survival is insured. That's security. And you can't be free without that kind of security.

By providing financial and emotional surety, the collective mediates and indeed releases workers' individual expressiveness. And workers use their freedom in very diverse ways—from searching for personal fulfillment to seeking a political revolution. In fact, the very diversity of their expressiveness—though it stems from the same workers at different times in their individual biographies, as well as from altogether different groups of workers—creates still other tensions and dilemmas for the group, even while it also constitutes one of the great strengths of the collective.

MAINTAINING THE STATUS QUO OR EXPANSION

There are two well-established and opposing tendencies in the collective: first, an inclination to see one's personal expressiveness fulfilled mainly outside the store; and, second, an inclination to see the store itself as the principal arena for one's creativity. A very small group of workers is permanently inclined toward the first tendency; another small group toward the second. Most workers fluctuate between the two viewpoints. The groups that emerge at any given time have sharply varying definitions of the place of the store in their present lives and varying images of what the future of the store should be. Both tendencies, I think, contribute in important ways to the success of the collective.

For periods of their lives, many Cheeseboard workers become caught up in the quintessentially Californian search for self-discovery and self-fulfillment. Some define themselves as artists and indeed work hard at music, painting, or writing. Others are engaged in a quest for spiritual or emotional enlightenment and spend considerable amounts of time meditating or engaging in philosophical discussions with close friends, trying to puzzle out the meaning of their lives. Still others are simply drifting and dabbling in a variety of activities, hoping to discover their life's work. For workers in such phases of their biographies, the store is a network of friends, a place to earn a decent living while they find and develop themselves, a center where they can be connected with larger themes and events, including the more political work of their fellow collectivists, without having to divert precious time from their main concerns. If they had to choose between the Cheeseboard and their search for self-fulfillment, these workers would have to choose the latter. However, as they are quick to point out, this is not a realistic choice. They depend on the collective for their livelihood and for much of their social interaction; they are proud of their work and feel that it is a decent way to make a living. They see their jobs as vital, positive aspects of their social presentations of themselves. But their search for self-discovery is the principal arena for their self-sustenance and for their most significant self-definitions. There is no sharp compartmentalization between these two spheres of their lives; rather, each sphere in its own way makes the other possible. They have achieved an integration between work and life which simultaneously binds them to the collective and frees them for other activities.

Workers in such phases of their biographies do not necessarily oppose change in the direction of the organization, but they also do not initiate it. Because they have a sense of harmony and equilibrium in their lives, of a cycle between work and genuine leisure (de Grazia 1964), of a balance between necessity and freedom, they feel no need to alter the status quo. In addition, their material expectations are low—a fact true of virtually all workers in the store—and they are satisfied with a generally modest, low-consumption life-style. They are, I think, the principal sources of the Cheeseboard's remarkable organizational stability. They represent, in fact, the antithesis of the main occupational hazard of alternative collective work, what is generally known as burnout. Burnout is the experience of feeling constantly overworked, of having too much responsibility and not enough organizational support to carry it out, of never having enough free time for personal pursuits, of constantly being hassled, of, in one worker's phrase, "losing your soul." Because of their adherence to the organizational structure which provides balance in their lives, these Cheeseboard workers help buffer the organization against any precipitous changes which could engender burnout.

At different stages of their Cheeseboard careers some of these same workers, as well as other workers, see the organization and their relationships to it in a very different way. They are, first of all, critical of their colleagues who put their self-fulfillment ahead of the store. They feel that this suggests a lack of commitment to the collective and of an engrossment in private worlds with no sense of vision or of the larger political significance of working collectively. One worker expresses this very sharply:

[There's] too much emphasis on emotional needs, too self-centered. Not enough historical perspective. They don't see it [the collective] in relationship to the rest of the world, the rest of humanity. They see it within the limits of their own needs and, from that perspective, it's a good deal and people like being part of a good thing. People don't really believe in the collective. In their minds, it's become a postrevolutionary state, and the revolution is supposed to serve the individual. This is a problem for me. I wouldn't be happy if the collective didn't plow money into the community. See, the thing is people are into living their own lives. They're at the store twenty hours a week. And there's too much indulgence, and laziness, and therapy at the shop. Too much taking care of problems. So they're good unionists. They like the good deal.

In this view, which is ideological in its emphasis on activism but which conforms in a way to the nonideological principles of the store because it is nonsectarian, the main purpose of working collectively is to change the society, not to facilitate the pursuit of private fulfillment. Workers holding this view have been the moving forces behind the Cheeseboard's long and impressive involvement with the Bay Area community. I have already mentioned that the store gives 3 percent of its profits back to the community. In addition, in 1972, activist Cheeseboard members helped found, with money, labor, and expertise, the Swallow, a thriving collective restaurant in Berkeley; in 1974, they helped others begin the Juice Bar, a collective sandwich and snack shop, also still doing a booming business in Berkeley. Around the same time, they helped found a trucking collective and got the Cheeseboard to finance it entirely with a $3,000 noninterest loan. At their urging, the Cheeseboard gave a refrigerator outright to another retail cheese collective in a different part of California. Activist workers have also been key figures in publishing the informative *Bay Area Directory of Collectives* (Collective Directory 1977) and in getting the Cheeseboard to fund this project in its entirety. They are now planning to launch an accounting collective which will make its expertise available to all other collectives and which will be financed through the surplus from the Cheeseboard. In short, they feel that the sense of the collective depends upon its continual outreach to the larger community; only by such engagement in the world can a group identity be maintained.

This expansive outlook is tied to the view that one's growth and development occurs principally through the collective. Workers inclined toward this view feel that their own identities depend upon the Cheeseboard's providing a continually expanding range of opportunities for them. One worker illustrates this in discussing what makes her job worthwhile:

> For me [it's] being able to expand the store in different directions. It's not upward mobility, but it's being able to have other schemes. We could start another store if we want to. Or doing a directory of collectives and making the Cheeseboard into a kind of information center. Or we could start a cheese farm in the country; we have enough money set aside to talk about that seriously now. It's having that sense that's the most important part. The possibilities are large there; you're not just confined to cutting cheese.

Without new opportunities, the Cheeseboard cannot hope to hold those workers who regularly feel this way or indeed those who become (temporarily) disillusioned with the search for self-fulfillment outside the store and turn back to the collective for self-validation. Without either group the organization itself, at least as a collective enterprise, might be in jeopardy. Unlike large bureaucracies which can rely on sheer inertia to get things done, small organizations require a constant renewal of commitment to their goals by at least some members. Without the esprit de corps generated by such renewal, groups like the Cheeseboard lose their vitality, their cohesiveness, and their sense of purpose. It is both those workers most committed to the idea of the collective itself and its possibilities—those who generally see their own futures and, in effect, the key aspects of themselves bound up with the store—and those workers returning to the collective as to a haven to find themselves, who provide this constant renewal. Even though much of the appeal of the Cheeseboard and a great part of its success is due to the freedom it gives to its members to pursue their own outside interests, the collective must expand opportunities within the store to survive and to succeed as well as it has. In short, it must simultaneously stay the same and change.

CONCLUSION

The dilemma of simultaneously maintaining the status quo and expanding is typical of the many paradoxes that make up the Cheeseboard experience. Collective work cannot remedy the ambiguous contradictions inherent in the modern workplace. Indeed, as this essay points out, collective work deepens the ambiguity in many ways by making problematic things that are taken for granted in a typical work situation. Unlike most other work arrangements, at least in a capitalistic society where economic efficiency is the key goal, collective situations do not suppress the social and political character of work. Consequently, big and difficult issues such as individual conflict versus group cohesion, or personal autonomy versus group consensus come under continuous examination. Men and women who work in collectives, far more I think than those in the semiritualized, compartmentalized worlds that bureaucratic work shapes, need a kind of secular faith—a willingness to confront and to live with ambiguity and, in spite of it, the nerve to make and to keep commitments to institutions, to other people, and to themselves.

More than most collectives, the Cheeseboard both demands and fosters this spirit in its workers. The numerous conflicts in the store stimulate a sharp awareness among workers of the never settled character of social reality, but the group's efforts to settle those conflicts elicit commitments to the principle and to the practice of negotiation. The personal relationships of the friendship network in the store make even small matters complicated, but the affective ties between people are the principal source of the group's solidarity. The sense of the collective as a family creates extremely ambiguous roles, particularly authoritative roles, but the familial imagery symbolically expresses and reinforces the bonds between people. Finally, the great, though disciplined, freedom that the store allows workers to claim leads to an almost constant and bewildering struggle of personal wills and to divergent and competing loyalties, but the sense of autonomous control that this freedom brings creates in the collective a rarely matched resiliency. The Cheeseboard survives and flourishes because its workers keep this faith in themselves and in one another.

NOTES

1. In effect, the two owners helped buy the store from themselves. Of the $10,000 purchase price, only 60 percent represented the equity of the former wage-workers, and a full 40 percent was the owners' own money.

2. I have been unable to get comparative data that would place the economic growth of the Cheeseboard in a meaningful context. There is, to my knowledge, no local trade association of cheese dealers and therefore no easily obtainable statistics of regional cheese sales over the last decade. From the Cheeseboard's own data, it seems clear that increases in sales from 1967 through mid-1977, when the volume was $8,000 a week, represented real growths in demand. However, the $400 increase from mid-1977 to mid-1978 seems to be, according to the store's bookkeepers, simply an inflationary increase. If demand for imported cheese has, in fact, leveled off in the Bay Area, it will be interesting to see what impact a lack of economic growth has on the Cheeseboard collective. Clearly, one of the key reasons for the success of the store is that it came into an expanding market at exactly the right time. (See the research note and afterword for an additional note.)

3. "Food conspiracies" are a colorful name for food co-ops or buying clubs. For a detailed description of these buying clubs in the Boston area, see William Ronco (1974).

4. This means that, as a general rule, what the Cheeseboard buys for $1.00, it sells for $1.50; most other stores, given the same cost to them, sell the item for $1.80 or $2.00.

5. Tasting costs the store an average of $20 per workday. Workers feel that this substantial cost is justified not only for the reasons noted but also because tasting gives customers clear expectations, and these build loyalty to the store.

6. Conflict between workers themselves permeates blue-collar work, although it often goes unnoticed or unemphasized by researchers because of their interest in workers' alienation from actual work tasks and overall situations. See, however, Shostak 1969:60–63. In the white-collar world, many bureaucratic workplaces are best described as sites of jungle warfare: on clerks, see Jackall 1978:115–122; on managers, see Dalton 1959 and Jackall 1983; on professionals, see Bensman 1967:125–149. For a general treatment, see Bensman and Rosenberg 1960.

7. One can get a sense of this political divisiveness by examining the breakup of the cooperative federation in Austin, Texas, reported in *Communities* (May–June 1977). Similar situations have occurred in Minneapolis and in San Francisco.

8. Phone interview with the manager of Curds and Whey, Berkeley, California, July 18, 1977.

9. With only a few exceptions, wages in most collectives are quite low, often averaging below minimum wage standards. The average wage in collectives across the country is below $4.00 an hour (see Jackall and Crain, chapter 5 of this volume). This leads some to use the term *self-exploitation* to describe work conditions in the collective movement.

10. The hourly pay scale at Curds and Whey, the principal rival of the Cheeseboard, as noted in the text, was, in July 1977, as follows:

starting pay	$2.75
after one month	$3.00
after six months	$3.25
after one year	$3.50

after eighteen months	$3.75
after two years	$4.00
after three years	$4.25

Pay for most clerical work in the area is between $3.00 an hour and $5.00 an hour.

RESEARCH NOTE AND AFTERWORD

Most of the fieldwork for this essay was done in June and July of 1977. I interviewed seven of the fourteen working members of the collective in depth; each interview lasted an average of two and a half hours. In addition, I had numerous informal conversations both with those collective members interviewed and with other members of the group. I also attended several meetings of the collective, worked in the store for the better part of a day, and spent several days observing the collective at work.

I sent an initial draft of the paper to the collective in May 1978; in August 1978, I met with the entire collective for several hours to discuss it. On the basis of that meeting, both because I collected more data at the time and because the group persuaded me that some of my interpretations were inaccurate, I revised some aspects of the paper, although all the central themes remained the same.

I have maintained some contact with the Cheeseboard over the years. As the final editing of this volume began in the Fall of 1983, I contacted the collective to update as necessary the material reported in this essay. As it happened, one of the most valued members of the group, Renate Holdreith, had been killed in a late summer automobile accident. Her death not only caused grief in the collective (the group closed the store for a week to mourn her) but also prompted a rejuvenating internal appraisal of the collective itself. Both because of this self-examination and because of the imminent publication of this essay, many members of the Cheeseboard reread the piece. Several times in November and December of 1983, I interviewed by phone one member designated by the collective; this was to gauge the group's reaction to the essay after a number of years and to get more recent particulars. There have been a number of developments in the collective over the years that should be noted. These are:

1. There are now twenty-one members in the collective, ten women and eleven men. Eighteen of these are regular working members who work between 14 and 36 hours a week. The average number of hours worked per week is 26, and the total number of hours worked by the whole collective is 413 per week. The median age of members is thirty-nine years, with the youngest being twenty-eight and the oldest being seventy-nine.

2. The store now generates a weekly sales volume of $15,000, a 78 percent increase over 1978. Much of this growth has been due to the enormous increase in bread baking, the single most important change in the store since this essay was written. The Cheeseboard now bakes, in several shifts a day, hundreds of sourdough baguettes that draw customers from all over the Bay Area. The collective is as much a bread store now as a retail cheese shop. In terms of work structure, this has meant lengthening the morning shifts and adding one worker to each shift during the day. This change seems to have made the already complicated relationships described in the essay a bit more tangled. As is typical with the collective, the decision to commit the store to such extensive baking was not taken lightly, despite the very lucrative character of the enterprise. Because of the social ramifications of the move, the store proceeded very slowly and only after many discussions; even now the store's commitment to bread is viewed warily by some.

3. Wages are now $10 an hour with the prospect of another raise early in 1984. Benefits have increased as well. For example, the Cheeseboard now covers the entire cost of health insurance either through the Kaiser Health Plan or an alternate plan for those workers who put in at least twenty hours a week at the store; for those with fewer than twenty hours, the collective covers half the insurance. A similar kind of proportional coverage applies to dental care. Although there is no policy extending coverage to children, the collective does provide coverage for some children of members, depending on need.

4. The basic structure of the selection process for new members remains the same, although the perception in the collective now is that new members can be drawn from outside a friendship network. Still, in practice, new members seem to be known well by at least one other member of the collective. The probationary period and the token equity required of new members has become more standardized; now each candidate works forty hours in the store. If the candidate is then rejected by the collective, he or she is paid at the regular rate. If accepted, the forty hours of work becomes the new member's donation to the collective.

5. Two recent developments have extended in new directions the old tension between the impulse to political action, on one hand, and that toward self-fulfillment on the other. A sizable number of the members have become deeply involved in the antinuclear power movement, and some have been arrested at various demonstrations. The store has in fact given money to aid the antinuclear movement in the Berkeley area. At the same time, after much debate for a number of years, the collective purchased land in Mendocino County from its growing surplus. While the land belongs to all, it seems to be used

principally by collective members dedicated to creating a rural, self-sufficient utopia. There is some concern in the collective that both of these tendencies are centrifugal and harmful to the group as a whole.

6. After a period of troubling uncertainty, when money seemed to be regularly out of balance, one member of the collective admitted to stealing several thousand dollars from the store over a period of time. This person offered to, and did in fact, repay the money. The person was, of course, ejected from the group. The episode caused a great deal of consternation, anxiety, and feelings of betrayal in the collective. The significant sociological issue is how collective members construct, in retrospect, the relationship of the guilty person to the group. As collective members see it, the person had not been working much at the store and had not been active in the social activities of the group—meetings, parties, informal get-togethers, and so on. As a result, participation in the life of the collective has come to be valued even more highly than it was previously. The converse also seems to be true. Those groups members not participating in group functions are somewhat suspect.

In short, the significant changes in the collective's daily life since this essay was written are: (1) the complication of social relationships caused by the increased commitment to bread baking; (2) the active politicization of some collective members through their involvement in the antinuclear power movement paired against the press by others toward self-sufficiency symbolized by the purchase of land; and (3) the increased emphasis on group involvement caused by the stealing episode. If anything, however, all of these developments have only deepened the paradoxes observed in 1977 and reported in the essay.

ACKNOWLEDGMENTS

I want to thank Joyce Crain, Derek Jones, and Hank Levin, who carefully read an early draft of this paper and made many helpful suggestions. My special thanks to Janice M. Hirota whose critical and editorial abilities greatly improved the essay.

I am very grateful to the Cheeseboard collective for sharing their experiences with me. They are a rare group of people, and they have enriched not only my research experience but my life as a whole. I am particularly indebted to Sahag Avedisian who originally suggested that I do this study and to Georgia Neidorf who greatly assisted me in updating the materials. I owe the deepest debt to Renate Holdreith, whose enthusiasm for the project and whose critical acumen were great aids in my work. I want to dedicate this essay to her memory.

PART IV

Toward Larger Cooperatives

This section presents two further case studies of worker cooperatives, both of which are considerably larger than the small urban collectives discussed in Part III. The first is Christopher Gunn's study of Hoedads Co-op, a forestry workers' cooperative based in Eugene, Oregon. Hoedads has 300 members in the cooperative, broken into several smaller work crews of about 15 to 20 each. The second is Edward Greenberg's analysis of several plywood cooperatives in the Pacific Northwest; there are fourteen of these firms presently operating, ranging in size from 80 to 350 members. Greenberg studies several of these firms and presents data gathered from 280 cooperative workers and more than 150 workers in capitalist firms in the same industry. Both Hoedads and the plywood cooperatives have fared well economically. Hoedads now competes successfully with many lumber industry giants for government reforestation contracts in excess of $1 million. The plywood cooperatives as a whole are both more productive and profitable than conventional firms and provide higher earnings for their workers.

One of the most interesting facts to emerge from these studies is how larger cooperatives practice workplace democracy. The small collectives examined earlier are all essentially face-to-face groups which try to reach decisions through consensus. In the larger cooperatives, sheer size, and in the case of Hoedads, physical dispersion of workers across hundreds of miles, complicates decision making and makes consensus a very difficult and cumbersome process. Hoedads and the plywood groups each approach the challenge of governance differently.

Hoedads has developed a system that combines both participatory and representative democracy. Each work crew of fifteen to twenty people is organized collectively, and their dynamics are similar to small collectives. They strive for consensus in all major matters, a mode of decision making entirely appropriate to groups that live together intensively under difficult conditions, often for extended contract periods. Each crew delegates one representative to attend regular administrative meetings with other delegates and with the elected officials of the co-op. Quarterly, the entire membership of the cooperative comes together in general meetings to debate and to decide long-term directions for the firm. Hoedads thus combines consensual participatory decision making at the crew level with representative and direct town-meeting-style democracy at the co-op level. The result is a vibrant organization that is able to overcome great physical distance between its members and the fragmentation that could result from working on different projects.

Formally, plywood cooperatives are structured as representative democracies with all final authority vested in the general membership of the cooperative. In practice, the membership delegates responsibilities to the board of directors which is elected annually and/or to the general manager who serves at the membership's pleasure. Information about issues that affect the whole enterprise is, according to Greenberg, widely disseminated and vigorously debated; the representatives of the cooperative are sharply aware of workers' sentiments on all policy issues and take them fully into account in their decision making. This democratic spirit finds its way into shop floor practices as well. For instance, Greenberg discovered a great deal of information sharing and quality control among workers; it is especially worth noting that the plywood cooperatives have far fewer line supervisors than their capitalist counterparts. Workers' sense of ownership and responsibility for the enterprise gives them a stake in production that permeates their work and their attitudes toward their firms.

7

Hoedads Co-op: Democracy and Cooperation at Work

CHRISTOPHER GUNN

Hoedads Co-op, Inc., a reforestation cooperative of approximately 300 members based in Eugene, Oregon, holds a significant place in the history of American worker cooperatives.[1] In its internal decision-making process it sets high standards of commitment to egalitarianism and democracy. In its external relations, it has shown a willingness to devote energy and resources to progressive social, environmental, and political causes in the Northwest. Hoedads was the first major worker cooperative formed in the Pacific Northwest since the last of the plywood co-ops was formed in the early 1950s. It has not only demonstrated the ability to survive and prosper but it has also served as fertile ground for the formation of other co-ops.

ORIGINS, DEVELOPMENT, AND MEMBERSHIP

Hoedads is a part of the timber industry of the Pacific Northwest. Its principal reforestation activities are tree planting, precommercial forest thinning, seed collection, conifer release, and stand exams.[2] It is also involved in forest trail construction and maintenance, and in fire fighting. These services are performed under contract, generally for either the Forest Service of the U.S. Department of Agriculture, or for the Bureau of Land Management of the U.S. Department of the Interior. Hoedads, other worker cooperatives,[3] and private contractors compete for these contracts. Hoedads works throughout the West from

New Mexico to Alaska, although the majority of its work takes place in Oregon, Washington, and Idaho.

The first contract won by the partnership that became Hoedads Co-op involved three original members in a sixty-acre reforestation job in 1970. By 1974 the co-op had grown to 100 to 125 members who worked in seven crews, and by 1980 membership varied between 250 and 300 people in ten to fourteen crews. By that time, Hoedads was grossing over $2 million per year. Members tend to be between twenty and thirty years old, single, and college educated if not degree holders. Approximately 40 percent of the members are women, and several crews have been composed entirely of women. Minority groups are better represented in the membership than they are in the Eugene area population.

The work of the Hoedads is labor-intensive and seasonal. Planting contracts begin in the fall, extend through the winter if it is not too severe, and then pick up again in the spring. Summer planting is rarely possible, as dry conditions diminish chances for seedlings to survive and in many areas create a sufficient fire hazard to warrant closing the woods to any work. Trail construction and maintenance and fire crew work sustain those members of Hoedads who want employment during the summer months. Some members also find summer work outside of Hoedads.

Hoedads exists as a cooperative corporation under Oregon law. This is the same legal form shared by several Oregon-based plywood co-operatives. Hoedads has had to play an active role in developing legal status for co-ops, as the plywood cooperatives have, through working for judicial and legislative definition of the special characteristics that set this legal entity apart from more traditional businesses. The most recent example of this burden in the case of Hoedads is its battle with state authorities over the application of workers' compensation regulations to worker cooperatives, an issue that will be discussed in further detail below.

Hoedads originated in Eugene, a western Oregon city with a population of approximately 100,000. A combination of environmental concern, emphasis on outdoor life, a large number of transient young people, high unemployment rates, and a recent history of progressive responses to economic and social problems make Eugene a natural base for cooperative organizations. The countercultural reputation of Eugene has attracted, over the last decade, not only young people who need jobs but also those who want less constraining and less hierarchical work than that offered by the University of Oregon or local industry, such as the nearby timber industry giant, Weyerhaeuser. Lane County, Oregon, is home for approximately 250 alternative firms and community-based organizations, and Hoedads is one of the largest and most successful of these.

In 1970, three people with an interest in forestry came together to create a business that would suit their needs. Overcoming barriers that included lack of credibility with bonding agents (a surety bond is required for most federal contracts), skepticism on the part of the Forest Service and other contracting agents, and lack of capital, John Corbin, John Sunquist, and Jerry Rust won a contract to plant sixty acres of seedlings near Port Orford, Oregon. After successfully completing that first contract, they expanded their group, becoming the Cougar Mountain Crew, and worked as one crew for the following two years. A loose cooperative form suited their desires for just enough organizational structure to get the job done, but one that would allow for individual freedom and self-expression. The countercultural and anticapitalist thinking of the late 1960s helped shape the organization, and its early history seems to have been one in which progressive individualism prevailed. The Cougar Mountain Crew eventually created Hoedads Co-op. It fought the early battles for viability, put up communally held land for bonding power, and trained many of the new members to be tree planters.

With the recession in 1973–74, unemployment grew in Lane County, as throughout the country. In a "fit of idealism" the decision was made to expand the co-op. An advertisement for new co-op members in the alternative newspaper in Eugene brought 150 responses and enough new members to form several new crews, with names such as the Mud Sharks, Cheap Thrills, and Red Star. Co-op membership was doubled again the next year, and expanded steadily until 1977, when after considerable discussion it was decided to limit the size of the co-op. From a peak of 350, membership was adjusted by allowing departing members to outnumber new members for enough time to reduce membership to about 300. That process was not a difficult or lengthy one, since entire crews occasionally depart, and since membership turnover in the earlier years approached the rate of 50 percent annually. Since then, crew size has generally not exceeded 30, a number that allows the kind of communication necessary for collective decision making. Contracts that require a larger work force are sometimes bid, and if won, worked by more than one crew.

A special period in the development of Hoedads as a confident and cohesive organization stemmed from their first involvement with local electoral politics. Jerry Rust, the first president of Hoedads, decided in 1976 to become a candidate for Lane County commissioner. With a political organization that was largely made up of members of Hoedads, and one that had little experience or money, Rust was given little chance of success. He ran as an independent, and the bulk of his campaign fund was donated by the co-op and by individuals within it. As it happened, Rust defeated a fourteen-year incumbent in a stunning upset. The impact of that election on Hoedads was strong; the co-op learned that it could transfer its organizational energy to a broader political arena. Lobbying, herbicide and pesticide research, "brush-ins" (in which members voluntarily help communities clear brush rather than use herbicides), and energy for linkages with other forest workers have in part grown from that realization.

The history of Hoedads has been one of continuous change. That is true of most organizations, but it is especially true of one that is run by all of its members. The early form of the co-op was largely established and maintained by its founding members in the Cougar Mountain Crew. With the 1973–74 expansion, the politics, structure, style, and process of the co-op changed. The change was gradual, but in total it was one that provided for more structured forms of democracy and a more coherently left-leaning political orientation. Founding leaders no longer automatically became the officers of the co-op, and new leaders emerged who consciously sought to expand democratic control of the organization. As a result, a formal set of bylaws was adopted in 1974, and the officers of the co-op began to play more of a coordinating and facilitating role than a directing one. The co-op also created a council, a treasury, bidding committees, as well as other representative groups to carry on its affairs. The organization has continued to develop and to change, but it has done so within an organizational framework that has provided a base for structured and democratic evolution. It is useful to explore this structure in some detail.

ORGANIZATION AND DECISION MAKING

The organizational structure of Hoedads has evolved in an attempt to maximize individual and crew freedom in daily work decisions, and at the same time to protect and sustain the co-op as a whole as well as to enable it to operate efficiently. These sometimes contradictory goals have been pursued by means of co-op-wide representative democracy, augmented by members' town-meeting-style direct participation in quarterly general meetings, and by direct democracy at the work crew level. It should be noted that the organizational and decision-making structures are related in important ways within Hoedads. Initially, I will focus on democratic processes within the co-op as a whole and within crews, and then on crew and work life.

THE ORGANIZATIONAL STRUCTURE AND DECISION-MAKING PROCESS

As a cooperative corporation, Hoedads must comply with a state mandated structure. The legal and practical board of directors is its council, which consists of one member from each crew, each with one vote regardless of the size of the crew. Formal responsibilities of the council include:[4]

  a. Setting policy for the co-op
  b. Setting the budget for the co-op
  c. Reviewing recommendations of the bidding committee
  d. Approving officers' recorded hours of work (logged hours) and work content, and determining compensation for other members who render service to the co-op
  e. Allocating work to crews
  f. Determining and controlling administrative functions
  g. Setting and administering special elections and referenda
  h. Limiting the size of the co-op

Policy decisions are carried out by a president, a secretary, and a treasurer, who are nominated by the general membership and elected annually by the council. The president and treasurer take office each January, and the secretary takes office in June. These officers are ex officio members of the council. Candidates for these offices, plus those for the two positions of treasury assistants and that of office coordinator, announce their desire for positions in *Together*, the quarterly newspaper of the Hoedads. Then they must be nominated by a majority vote of the council. This election process has evolved both in response to the needs of the co-op and in part to meet Oregon Cooperative Corporation statutes. Members seem to feel that the council tries hard to reflect general membership sentiments, as indicated in the nominating process when it carries out its final vote.

Co-op officers' roles are clearly defined in the bylaws of Hoedads, although there is considerable latitude given to the interests and personal style of particular officers and to the team functioning of a group of officers. Officers have little impact on the decision making of work crews, but they can of course affect co-op-level decisions through their analysis and presentation of information used for decision making. Their tasks require not only technical and interpersonal skills but also a commitment to cooperative principles to see them through times when it would be easiest simply to make decisions autocratically.

Information flow is the lifeblood of any democratic organization, and this is particularly true of a reforestation co-op, where members are often separated by hundreds of miles in their work and directly involved for long periods of time with only their work crews. Hoedads has, therefore, several regular internal publications to address this need. These are:

a. The weekly Council Minutes and the Newsletter which report where crews are working; how many hours co-op staff members have logged in the previous week and generally how that time was spent; names of members who have resigned; general announcements; and a suggested agenda for the upcoming weekly meeting. The Council Minutes and the Newsletter are written by the co-op secretary, posted in the Eugene office, and sent to each crew and any member requesting them.
b. A quarterly newspaper entitled *Together* is published before each general meeting and distributed to all members. It includes crew reports, members' individual letters, articles on matters of concern to the co-op, short stories, cartoons, officers' reports, tips on work health and safety, general membership meeting agendas, announcements, letters from candidates for office, and more. This tabloid newspaper of approximately thirty-two pages is compiled through a collective effort, generally involving upward of a dozen Hoedads. The office coordinator and secretary are involved in the production of each issue.

In addition to these written forms of communication, considerable office time is spent in maintaining telephone communication among crews and members. With crews often miles from the nearest telephone or post office, the office of Hoedads is their central communications network. Members use it to catch up with their crews, receive calls from family members, get messages to friends, and seek information on work conditions—the variety of calls is endless. If the recipient is not regularly near a phone, messages are logged, then relayed to their intended recipient or read over the phone when that person calls in. Officers and the office coordinator rotate the task of call forwarding, which includes receiving and logging calls at home when the office is closed. The 1979 operating expenses of Hoedads indicate that as much as 30 percent of their overhead can be attributed to disseminating information throughout the organization.[5]

The overall organizational structure of Hoedads in 1980 can be most clearly described with the help of the organizational chart that appears as figure 7.1. The co-op as a whole is made up of individuals who are also crew members. At the center of the co-op are several administrative bodies and staff members through which Hoedads func-

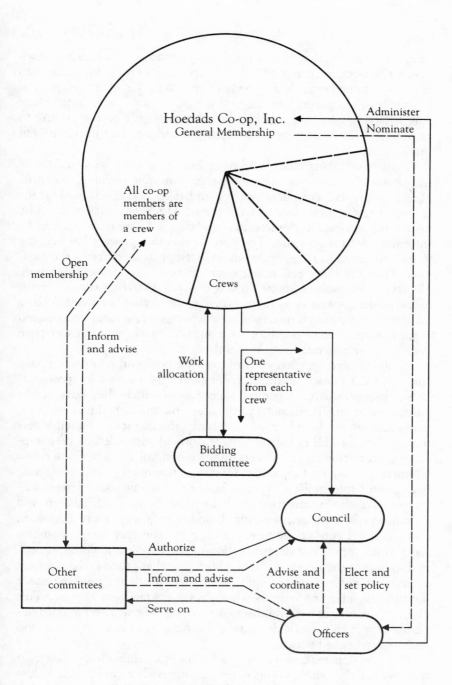

Fig. 7.1 Hoedads Co-op Organizational Chart[6]

tions as a cooperative enterprise. The governing apparatus is shown below the circle, representing the co-op and its crews and, although it is diagrammed outside the body of the co-op for clarity of presentation, it is, of course, internal to the organization. Lines in the chart vary between solid and small dashed lines, roughly corresponding to greater and lesser degrees of authority, oversight, and informational linkages.

Council members meet weekly in Eugene during busy periods of the year and less frequently during the more quiet summer months. Meetings involve considerable give and take among the various interests of representatives and their crews. Minority positions are fully heard and reported in the minutes, and decisions are usually taken by informal vote on an issue. The council meeting process has become more structured in recent years in an attempt to accomplish the business of the week in three to four hours. Efforts to make meetings more efficient have included more strictly observing starting times, clearer agendas, and attempts to focus on issues until they are dealt with to all members' satisfaction. Crews are encouraged to rotate their council representatives over periods of six months or more, so that short-term decision-making continuity is maintained.

Members exercise their control over the co-op on an ongoing basis through their choice of and influence over their council representatives, through quarterly general meetings in which they have direct participation in discussion and debate, and through direct vote on issues and referenda presented to them by the council. Council meetings are open to all members but are normally attended by crew representatives, the co-op officers, and a handful of other observers. Council procedure frequently involves introducing and providing background information on new business, having council representatives take the information back to their crews for discussion and formation of a position, if required, and then having more discussion and a council vote at the next meeting. At the crew level, members have direct input into determination of the decision-making process, and then into the decisions reached through that process. Referendum voting has been usually employed for decisions that must be made during busy planting periods when crews are far from Eugene. This process involves crew-level discussion of the issue at hand and a telephone report to the officers, citing the number of crew votes for and against a proposed action.

The decision-making process faces its most difficult challenge at the level of the whole co-op when dealing with complicated, value-laden decisions, especially those that are politically controversial. Where a small decision-making group in a hierarchical organization might spend a week reaching a decision of this kind, Hoedads and other democratic groups may be at it for months. A case in point for Hoedads has involved decisions concerning workers' compensation. As co-op members, Hoedads has been exempt from mandatory workers' compensation coverage by provision of a state administrative ruling. The Association of Reforestation Contractors (a trade association of reforestation contractors, and the arch rival of the co-op), arguing that the exemption provides co-ops with unfair competitive advantage, brought suit against the state board that administers the insurance plan for supposedly not enforcing the law. The Oregon co-ops in the Northwest Forest Workers' Association (NWFWA) decided to launch a legislative effort to have co-ops specifically excluded from mandatory coverage under the state law. Their bill made it to the senate floor, where it was defeated. The lobbyist for NWFWA, the president of Hoedads, and other co-op members devoted considerable time and resources to that battle.

Hoedads and another co-op prepared to defend themselves in court. They felt that it was important to win this case for a number of reasons.[7] But, for many within Hoedads, this was the wrong battle. They argued that Hoedads should have had workers' compensation coverage and that the energy and resources of the cooperative could then have been devoted to reforming the state system to reduce its bias against co-ops. Such a highly controversial issue can paralyze a co-op, and it is in negotiating cooperative solutions to difficult issues like these that cooperative structures face their greatest test.

It is in the individual work crews of Hoedads that the organization has the opportunity to develop decision making furthest in the direction of a collectivist democracy[8]; it is there that Hoedads uses a consensus process involving crew members in the collective formulation of problems and negotiation of decisions. At the crew level, several factors operate to create the opportunity for heightened forms of democracy. Through the screening of new members, crews informally assure a greater homogeneity of interests and philosophy than the co-op as a whole can achieve.[9] The small size of the crew, and the fact that most crews live together and share certain life and work support responsibilities, allow for close interpersonal communication. Crews, which work as a team, share common material incentives in order to complete contracts and a common concern to keep crew costs within some group-defined limits.

Crew meetings sometimes last all day. Most crews hold a meeting before each contract begins. It usually deals with the prework conference held between the contractor and the nonplanting foreperson, as well as with the strategy for planting, logistics of the crew camp, provisions, equipment, and the like. This meeting tends to focus on the work confronting the crew, and it is usually relatively businesslike.

Meetings that deal with interpersonal problems within the crew—for instance, personal styles of work, personal power and its use within the crew, or sexism in the work or living situation—can be most difficult but potentially also the most rewarding. There is a feeling held in common among the Hoedads that, however tortuous and personally painful crew meetings are, they are one of the focal arenas for personal and organizational development. It is there, for instance, that prejudices and power relationships are confronted. Crew members know that they have to work together often within hours of their crew meetings and that such difficult issues will not go away.

Variations in crew-level decision making are many, but the process is usually based on some mixture of consensus decision making and parliamentary procedure. Issues are broadly and sometimes intensely discussed. Voting is used in some decisions by all crews, but when it is, members typically discuss how strongly they feel about their vote on a particular issue. Crews might use a soft or modified parliamentary process, where a chairperson leads the meeting through an agreed-upon agenda, maintains the focus of the meeting, conducts whatever voting procedure has been agreed to, and in general directs a meeting more than a facilitator in a consensus decision-making process might. Under this modified parliamentary process, the meeting generally ends with a criticism/self-criticism session. I observed a crew meeting that operated in this way. The chairperson, who was in part drafted and in part volunteered, was not particularly experienced at the task. Other crew members helped him at times, and the business of the meeting was accomplished using an assortment of meeting procedures. When the meeting became chaotic or drifted from the subject at hand, the chair reexerted informal control. Crew members had frequent opportunities to make their views on issues known, and simple majority rule did prevail on several issues where those with opposing viewpoints did not feel strongly enough about their positions to challenge the majority. Difficult policy issues on which the crew could not reach relatively easy decisions—such as how many new members to take into the crew and whether they should be female or male, minority or white, experienced or inexperienced, and so on—were put aside for another meeting. This sort of issue would probably take up most of a four- to five-hour meeting, or possibly several meetings. These difficult issues are the kind on which the crew strives for consensus, precisely because they are the types of issues that could break a group apart.

Crews have typically made a conscious effort to avoid the individualistic and competitive relations that accompany traditional parliamentary process and majority rule. Some have developed very consensual processes based on collectivist, feminist and antiauthoritarian crew philosophies. Ground rules for a modified parliamentary process are currently being developed by the council and by some crews, as they search for a concise but cooperative and democratic decision-making process.

Crew meeting process is, of course, linked to how crews carry on their day-to-day work between the meetings. Crews differ in the kind of independent decisions that an individual can make on the job, in how much authority the nonplanting foreperson has on the job site, and in how and what kinds of decisions can be reached over dinner or at some other time when the crew is informally together. The system of pay within the crew is also linked to these crew process issues.

At the co-op level, Hoedads is in the process of more formally assembling task force committees to deal with issues that require co-op action but for which significant research and organizing of information is necessary. There is no requirement that each committee have a representative from each crew. Sign-up lists for any task force that has been created by the council hang in the offices and meeting place of Hoedads. Committees are responsible for bringing well-organized information to the council or general membership. The task force committees are open to any members who want to serve on them, and especially to those who have, as it is stated in a set of council minutes, "gripes or energy to make changes." During the summer of 1979, task force committees were working on internal issues, such as health and safety, new member education, pay systems, and insurance and disability benefits. Voluntary and committee representatives also interact with the Northwest Forest Workers' Association and the Forest Workers' Organizing Committee.

Task force committees do not make policy decisions, but they clearly have important power, as officers do, insofar as they can choose how to present an issue for discussion and decision to either the council or the general membership. The committees walk a fine line between helping to provide leadership and informational input for long-term planning and for policy and operating decisions on the one hand, and impeding the democratic process of the co-op on the other. Members seem well aware of this and stress the need to keep committees open in membership and advisory in role.

The major opportunity for face-to-face communication among all Hoedads occurs at the organization's general meetings. Summer meetings in particular are special events, and members come from near and far to set up camp, talk, argue, listen to reports, and vote on matters vital to the co-op. These meetings involve constant work on democratic process for decision making, as well as efforts to overcome sexism, and recurring philosophical and practical debates about issues such as co-op size, growth, obligations to further the co-op movement, and the level of administrative overhead for the co-op.

Decisions that are brought to a vote at general meetings tend to be policy issues that are known to be controversial by the council, decisions that involve new commitments of over $1,000 of co-op funds, or rules that would make anything compulsory. Meetings include criticism/self-criticism periods, and although there is an agenda determined by council, that agenda is open to change at the beginning of the meeting. General meetings are chaired by the officers, crew representatives, and other members who are good facilitators. Since these meetings can be long and exhausting, the co-op has learned to arrange a summer gathering site where several hundred people can work and play together. The June 1979 general meeting lasted for three days, one of which was set aside for play. Winter meetings are frequently held in the Woodsmen of the World (WOW) Hall, a community center in Eugene with historical ties to forest workers' labor organizations.

The complicated and multilayered organizational structure of Hoedads is thus best understood as an evolving attempt to maximize individual and group freedom within the organization while preserving and fostering the organization itself. The unique combination present, of consensual direct democracy at the work crew level and of both representative and direct town-meeting-style democracy at the level of the whole co-op, gives it the flexibility to accomplish both of these goals. To be sure, the cooperative decision-making process is cumbersome when it comes to solving multifaceted, value-laden issues, whether at the co-op or the work crew level. But it is also precisely these kinds of decisions that push the co-op to devise new methods of problem solving that enhance its flexibility and ensure its long-term cooperative survival.

CREWS, NEW MEMBERS, AND WORK LIFE

The semiautonomous work crews of Hoedads form the backbone of the co-op. The bylaws specify that crews can be created from the general membership of Hoedads, or in other words, by members of already existing crews. They can also enter the co-op as already formed units. The first major expansion of the co-op in 1973 included the entry of Thumb Forestry, an experienced crew that had formerly worked in northern California. More recently Hoedads accepted an entire crew with the understanding that they would learn the business from Hoedads, and then split off. New crews must be approved by a two-thirds vote of the council. Crews can be removed from Hoedads as well, and that involves both a two-thirds vote of the council and a majority vote of the members at large.[10]

Crew responsibility to the co-op includes: providing a council member, providing a crew treasurer who will maintain the crew bank account and a working relationship with the co-op treasury, and providing a member of the bidding committee who shares the responsibility for bidding the work. The bylaws of Hoedads also specify that the logistical support for the crew and responsibility for crew expenses rest solely with each crew.

After these responsibilities to the co-op are met, crew autonomy is well protected. Crew rights that appear in the bylaws include: determination of crew membership as well as member entry and termination conditions; determination of the nature of logistical support (e.g., is crew food handled collectively or individually, etc.); determination of the division of labor and organization of work for the crew; and determination of the crew's council member by whatever means and for whatever term (up to a maximum of three years) the crew chooses. Crews cannot be forced to work on any contract that they do not want to participate in, as long as they have made their crew's refusal clear prior to bidding for contracts.

Membership in Hoedads begins with the individual joining a crew. After being accepted by a crew, the new member signs a statement acknowledging that she or he has read and understood the co-op bylaws and accepts liability for the membership fee of $2,000. That fee can be paid upon joining, but it is almost always paid over time from a member's earnings. The full fee is returned to those leaving the co-op except in cases when members depart before $50 of the fee has been paid. Membership is fully established upon acceptance of an individual into a crew and the recognition of the individual's legal obligation to Hoedads for the membership fee.

The Eugene-based office and administrative staff refer individuals seeking work to crews, and learn later whether an individual has been accepted into a particular crew. With crews sometimes hundreds of miles from Eugene, this is a cumbersome process for the prospective new member, but one that probably discourages the marginally interested. A prospective member's communication with crews working outside of Eugene usually begins with a meeting with a crew's council representative when the representative is in Eugene for a council meeting. If that meeting goes well, the prospective member may be invited to the work site, possibly to attend a crew meeting. If the crew decides to take on the new member, and that member is willing to either pay or incur liability to Hoedads for her or his membership fee, then the initial entry is complete. The informal role of the administration and office staff in this search and screening process cannot be overlooked. Office staff members have knowledge of which crews are seeking new members and of the specific characteristics of various crews. Then they can informally determine how much effort to put into bringing the potential new member into contact with a crew, based on their impression of the individual.

The process of work training, socialization to camp life, and development of a full role in the decision-making process of the crew varies among the crews and with each member as well. It is the common practice that the new member's sponsor sees that he or she has basic knowledge of what the work entails, what an individual's responsibility to the crews is, and what equipment and clothing should be taken to the member's first contract job. When the new member begins work, she or he usually spends a few days with the nonplanting foreperson on the crew, learning basic planting techniques. From that point, training continues with many members of the crew offering advice on how to work efficiently and minimize risk of injury. In the past, new members have learned about the history and operation of Hoedads from informal discussion with older members.[11] An education task force within the co-op is currently developing written materials that will help to acquaint new members with the co-op more quickly. New member involvement in crew decision making can come very quickly and is probably heavily dependent on the initiative of each new member. In one crew meeting that I observed, two members who had been a part of the crew for only two weeks were playing a very active part in the discussion and decision making.

A significant task that may be assigned to relatively new crew members who have demonstrated a threshold level of responsibility and competence is that of crew treasurer. The crew treasurer maintains the crew bank account, which is the conduit both for paying crew bills and for distributing crew earnings via the co-op treasury. As a task that requires routine attention to detail, it is an anomaly in the freewheeling environment of camp life. A new crew member may find it a challenge to learn both tree planting and the business practice of the crew, although she or he learns quickly through this job about the individual crew's business operations, and also the workings of the co-op treasury. This crew member is involved at the co-op level of activity on an ongoing basis, as are the crew's bidding committee member and its council representative. Crew treasurer duty may last from several months to a year or more. Training of the new crew treasurer is the responsibility of the outgoing crew treasurer, and it is augmented by the co-op treasury staff. The crew treasurer is rewarded through reimbursement by the crew for time lost from contract work. The task is considered a burden by many who perform it, yet it is vital to the smooth functioning of the crew and the co-op. The cost in training time compared with having one person perform the function of crew treasurer on an ongoing basis is obvious, yet for those who take on the duty it is also an empowering process, providing knowledge which can enhance the relatively new member's ability to participate in crew and co-op decision making.

Members who are new to tree planting can expect to spend $150 to $250 on personal equipment. This includes a hoedad, a tree bag, boots, and rain gear. At least part of this equipment may be acquired secondhand or bought over time as the new member gains experience and income. It is not uncommon for everything but the hoedad to need replacement after a planting season. Experienced tree planters tend to acquire their own rig—a truck with camper, a small trailer, a panel truck, or some other dependable vehicle—equipped to serve as home while at or traveling between camps.

Tree planting is labor-intensive in the extreme.[12] A typical day's work for one planter involves planting 500 seedlings, with variations from 300 to 1,200 seedlings. The tools of the trade are basically two: the hoedad, an adzlike tool that resembles a cross between a pick and a narrow-bladed shovel; and a tree bag and waist belt, with which seedlings are carried on the back of the hips. In addition, a hard hat may be worn, sturdy boots are a necessity, and gloves and rain gear are used regularly. Rain is a constant reality for planters, since rainfall usually measures over 100 inches annually in areas of the Northwestern Coast Range.

A tree planting contract entails a crew being on site in the forest for one to four weeks. Once on site, a crew must decide how best to approach the planting of the clear-cut land area under contract. The strategy is discussed among crew members, and the teamwork of a crew in planting, called *patterns* or *maneuvers* by many tree planters, centers on how to get the job done most efficiently. Measures of efficiency include how many trees can be put down in a unit of time and at a density that will just meet the contract specifications. This usually entails questions of how irregular terrain can be covered with a minimum of walking on the part of the crew. The considerations here are the size and shape of the unit, crew size, amount of time available (before the end of the day, week, contract time, etc.), road access or walking time to the unit, steepness of the grade, or other complicating factors. Inspectors, the field representatives for the contracting agencies, make day-to-day decisions about whether work is meeting contract specifications. A crew generally designates one member to be the nonplanting foreperson, a position that is rotated. The nonplanting foreperson coordinates a crew's work and serves as liaison with the contracting agency and its inspector.

Crews strive to make maximum allowance for the individual crew member's planting style without jeopardizing the well-being of the crew as a whole. Efficient planning helps a crew finish the contract more quickly. It can then enjoy a break and the amenities of town life for a longer period of time before leaving for the next contract.

Crew members live together in various levels of sharing while on the job, and their work process decisions are influenced by and have an influence on their crew living situation. Tree planting is difficult work, and the refocusing of energy that takes place in the evening at camp is important to getting the job done. Camp life provides relief in the form of companionship, food, and shelter. Camps are usually set up in forest clearings or gravel pits and left in the same location for the duration of work on the contract. Most crews have come to use a yurt (modeled after the round, folding structure developed in central Asia) as their important common space and the place where meals are prepared and served, if the crew shares meals in common. Tree planters have to be nomadic, and the individual shelters used by many members show a wide variety of individual tastes and levels of personal energy and financial investment. Tents, trailers, vans, and tepees are all common. The crew yurt and its wood-burning stove get transported in the *crummy* (an old Northwestern lumber camp term—derivation unknown) as do much of the crew's gear and tools, and some of the members. The crummy is generally a refurbished small school bus or large van, and it is the major piece of equipment owned by the crew.

The close relationships of crew life give way to larger scale forms of interaction at the co-op level. The co-op has numbered over 400 members in the past, and members' concern with becoming too large and impersonal to function effectively as a cooperative unit led to a bylaw that charges the council with responsibility for limiting membership. As noted earlier, an informal consensus has emerged around a co-op size of 300 members.

One means by which the size of Hoedads is held down involves individuals, and at times whole crews, leaving the co-op to join or form smaller reforestation collectives and co-ops. Departing members take with them knowledge of the benefits and problems of cooperative work, a very real awareness of the joy and misery of tree planting, and nuts and bolts knowledge such as how to bid for contracts. In addition to experience and knowledge, the departing members also take with them their accumulated membership fees. The inspiration for the new co-op, the expertise to make it work, and at least some of the capital to get it started flow out of the departing members' years of experience with Hoedads. In this sense Hoedads has served as an organization helping to generate other co-ops in the area. Several of these other co-ops now number from twenty-five to seventy-five members, and they compete for the same contracts that Hoedads bids for. The departure of the core groups for these co-ops is viewed as a natural process that keeps the growth of the Hoedads within acceptable limits, while it helps to strengthen the co-op movement in the Northwest.

FINANCIAL STRUCTURE AND OPERATION

The organizational structure and the decision-making process do not exist in isolation from the financial structure of an organization. The organizational democracy and cooperative spirit of Hoedads reflect in part the egalitarian economic commitment of members to the co-op, but perhaps more importantly they reflect an organizational form that has broken the link between the level of financial contribution to the organization and the level of power that each member wields within it.

Both Hoedads themselves and outsiders familiar with the co-op tend to think of it as a wealthy organization. With annual contract income exceeding $2 million, they have been referred to as "the millionaire hippies," a title that obviously could not be applied to any of them individually. The cash reserves of Hoedads can be in the neighborhood of $250,000 to $300,000. These reserves originate from membership fees and a special fund—an additional assessment on members' earnings created when the membership fee was $1,000. The reserves serve several purposes related to the nature of the work that the Hoedads perform. They qualify the co-op for bonding, provide a basis for a bank line of credit to the co-op, and offer a means to smooth the cash flow irregularity in this seasonal business.

As a cooperative corporation, Hoedads engages in business to provide its members with the opportunity and material conditions for work. The earnings of worker cooperatives are not profits; they are called *net surplus*, and the co-op is legally obligated to return those amounts to members on a patronage basis. Legal principles that have evolved from the Rochdale Society of Equitable Pioneers, and that were most clearly applicable to consumer cooperatives, have been more recently applied to worker cooperatives in this country. Specifically, a 1976 court ruling clarified that a worker's patronage or "business done" with a worker cooperative is "work."[13] The net earnings (patronage dividends) of the cooperative from business with or for its patrons (worker-members) may be excluded from its taxable earnings. The earnings are distributed to worker-members on the basis of their relative patronage, which is defined in terms of hours worked in a given accounting period.

Two options for how earnings are paid out to members are available to worker cooperatives in the United States. The more traditional is the one described above. It involves a regular payment of a *patronage advance* on anticipated members' earnings. Worker cooperatives can also pay hourly wages to their members and deduct them as business expenses for tax purposes. Remaining co-op earnings at the end of an accounting period are then distributed to members as their earned individual income, and the total earnings of members are subject to personal income tax. As in the case of patronage dividends, these earnings are not taxable income for the co-op.

Hoedads Co-op collects contract earnings for its members, deducts an estimated percentage to cover the operating expenses of the co-op (called the *administrative rake-off*), deducts individual members' payments toward their membership fee, and deposits the remainder in crew bank accounts. There has been no co-op-wide rule for the distribution of income to individuals; that decision has been made at the crew level. Most crews have traditionally distributed income by a piece rate system, according to the number of trees that a member plants. There are signs of change in this practice, and variations among crews in methods of income distribution will be discussed below.

Capitalization of Hoedads has taken place through payment of the membership fee. The fee is payable upon entry but is usually paid out of earnings at a rate of 8 percent of a member's earnings until the full amount is paid. This is a matter of necessity for many members who enter the co-op with very little money. It also might be thought of as a rational choice, since there is no interest assessment during the period of payment and no reduction in the fee or other incentive for payment of the fee upon entry. Cases of membership fee repayment are subject to a forty-five-day period during which departing members continue to share liability with ongoing members for any claims or judgments against Hoedads. The total liability of each member is limited, as it is for any cooperative, to the $2,000 membership fee. This liability exists for new members who have not fully paid the membership fee as well as for those who have paid it in full.

In the late 1970s, the co-op was financially secure enough that the departure of a number of members at one time did not lead to a financial crisis for the organization. A case in point was the departure of the entire Mud Sharks crew in the summer of 1979. Their withdrawal to form a smaller co-op meant the loss of $38,000 in membership fees and accumulated funds. That amount was available on demand to the crew. This ample financial base has not always existed, and it was the task of the early members to accumulate liquid assets to the point where the co-op could function smoothly.

The early financial history of Hoedads is best understood in light of familiarity with the financial aspects of reforestation contracting.

Contracts are let for public lands, and also by private forest products corporations for their own land. Hoedads works almost exclusively with agencies of the federal government. Although private timber companies will let contracts to some small, less political co-ops, they have generally refrained from contracting with Hoedads and most other NWFWA member co-ops.

Federal contracts impose two financial burdens on the contractor. First, a surety bond has to be posted by the contractor. This bond insures the contracting agency against loss resulting from the con-tractor's negligence or failure to complete a contract. Hoedads has worked with one bonding agent long enough to have established a very sound track record of contract completion. The cost to the co-op for bonding was $9 per $1,000 of coverage on each contract in 1980. Second, the contractor must be prepared to pay the crew and cover its operating expenses during the work period and up until the time when payment on the contract is forthcoming. The payment period is sometimes as long as three months after completion of work. This twofold need for bonding and for financing over periods of little or no cash inflow has proven an insurmountable barrier to a number of reforestation co-ops.

The first contracts awarded to Hoedads were won using collectively held land, old Volkswagen buses, and even personal belongings such as backpacks for collateral with a Eugene-based representative of a national bonding agency. Founding members used income from a va-riety of sources to sustain themselves while planting and waiting for payment on their few, early contracts. Tools were acquired with funds from part-time work, and members lived in cars, tents, and under any form of cover while at the site. Establishing cash reserves for bonding collateral and for operating capital became a major objective. During the slow growth period of 1970 to 1973, the original partnership struggled to establish sound working relationships with both the bond-ing agent and the bank. Those relationships were threatened when a 1974 contract for trail building in the Olympic Peninsula of Wash-ington proved much more difficult than anticipated, and the crew working it could not complete it within the contract period. Default would have jeopardized the bonding power of Hoedads for the fall contracts of that year and could have spelled the end of the co-op. Several days before the contract deadline, seventy-five co-op members responded to the crisis by arriving at the work site with $2,500 in tools and food. Through a collective effort they completed the contract on time. The teamwork involved and the joyous celebration that followed helped to reinforce members' understanding of what the Hoe-dads Cooperative was all about.

With growth in membership and the gradual accumulation of membership fees, by 1975 the co-op treasury reached sufficient size to assure the continued smooth operation of the contracting process and to enable regular payments to crew members who were on the job. Today those payments take the form of advances from the co-op treasury to each crew account. Those funds are repaid to the co-op treasury when the contract income is received. Because of the large number of contracts now worked by Hoedads at the peak fall and spring periods, the co-op uses an assignment-of-claims process with its bank in order to keep payments to crews flowing on a regular basis. Future income from completed contracts is assigned to the bank, and the bank loans 80 percent of the gross amount of the contract payment to the co-op at an interest rate slightly below the current prime rate. When the contract income arrives at the bank, the balance due Hoedads, less the interest charge, is forwarded to the Hoedads's account.

The seasonal nature of Hoedads's income creates a cash surplus during the summer months. In summers up through 1978, liquid assets were in large part left in the co-op's savings and checking accounts at a state bank. A more sophisticated cash management plan was implemented in 1979, one that not only involved greater interest income to Hoedads, but one that also put their liquid assets more directly to work in the Eugene community. Funds were loaned to Starflower, a feminist collective and regional food distribution company, on a short term note at 2.5 percent above passbook interest rates. Other funds were deposited in the Oregon Urban and Regional (OUR) Credit Union which serves low income area residents. And a substantial part of the $150,000 to $200,000 in summer liquid assets was loaned to the Lane County School Employees' Credit Union at 7.5 percent. Although cash in this magnitude could obviously be invested in money market funds, certificates of deposit, or other short-term investment opportunities, none of these is an attractive alternative to members of Hoedads. Placing the funds with community-based organizations and receiving some premium over passbook interest rates satisfies the co-op's desire for both more economically astute and more socially desirable cash management.

In the following diagram the flow of income through Hoedads is represented (see fig. 7.2). This diagram serves to highlight the special aspects of the co-op financial structure, one that is created to serve working members of the organization. Unlike a private corporation, the people working in the co-op are not a peripheral expense as funds flow through the organization to expand owners' capital. In the case of Hoedads, membership fees finance the organization (cash reserves), and the administrative costs of the organization (mainly hourly wages to staff members who are themselves co-op members) are paid directly out of members' income.

The financial structure of Hoedads has evolved with the develop-ment of the co-op, and it has thus far served that development well. The primary financial needs of the co-op have been to provide for working capital rather than the investment capital that would be required to equip a less labor-intensive work process. A significant body of theoretical literature and empirical evidence on appropriate financial structures for labor-managed firms indicates that choices made in this area of co-op structure can play a vital role in determining the ability of a firm like Hoedads to survive over time.[14] The principal findings of that literature are that members' funds that are used to finance a firm should be recoverable when the members leave the organization or retire, and that firms of this type should pay a scarcity-reflecting rent (interest) on funds supplied by members. Both of these conditions are designed to guard against the problems, historically common to co-ops, of small size and undercapitalization. Both help to overcome what have traditionally been investment disincentives for members, and both are compatible with a complete separation between the amount of capital a member may have invested in the co-op and the amount of voting influence each member would have.

Hoedads meets the first of these conditions, in that membership fees are returned to departing members. The second of these condi-tions, that interest be paid on members' contributed capital, is not met by the co-op. Mainstream economic theory indicates that this could create an incentive for members to slowly reduce their numbers and share "returns to capital" among a smaller number of members.[16] Hoedads uses very little capital in its principal work process. Planting trees involves minimal equipment; therefore Hoedads may avoid this historical tendency of worker cooperatives largely because of the labor-intensive nature of its work.

The fact that the members of Hoedads voted to increase their membership fee from $1,000 to $2,000 indicates that the co-op has avoided a second financial problem common to worker cooperatives. That problem is also associated with not paying interest on members' invested capital. Members acting in accordance with mainstream eco-nomic assumptions of rational capitalist behavior would seek to invest their money in ways that would provide them with maximum monetary return on those funds. This would theoretically have members seeking to avoid investment in their own co-op when interest-paying savings or investment opportunities were available to them. This would leave the co-op consistently deciding against new investment.[17] In the cap-italist market environment in which the co-op is normally assumed to operate, this tendency would lead over time to undercapitalization, or to too low a capital-labor ratio for the co-op to be competitive in its industry.

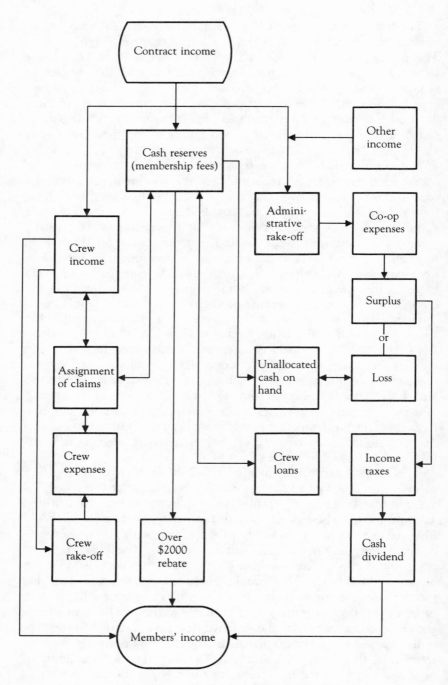

Fig. 7.2 Hoedads Co-op: Flow of Income[15]

Hoedads has avoided the problem of undercapitalization for several reasons. First, its financial needs are primarily for working capital; the level of need in this case is determined by forces external to the co-op. The co-op's bonding agent and its bank determine the amount of funds that Hoedads will require, given the volume of work it plans to perform. A second and very important reason why failure to pay interest on members' contributed funds has not adversely affected Hoedads Co-op has to do with members' motivation and behavior. Members consider their membership fee to be their contribution to their own organization of work, one that yields them a vitally important nonmonetary reward in the form of a viable and liberating work environment. The membership fee is also considered a form of enforced savings and, despite the ravages of inflation, is considered a service by many members. Other members, in perhaps more rational economic thinking, point out that the pool of membership fees not only assures them of the ability to get work but also helps smooth their income flow from that work. One person explained that she and others would have to borrow money (and pay interest on it) while waiting for sporadic payments from completed contracts. She argued that in effect the co-op's pooled capital enabled her to take interest-free short-term loans that compensated for the lack of a regular interest payment on her paid-in capital. She did recognize the occasional expense of using the co-op's assignment-of-claims process to accomplish this, but she argued that many members might not have access to loans individually, whereas the co-op as a whole does have that access. In short, it appears that thinking of this kind is not well addressed by economic theory that would have individuals behaving as capitalist financiers. Although monetary interest is not paid on the membership fees at Hoedads, the fees are seen as providing rewards (which some economists might call *income in kind*) to members that counteract or neutralize any tendency to not invest. Neoclassical economic theory is based on assumptions about human behavior where that behavior is conditioned by a capitalist environment. Although the macroenvironment in which Hoedads is located is clearly capitalist, Hoedads and similar organizations may be able to create an organizational environment that reinforces noncapitalist behavior on the part of their members. Where that has been accomplished, analysis of those organizations based on neoclassical economic precepts must proceed cautiously.[18]

In summary, the financial structure used by Hoedads and the level of consciousness of its members guard against the worst of the economic imperfections that have historically been associated with workers' cooperatives. If the future diversification of Hoedads leads it in the direction of more capital-intensive work processes, and if it desires to or has to capitalize itself primarily from membership fees rather than from external debt, then it will face an important decision about whether to pay interest on members' funds or not. That decision should be informed by lessons from other worker cooperatives, but its proper resolution will depend largely on the particular needs and on the level of cooperative consciousness within Hoedads itself.

The financial structures of crews within Hoedads vary considerably because of differences in crew philosophy and practice described earlier. Most crews own at least some basic equipment in common, such as one or two crummies, a chain saw or two, some hand tools, and a yurt and woodstove. This equipment is typically paid for out of the crew rake-off—a mutually agreed-upon percentage deducted from crew members' income to pay for crew expenses. The useful life of most of this equipment is two to three years at best. If members of a crew are leaving, and those people have been with the crew long enough to have paid significantly toward equipment, a negotiation process might determine a fair price for their share. In the summer of 1979, for instance, a crew named Full Moon Rising divided approximately $5,000 in property held in common. Some members were staying with Hoedads to form a new crew, while others were leaving to join another reforestation co-op in Seattle; nonetheless the equipment was disposed of to the members' satisfaction.

Most of the investment decisions made by crews involve equipment that determines how well they live while working a contract, rather than how much equipment crew members will use in production. This is especially true of the crews that live more communally. In general, then, individual investment in crew equipment is recoverable through informal negotiation, and it does not receive a scarcity-reflecting rent.

Treasury estimates of the cost to capitalize a new crew of ten to fifteen members in 1980 indicate that a crew could be outfitted for as little as $3,000, with some need for working capital beyond that figure. Most of the capital expense would be for acquisition of and conversion work necessary on a vehicle suitable for the crew's crummy. A crew can borrow most of the initial capital needed from either the local credit union (with the co-op's backing) or the co-op's cash reserve fund.

The personal income of Hoedads's members varies within a range of $2,000 to $20,000 a year, with an estimated mean of approximately $8,000 a year (1980 dollars). This estimate represents members who have worked both of the primary seasons in the year and probably some of the winter or summer. The current estimates of the hourly wage earned by a member while working a contract is $7 per hour. Individual variations in income result from individual choice as to both the duration and the intensity of work. Crew decisions on their work schedule and work load affect these variables as well.

The officers and office staff members have little time to work with their crews, but they do make a point of maintaining involvement with them. Officers of the co-op, as well as treasury assistants, bidders, the office coordinator, and any members who work on special projects approved by the council, all earn equal hourly pay. The rate in 1980 was set at $7 per hour. Logged hours for regular officers and staff members average approximately thirty per week, typically for forty-five weeks per year, giving them approximately $9,500 in income, with fewer free weeks than most members who are working contracts. Officers and other workers frequently log fewer hours than they actually work.

Pay systems within crews have typically followed one of two alternatives. Contracts frequently pay planters on a per tree basis, and most crews have used a similar piece rate system to allocate income to members. Other crews have paid themselves on a per share system, which is based on each member's hours of work reported at the end of a workday. The implications of each method for development of individualistic versus cooperative work relations within crews is a topic of considerable debate. Those who argue for the share (hourly) system stress its importance in helping to neutralize differences in physical ability and stamina among crew members, and its positive contribution to work crew solidarity and sharing. Defenders of the per tree system like the freedom it imparts—freedom for an individual who wants to or has to earn more money to work hard and to receive the direct reward for her or his work, or freedom to take it easy without feeling group pressure to do more. Others think the work incentive of the piece rate system is a necessary evil in a large co-op that has only minimal criteria for entry of new members. A co-op task force is studying whether the co-op as a whole should adopt a uniform pay system. The proposal that appears likely to emerge from this group would involve a blending of the two systems. Half a member's pay would be based on hours worked and half on the number of trees planted. There seems to be widespread support for such a method of combining both individual and collective material incentives and, if chosen by members as a co-op policy, it could represent an important step toward strengthening collective consciousness within Hoedads.

The co-op's financial history to date has been one of growth, then achievement of stability in financial transactions and, by the late 1970s, refinement of the central treasury operation in response to the challenge of operating an increasingly complex organization in a co-operative way. With a period of rapid growth behind the co-op, a financial structure is in place that will enable Hoedads to deal with the more steady-state period that seems to lie ahead. Hoedads is beginning an effort to diversify into more technical forest-related contract work, such as stand exams, phenotypic surveys, and erosion control. The financial health of the co-op will provide a solid base for these new developments.

THE SIGNIFICANCE OF HOEDADS

The history of worker cooperatives in the United States is one in which prototype co-ops have played a significant role in the formation of other co-ops. In the 1860s and 1870s in the Minneapolis area, the Cooperative Barrel Company served as a prototype for other cooperage co-ops. In the Pacific Northwest, Olympia Veneer, formed in 1921, served as a model for the plywood co-ops that followed.[19] Hoedads Co-op has been such a model for forestry worker cooperatives in the northwestern United States. In some cases the other forestry worker cooperatives have been formed by people who were formerly Hoedads, and in other cases they were begun independent of the direct influence of Hoedads but with knowledge of its structure and early history. Hoedads was the first; it has grown and served as a learning base for founders of other co-ops; and it remains the largest reforestation co-op.

Several characteristics set Hoedads apart from earlier worker cooperatives founded in the United States. One is that Hoedads has achieved a level of internal democracy that, given its size, clearly exceeds earlier examples. The most obvious comparison with Hoedads at its co-op level is that of the plywood co-ops. In those co-ops (and in most other historical examples of worker cooperatives as well), nonmember workers are employed by the co-op. Full membership in most of these co-ops entailed paying a membership fee or supplying capital in some other form *before* gaining full membership rights. Members of Hoedads do pay a membership fee, but the fact that a prospective member does not have that sum of money does not preclude her or him from attaining full rights upon entry into the organization. In addition, only working members participate on an ongoing basis in managing the organization. Capital has been eliminated as both the ticket of entry and the vehicle of control within the organization.

But Hoedads also takes democratic decision-making principles a step further than representative democracy and participation in periodic general meetings. Their ongoing attempt to develop consensual and cooperative decision-making processes at the crew level creates the potential for realization of organizational processes normally attainable only in small collectives. Several of the smaller forestry worker cooperatives have chosen to remain small in an attempt to better approach this organizational ideal. The structure of Hoedads allows room for this development at the crew level, and then uses representative and direct, town-meeting-style democracy to control and guide a larger, democratically centralized body. The results are small, human-scale work groups, considerable room within the organization for participation and personal growth, and the combined strength of 300 united working people.

Another characteristic of Hoedads that sets it apart from many historical examples of worker cooperatives is more elusive and more difficult to label clearly. It involves the fact that energy and resources flow out of the co-op in support of cooperative political, social, and economic causes in the Northwest. Hoedads is an activist co-op. It is linked with a dozen other forestry worker cooperatives and collectives through the Northwest Forest Workers' Association (NWFWA). NWFWA funds the Northwest Coalition for an Alternative to Pesticides, which is sponsoring some of the most significant research being done on the human and environmental hazards of chemicals used in forestry, and on economically viable alternatives to herbicides and pesticides. The lobbying efforts of Hoedads and NWFWA in the Oregon legislature were instrumental in the state's decision to severely limit the use of chemicals containing thiram in Oregon forests. Hoedads joined with other groups in a court suit aimed at halting the use of sprays containing known toxic substances in the Siuslaw National Forest. The Forest Workers' Organizing Committee (FWOC), a caucus with NWFWA, has responsibility for investigating the potential for an industry-wide organization of reforestation workers, for workers who currently have no union representation.[20] Through its active support of other cooperatives, forest worker advocacy, and involvement in the Eugene community, Hoedads has set itself apart from many co-ops that have preceded it in the United States. Rather than being content with an organization that provides the work setting they want, its members are willing to fight the battles that will help define a special place for worker cooperatives in the economic and social fabric of the Northwest.

Can Hoedads serve as a model for other organizations beyond the forest industry of the Northwest? Despite some of the unique characteristics of Hoedads—the labor contract thrust of its work, the age and character of its members—it is readily reproducible as an organizational form. Hoedads has refined a way for people to work together democratically, to control their internal work process completely, and to sustain an environment that encourages the growth of individuals

168

and of community. This is a remarkable achievement, and one that can both inspire and provide practical lessons for others pursuing the same goals.

But worker cooperatives, no matter how successful they might be, cannot be seen as an end in themselves when they are located within a capitalist economy. In the best of circumstances, the forestry worker cooperatives of the Northwest may provide examples of something more vital—of how people who organize in cooperative and egalitarian ways can reach out to more oppressed and exploited people around them and demonstrate a viable alternative to traditional work organizations. That process need not and should not involve an evangelical mission for worker cooperatives alone; at best it will include a flexible and sophisticated attempt to meet people on their own ground and to work with them toward goals of a democratically controlled workplace, labor movement, and economy.

NOTES

1. The co-op as a whole and individual members are known as Hoedads. The name comes from the hand tool used in planting tree seedlings.

2. Reforestation is a term that applies to specific timber industry processes in the Northwest. Most harvesting of conifers (primarily Douglas fir) in the region takes place by clear-cutting. Cut-over sites are prepared (cleared of some debris from the logging operation) and then contracts are let for planting. Seedlings are planted, and after a few years, nonconifer vegetation may have to be cleared (manual conifer release). When the planted conifers reach pole size (10 to 14 years), they may have to be thinned (precommercial thinning). When mature trees are harvested, this cycle is set in motion again. Seeds for the nursery stock are gathered from the forest (seed or cone collection), and contracts are also let for plantation surveys (stand exams or phenotype surveys). Manual reforestation over steep mountain terrain is essential to new timber production, and in most clear-cut areas it constitutes the defense of, or restoration of, forest ecology.

3. Hoedads is not the only forestry worker cooperative in the Northwest. By the end of the 1970s, there were approximately fifteen of them in Oregon and Washington. Some are more politically homogeneous than Hoedads, others are more involved in working out collective internal process, and all are smaller than Hoedads. Total membership of the co-ops in late 1979 was estimated to be close to 1,000 worker-members, while private contractors employ from 7,000 to 14,000 forest workers, depending on seasonal demand. See J. Walker 1979.

4. Hoedads Co-op, Inc. Bylaws, December 1978, Art. IV, pp. 3–4.

5. Calculated from operating expenses for January to June 1979. See Gunn 1980.

6. Ibid., p. 174. This chart was constructed from the author's field notes.

7. Aside from the problems with the Oregon workers' compensation system itself,

the case by the Association against the co-ops is in part based on the claim that an employer-employee relationship exists in the co-ops. That is a fundamental challenge to the co-ops, and one they feel will be both easy and important to negate in court. Other reasons that co-op members do not want to be subjected to mandatory workers' compensation coverage include: (a) For their first eighteen months of coverage, the cost to each co-op member will be 13.5 percent of earnings; (b) only after that eighteen-month period will the safety record of Hoedads, one they feel is far superior to the state average, be considered and the premium for the co-op reduced; (c) the state system, according to Hoedads, provides too little reward or incentives for safety on the job; (d) the high costs of the system in part reflect the swollen bureaucracy that administers it, one rife with political appointees in high-paying jobs, and a director who is reported to be a major stockholder in the largest private insurance carrier in the state system.

8. Rothschild-Whitt 1979:512.

9. Crew homogeneity does not necessarily assure co-op homogeneity. Some members feel that the co-op as a whole should develop criteria, such as specific skills or commitment to co-op principles, that would be used to screen new members. One former officer of Hoedad characterized the current new member entry process as "extended family nepotism," one in which crew members bring in their friends.

10. Hoedads Co-op, Inc. Bylaws, op. cit., Art. III, pp. 2–3.

11. Recently more formalized training in forest work has been made available through a CETA-funded independent forestry training program offered at Lane Community College. The training program was designed and is being taught by several past and present Hoedads.

12. Planters first prepare a place for a seedling by using the hoedad to clear away vegetation in an area about one foot square (known as a *scalp*), and they then loosen the soil and sink the hoedad deep enough to create a hole for the seedling roots, usually 8 to 12 inches. The seedling is inserted and the soil is packed back around its roots. Roots must be at the proper depth, and pointed downward, not curved sideways or upward. Planters refer to good planting conditions (soft soil, not much debris or brush) as *gravy*, and poor conditions as *slash*.

13. Alvarado-Greenwood et al. 1978:85.

14. Vanek 1977*a*; Jones and Backus 1977; and McGregor 1977.

15. See Gunn 1980:192. This chart was adapted from one appearing in Hoedads's *Together* (Summer 1979):10.

16. Mainstream economic theory of the firm assumes that capital is productive and that its owners should therefore receive income in the form of profit for its use. The economics of the labor-managed firm has neoclassical roots, but all income to this firm belongs to those who work in it. There are neither hired workers nor profit-seeking investors in this firm; its member-workers share all income to the firm net of operating expenses and taxes. The labor-managed firm is assumed to pay a "scarcity-reflecting rent" (interest) on the financial assets that it uses, whether they are supplied by its members, by outside lenders, by a trust in some form of social ownership, or by a governmental agency from public funds. For a detailed elaboration of the economics of the labor-managed firm, see Vanek 1970, 1977*c*.

17. See Vanek 1977*a*, Jones and Backus 1977, and McGregor 1977.

18. This issue is discussed in greater detail by Gunn (1980:197–200, 230–232, 235–237).

19. See Jones 1980*b*.

20. The Forest Workers' Organizing Committee is exploring various forms of liaison with the International Woodworkers of America (IWA). More radical in Western Canada than in the United States, the IWA is the successor of the International Workers of the World (IWW).

RESEARCH NOTE

Research for this article involved preliminary fieldwork in July 1979 and more formal inquiry, interviews, and collection of data in August of that year as well as in July 1980. The author has had access to minutes of weekly council meetings and quarterly general meetings and to written documents and financial records of the Hoedads Co-op. The article does not reflect changes that have taken place in Hoedads since 1979–1980.

This article is based in part on material from chapter 5 of the author's "Workers' Self-Management in the United States: Theory and Practice," Ph.D. Dissertation, Cornell University, 1980. Dissertation research was supported by U.S. Department of Labor-Research and Development Grant no. 91–36–79–47. The author wishes to express his gratitude to many Hoedads, past and present, for their assistance, and especially to Jonathan Walker, Lauri Patterson, Greg Nagle, Robbie Vasilinda, Debbie Traynor, Gail Slentz, Ken Miller, David Straton, and Tim Schottman. Thanks also to Hazel Dayton Gunn and Robert Jackall for their helpful comments on earlier versions of this article.

8

Producer Cooperatives and Democratic Theory: The Case of the Plywood Firms

E D W A R D S. G R E E N B E R G

INTRODUCTION:
WORK ORGANIZATION AND DEMOCRACY

Industrial enterprises might reasonably be understood as political systems as well as economic entities. It is possible to make such a claim because of the widely recognized fact that so-called private enterprises affect, for better or worse, many third parties outside of their immediate environment, help shape the contours of social life in general, and broadly determine the boundaries of what is possible for both citizens and government. This role of the firm as an *authoritative allocator of values*, in the terminology of modern political science, is increasingly recognized (Bachrach 1967; Dahl 1970). Much less evident, and only rarely analyzed in scientific terms, is the degree to which firms are themselves minipolitical systems, comprised of an inner social life in which decisions are made, bargains struck, power exercised, ideology formulated, and order enforced. They are systems in which the drama of political struggle and of accommodation take place daily.

In most advanced industrial systems, of course, political life within enterprises more closely approximates authoritarian forms rather than democratic ones, a generalization that holds for both capitalist and socialist societies. The continued vigor and vitality of authoritarian forms within the work setting is impressive and stands in vivid contradistinction to the democratic rhetoric that tends to surround and serves to justify most social systems. The paradox of enterprise au-

171

thoritarianism operating within a formally democratic political system is particularly marked with respect to the United States, a system in which the fewest advances have been made toward practical experiments in industrial democracy (in sharp contrast to the lively activity in this sphere in western Europe [Garson 1975; Jenkins 1974; Vanek 1975a]) and in which the distribution and practice of formal democratic rights and liberties are theoretically the most widespread. It has often been pointed out, in fact, that American workers must, as a condition of gaining their livelihood, give up their accustomed rights and privileges of citizenship upon crossing the threshold of the factory gate or office door. Within the boundaries of the business firm, that is, with respect to the internal life of private enterprises, the historic rights of free speech, free association, election of leadership, and general control of collective policy, so central to most definitions of the democratic polity, are not generally considered to be in effect. It is widely assumed by all parties concerned, whether employees or business managers, unions or government officials, that the *wage relationship* which forms the core of economic life in capitalism axiomatically implies an unequal, hierarchical relationship within the firm. In this relationship between an employer and an employee, managers retain the right, subject to relatively minor restrictions and standards set by government and by labor unions, to direct and to coordinate enterprise production in the interests of the aggrandizement of capital. It is generally understood that hired employees must conform both to the purposes of the enterprise and to its internal order. The only residual right that is retained (and it remains an important one) is the freedom to leave the enterprise and seek other employment. That is, the exercise of choice is external to the life of the enterprise, not internal to it.

There are, however, some notable exceptions to the above generalizations. There have been historical cases and there remain in existence today some enterprises organized along radically different lines, enterprises in which the people who work within them, retain full power of determination over the general directions of production and distribution, as well as the particular procedures and arrangements whereby production and distribution are planned, executed, and monitored. These enterprises are commonly known as *producer cooperatives,* firms that are owned, operated, and managed by the people who work in them. As a general rule, responsibility for the formulation of overall production and sales policy ultimately resides in a general meeting of the membership of the cooperative, customarily called *shareholders.* Technical and managerial specialists are most often "hired" and subjected to the direction and bidding of the shareholders.

Producer cooperatives highlight and bring to our attention basic questions about the governance of industrial work life, questions about the proper and/or most attractive forms of internal enterprise governance. Examination of the internal practices and processes of producer cooperatives provides a reasonable method to consider the possibilities and limitations of democratic life within workplaces. The purpose of this paper is to undertake just such a task, to focus attention on the internal governance and politics of operating producer cooperatives, and to raise questions about the promise and performance of one important form of self-governing work community. To this end, I shall focus most of my analysis on the large plywood firms located in the Pacific Northwest.

DEMOCRATIC GOVERNANCE

What most sharply calls producer cooperatives to our attention is their self-governing quality, the fact that those who work within these enterprises generally run them. It is this quality that most clearly sets the producer cooperatives off from other firms that share a similar technological organization and product mix. It is also this self-governing quality, amid the growing concern about the seemingly inescapable and expanding problems of work alienation, workplace indiscipline, absenteeism, and the like, that has attracted scholars, public officials, and business leaders to the cooperative model of work organization.

Self-governance, of course, immediately raises the issue of democracy. What we want to know about producer cooperatives and about formal democratic communities, is the quality of the actual democratic life within them, and the effects that a self-governing workplace has upon the people who work within them. We want to know what self-governance looks like up close, how people participate in this formally democratic setting, and how this way of life compares specifically with the internal processes of more conventional enterprises. In short, in looking at producer cooperatives, we want to understand the degree to which its governance and political interactions approach what we know, in nonenterprise governance and politics, as democracy.

There are two sharply competing historical models of democracy which this essay will use as guides in examining the governing processes of producer cooperatives: direct (participatory) democracy, and representative democracy. Central to the notion of direct democracy is the idea of participation. At the heart of this model is the idea that perfectly ordinary human beings, given the proper education and environment, can be responsible and reflective and govern themselves wisely (Pateman 1970; D. Thompson 1970). On the surface at least, it seems that the internal life of producer cooperatives closely resembles this model of democracy. That is, in theory, the cooperatives are comprised of people who are participants in the direct, interactive, citizenship type of activities by which the collective enterprise life is carried on. In this paper, I shall look closely at the internal life of cooperatives and try to make judgments about the "closeness of fit" between the actual activities of cooperative members and the model of direct democracy. In particular, I will want to reach conclusions about the degree to which shareholders in cooperatives act as *citizens* in the classic Greek sense, where citizenship implied a notion of continuous involvement in the life of the community.

In the competing model of representative democracy,[1] not only are government and governed separated and distinct but the role of politics becomes not one of deliberation but one of forging instruments by which citizens exercise some control over government leaders and policy, over a governing class that is potentially alienated from the general citizenry. In this conception, people do not rule directly but indirectly through representatives authorized to make policy decisions in their name. While citizen participation remains an important constituent element, it seems limited in scope precisely to the periodic election of persons who act in the capacity of representatives and to the occasional transmission of instructions to them (Sartori 1962; Schumpeter 1943). A representative system is able to address two inherent limitations of direct democracy—first, the problem of optimal size for face-to-face deliberation and second, the constraints of time (Dahl 1970). There is probably an upper limit on how large a group may be and still remain both democratic and manageable; similarly, no political community can be in continuous session because of the normal demands of family and private life.

In the remainder of this paper, it is important to keep these theoretical models of democratic politics in mind as I compare the governance and internal political life of cooperative and conventional firms.[2] Again, my objective is to generate information out of this comparison that might help one think more cogently about the possibilities and limitations of democratic life within workplaces.

THE POLITICS AND GOVERNANCE OF PRODUCER COOPERATIVES

The examination of the political life of the self-managed enterprise in the United States has not been a matter of general concern to scholars, in minor part, perhaps, because of the overwhelming commitment of American intellectuals to capitalism and its conventional institutions. In the main, however, this lack of attention may be traced to the virtual absence of producer cooperatives or other types of worker-managed enterprises that might have called attention to these issues and provided a setting for scholarly investigation. An analysis of the paucity of these institutions as well as their historical instability and limited duration lies well beyond the scope of this paper and has already been touched upon by a number of scholars (Berman 1967; Bernstein 1976b; Blumberg 1968; Derber 1970; Jones 1977; Shirom 1972), but most certainly, the hostility of financial institutions, competing enterprises, and the rigors, discipline, and demands of the market have all played a part in their history.

Nevertheless, a close examination of the politics of self-management is possible because of the rather unique and remarkable concentration of fourteen worker-owned, and worker-managed industrial enterprises in the Pacific Northwest plywood industry. Since elaborate descriptions of these firms already exist in the literature (Bellas 1972; Berman 1967; Bernstein 1974), it would serve no useful purpose to devote extensive space to a similar exercise in this chapter. A few brief remarks about them, however, might serve as an introduction to what follows.

Most of the worker-owned plywood firms were founded in the years immediately following the Second World War. Several were started from scratch by lumber workers worried about the dismal employment prospects in their industry, several were the product of workers seeking to prevent the closing of a privately owned mill, and more than a few were created by promoters who took a healthy slice of initial profits for their efforts. Whatever their origin, it is important to note that most of these worker-owned firms, today ranging in size from 80 to 350 members, have been in continuous operation for over twenty years and appear to have the productive capabilities and market prospects to stay in operation for the foreseeable future. The firms now in operation, by the way, represent the residue of a steady process of contraction in this sector of the industry in which the number of worker-owned firms has fallen from twenty-one in the mid-1950s to their present number. This contraction process, I should add, is as much the product of success as it is of failure. While several firms have closed their doors because of business failure generated by a combination of mismanagement and the severe fluctuations in the plywood market, the majority ceased operations as worker-owned firms because they were absorbed by larger lumber corporations (ITT-Rayonier, Boise-Cascade, etc.) after cooperative members agreed to very generous per share offers. Almost without exception, these offers were tendered by large corporations because of the significant timber holdings enjoyed by the worker-owned firms. It is also important to add that the remaining worker-owned firms account for over 10 percent of all plywood production and are generally conceded to be the source of the highest quality product in the industry. Finally, and without exception, studies of the plywood industry indicate that the worker-owned firms are characterized by higher levels of productivity than those in conventional firms. Several reports suggest, in fact, that when measured in terms of square feet of output per man-hour, worker-owned firms are from 25 to 60 percent more productive than conventional ones (Bernstein 1974).

This analysis of the governance and politics of American producer cooperatives will depend almost entirely upon these plywood firms, with occasional references to the experience of other producer cooperatives, most often to those relatively small firms in the service and handicraft sectors. The plywood cooperatives will remain the center of this analysis because the number of operating firms and the size of their work force make intensive, careful, and analytically sophisticated examination possible.

FORMAL GOVERNANCE

Unlike most of the smaller service and handicraft cooperatives, formal rules of governance are universal in the plywood cooperatives. The smaller cooperatives are usually of such a small size that they are, in fact, face-to-face groups which conduct most of their affairs in quite loose, informal, and very often intense and chaotic ways (see the essay by Jackall and Crain, chap. 5). Given their much larger membership (100 to 250 members) and the scale of their production, such informal procedures are impossible in the plywood cooperatives. Consequently, they are all characterized by formal rules of organization and procedure. It is important to add that because of the requirements of business law, and because of the cooperative tradition itself, these formal arrangements look quite similar across all of the plywood firms.[3] The following chart gives a convenient overview of some of these formal organization features.

The most important single feature in the formal organization of the worker-owned firm is the vesting of ultimate and decisive authority and responsibility on all matters in the general membership of the cooperative, expressed concretely in the annual or semiannual general membership meeting. While this meeting in practice may choose to delegate many of its responsibilities to the general manager and/or the board of directors, in a formal sense the purview of the meeting is unlimited, responsible as it is for the total governance and direction of the enterprise. If they so choose, shareholders at these meetings may decide to fire the manager and hire a new one, or alter hourly

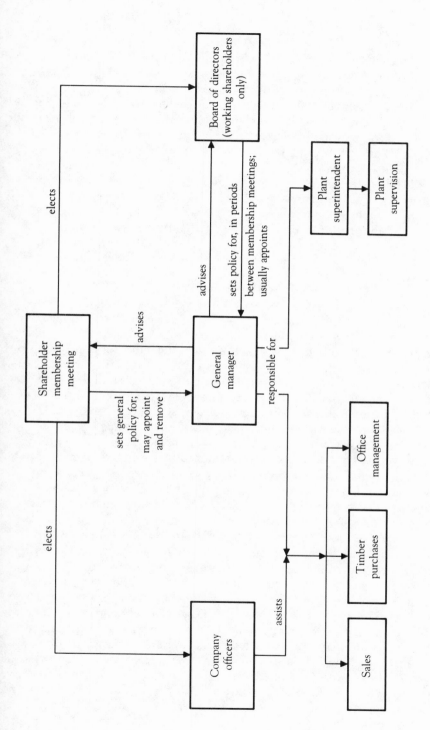

Fig. 8.1

wage rates, or build a new plant, or whatever else seems appropriate
to the general membership. Traditionally, membership meetings are
responsible for periodic reviews of company financial performance, the
division of the annual enterprise income between investment (capital
equipment, buildings, machinery, timber purchases) and distribution
to working members, review of managerial performance, and election
of a board of directors. In such membership meetings, each shareholder
is entitled to only a single vote even if, as in a few exceptional cases,[4]
he owns more than one share.

At these meetings, an entirely new or partially new board of directors is elected from among the shareholders themselves, a body for
which all members are eligible. This board is charged with general
policymaking in the interim between general membership meetings.
The board is not entirely free in policy matters, however, since all of
the firms require the board to gain permission from the general membership for any expenditures beyond some specified maximum figure.

Other features common to the formal organization of the plywood
cooperatives are worth noting. All, for instance, operate on the principle of equal hourly wage rates among the shareholders regardless of
the number of years on the job or skill level. All divide the annual
surplus (the amount that remains from total income after hourly wage
rates, operating costs, taxes, investment, and savings have been deducted) to the shareholders as workers rather than as dividends on
capital. That is to say, nonworking shareholders are not entitled to a
portion of the surplus. All hire a management team (a general manager
and his assistants) which is responsible for the day-to-day operations
of the firm, subject to the guidance of the board of directors (which
usually meets biweekly) and the sufferance of the general membership
meeting. All insist that potential new worker-owners spend a probationary period working in the plant, and that their membership be
formally accepted by either the general membership meeting or the
board of directors.

To be sure, some important differences in formal arrangements do
exist among the plywood cooperatives. For instance, while all firms
hold to the principle of equal hourly wage rates, they tend to vary in
their willingness to allow differentials in the total hours worked over
the course of the year. Some firms allow their members, given the
availability of such work, to work as many hours of overtime as they
wish, while several firms attempt to strictly limit the differentials in
total hours worked among its members. Whereas the latter system
guarantees a rough equality in annual member compensation, the
former allows very wide disparities, given both the time-and-a-half
provisions for overtime work and the division of the annual enterprise
surplus according to total hours worked. Or to take another example,
most of the cooperatives hire general managers from the outside who

are not shareholders, while a few allow shareholders to hold such posts. Finally, firms vary with regard to whether they allow shareholders to hold supervisory positions in the plant.

Nevertheless, despite these variations, what is most immediately striking is the degree to which the formal organization and rules of procedure are identical among the plywood cooperatives. What differences are evident are simply minor deviations in an otherwise relatively uniform picture. To put it in another way, when compared with the formal organization of conventional firms, the general similarities among the plywood cooperatives are more evident than their differences.

THE ANALYSIS

While an understanding of the formal organization of the cooperatives is obviously an important first step in an understanding of them as institutions, it certainly does not take us very far. Were one to stop here, one would have only an understanding of the skeleton, but not of the flesh of the dynamic processes at work within the body of the cooperative. The formal structure is simply the framework within which the colorful and rich life of human interaction takes place. The task then is to turn to an examination of these more elusive yet vital aspects of cooperative life. The remainder of this paper is designed to make just such explorations.

This analysis of the dynamics of enterprise governance will take the form of a comparison between the internal political life of worker-owned enterprises and conventional enterprises in which, insofar as possible, all variables other than plant organization have been controlled. That is to say, I shall be comparing cooperative and conventional firms within the same industry (plywood), all of which are characterized by an identical technical division-of-labor within the plant, roughly similar size, location within the same geographical region, and similar work force demographics (e.g., racial, sexual, and age distribution). Differences that are discovered in their internal political environment and governing processes will be mainly attributed, given their nearly identical characteristics on all other major variables, to differences between cooperative versus conventional work organization.[5]

JOINING A COOPERATIVE

What is most immediately evident about motivations for joining the plywood cooperatives is the very low, almost nonexistent political dimension. That is to say, the strongest motivations for becoming members of these enterprises are almost universally financial in nature, with little thought given to matters such as self-governance, the relatively pleasant work environment, or the unique social relations within the plant. This, by the way, stands in vivid contrast to the small handicraft and service cooperatives that have blossomed in several urban areas over the past decade. Almost each and every one of these new cooperatives, whose business activities range from groceries, to woodworking, to baked goods, to health food outlets, to health clinics, and the like, were formed by small handfuls of people, many of whom were of upper-middle-class and college-educated backgrounds, active in either antiwar, ecology, or countercultural politics, with the explicit purpose of establishing businesses of a distinctly different type. That is, their motivations to form small cooperatives that would both serve the community and provide a work environment devoid of the "hassles," hierarchy, and "rat race" of the conventional business world, were inherently political. While very few of these cooperatives hold to a specific and narrow political line, each represents an attempt to create a work environment in which the normal internal politics and governance are altered toward more democratic directions, and in which the goals of the enterprise include linkages to and concern for the surrounding community and its development.

In marked contrast, the primary motivation for joining the larger, more established producer cooperatives in plywood is connected, in one way or another, to the desire for financial gain and job security. It should be remembered, of course, that the people who join these cooperatives are distinctly working class in origin, many of whom have had periods of economic difficulty in their lives and have experienced significant periods of unemployment—47 percent have been unemployed, with 46 percent of that total experiencing over five months of unemployment. The fact that a member of a cooperative is guaranteed a job as long as the firm remains in operation, is no small attraction to people who worry about financial security. Furthermore, given their limited ability to save and given the declining opportunities in the small business sectors, the producer cooperative becomes one of the few outlets that working-class people have for making a small financial investment. Jobs and investment are thus the recurrent reasons for joining the plywood cooperatives. These reasons are evident in the figures below which represent the responses of shareholders when asked to judge the degree of importance of the following factors in encouraging them to first join a cooperative.

What is most evident in table 8.1 is the degree to which investment assumes the dominant position with respect to motivations for joining a cooperative, closely followed by the importance of good wages and job security, and conversely, the dismal showing of those items related

TABLE 8.1

How Important Were Each of the Following in Your Decision
to First Become a Shareholder in this Cooperative?
(percentage answering very important; total = 280)

Heard that workers in the plant got along well with each other	17.9%
Heard that supervisors and workers got along well	17.1
Thought it would be a good financial investment	66.4
Wanted an opportunity to help run a company	12.5
Wanted a guaranteed job in case times got hard	42.1
The wages were good	48.2
There were no other jobs available at the time	15.0

to the internal governance and political processes of the cooperative. These figures are strongly buttressed by shareholder responses during the in-depth interviews. As far as I am able to determine, not a single respondent, spontaneously and without prompting, even vaguely mentioned political or ideological grounds for joining these enterprises. Almost all were quick to mention the investment and job security aspects, a surprisingly large number mentioned the desire to escape labor union-company tensions and uncertainties, and not a few seemed to have accidently wandered in for no particular, premeditated reason. Political motivations were notable for their absence.

I thought of it . . . as an investment . . . that shares would go up.

Well, it was just the idea of getting higher wages than I had before.

Of course money is probably the primary issue.

Buying a job . . . it was a job. The plant's running seven days a week, twelve hours a day ever since I've been here. So, if a guy wanted to really get in to work, he could make all the overtime he wanted. So he could actually bring home a pretty good check.

And I was getting a little tired [of seasonal work]. So I came down here. . . . These guys work 365 days a year . . . and so I thought more or less buying a share was a good security for a job . . . good chance of staying, you know, instead of getting caught in a layoff.

Well, I thought I wanted to buy into a small business . . . be my own boss. And my brother-in-law convinced me that would take too long and it would be more risky than [this].

GENERAL TONE/MOOD OF
PRODUCER COOPERATIVES

If self-governance is notable for its absence as an initial motivation for joining the plywood cooperatives, it very shortly comes to assume a position that is at least coequal with that of financial returns and job security. No matter the initial grounds for buying a share, almost all co-op members come to appreciate the special environment that these enterprises offer to those who own and work in them. This is not to say that there exist no interpersonal tensions, general grievances, dissatisfactions, and the like, but that an overall appreciation tends to develop for the cooperatives' unique set of mechanisms for working such problems out and attenuating their effects. While their use is not always successful, to be sure, it is generally understood that these mechanisms exist for the use of interested shareholders.

A theme that constantly recurs in the interviews is the very strong sense that it is the shareholders who run the enterprises, who are responsible for what goes on in it, and who have the opportunity, within certain boundaries, to make of their environment what they will.

> Well, essentially, I mean, if it comes down to it, the stockholders have absolute rule down there. In fact it has happened in this mill before . . . if things get too bad, the stockholders can just break down and say, "Wait a minute . . . we are going to change this." And if they have enough of them, they can do it, if enough guys get together. I think that's great because there's a lot of companies that . . . take advantage of the workers . . . and there's nothing that can be done about it.

The contrast to the situation in the conventionally run mills we examined, where workers are essentially apart from the decision-making process, could not be more marked. Within them, people feel, quite correctly, that they are beings who are acted upon by distant and inaccessible decision makers.

> There's a strange relationship between the management and the people that work in the mill down there. There's a certain aloofness by management, you know. They don't have a close association with the men.

> [In response to a question about possible layoffs] we asked and tried to find out what they had in mind, but it was all kind of hush, hush, hush, and no one was saying very much . . . nobody ever found out.

> [about breaks] It's all set by the company.

[about the future of plant] Well, like I say, we don't know what kind of decisions they will make. Like in New York, maybe they want it for a tax write-off some day. . . . Unless it's a high level decision, this place will go on for a long time. So if it's going to go down it's going to be because somebody wants it for a tax dodge or to sell the property for a marina or something high-money level.

But we never see any high-level guys that would let us know what's going on. So I don't know where the major decisions come from.

This sense of distance from decision making, this sense of being an object rather than a subject in the workplace, is a constantly recurring theme among workers interviewed in the conventionally organized plywood mill.

This contrasts sharply with the general feeling in the cooperatives captured by the following observation by one of the older members:

I don't think I'd ever give it up. . . . It's been good to me and it's. . . . There is a certain feeling to know that you own part of what you're working for. I mean, it's better than working for somebody else. . . . I've always gone to all the stockholder's meetings and . . . I enjoy it.

I've never had so much fun! Hell, we run this operation all by ourselves.

This overall sense that they are their own bosses, that they are the people who run the enterprise, and that, in addition to making a decent living at it, they are also enjoying themselves, is a complex of themes mentioned spontaneously by many of the shareholders.

Not surprisingly, while there remains a great deal of variation among the shareholders in their degree of participation, the pervasive participatory environment of these places fosters an extremely strong sense of collective responsibility and mutuality.

You just find it's kind of a big family attitude, you know. Those that can put out, put out, and you don't feel too bad about the guys that can't.

[In response to a question asking why he supports the concept of equal wages] I think they all got to equalize out . . . they all got to eat.

It's altogether different here [compared with his former job.]. It took me a little while to get used to this because where I worked over there, there was a union and you did your job and you didn't go out and do something else. Here you get in and do anything to help. . . . Everybody pitches in and helps. . . . The people stick together, that's the reason we've gone so far and production is so high, 'cause everybody works together.

TABLE 8.2

WHICH OF THE FOLLOWING STATEMENTS BEST DESCRIBES YOUR
ATTITUDE ABOUT WORKING HERE?

	Producer cooperatives	Conventional firm
I do as little as possible	0%	0%
I do an average day's work	11.6	12.7
I do the *best* work I can for the time I'm paid	33.7	50.3
I not only do the best work I can, but I do whatever extra needs to be done	54.7	36.9
	N = 276	N = 257

(Chi square significance = .001)

The strong commitment by the shareholders to the work of the collective enterprise in the cooperative comes out very explicitly in a
comparison with workers in the conventional plant (see table 8.2).

Note that the bulk of workers in the conventional plant fall into
what might be called the wage-labor category—that is, they express
a stated willingness to work diligently for the time they are paid, but
not more; whereas the bulk of shareholders fall into the category that
implies a collective responsibility to the enterprise beyond a straight
trade of pay for hours worked. One can see this general attitude
reaffirmed, and the contrast with workers in conventional plants reinforced, by the response patterns to items asking about each respondent's sense of responsibility for his work-group and the plant as a
whole (tables 8.3, 8.4).

This strong sense of mutuality, caring, and cooperation seems to
come strongly to the fore during crisis times, a seemingly recurrent
state of affairs for all of the plywood firms, given the instability of the
industry in general. While crises tend to bring forth much ill will and
interpersonal antagonism, to be sure, paradoxically they also seem to
call forth the powerful social bonds within the institutions and best
highlight the difference between these firms and conventionally organized ones.

[Interviewer: Did you ever think of getting out during bad times?]

No . . . instead of giving up, you fight all the harder. I mean, if things
get tough, you know, why you don't all of a sudden go to work and
somebody says . . . notice up there saying plant shutting down tomorrow
because we're losing money. Here if we got to that point where it's shut

TABLE 8.3

To What Extent Do You Feel Responsible for the
Success of Your Own Work Group or for the
Success of the Whole Plant? Production Line?
(in percentages)

	Producer cooperatives	Conventional firm
Hardly at all	1.2	2.7
Somewhat	18.9	30.8
Very much	79.9	66.4
	N = 249	N = 146

(Chi square significance = .01)

down or something, they call a stockholder's meeting. They'd say, now look if we take a 50¢ an hour cut in pay, we can keep going. Let's have a vote on it. So, we'd keep working. Everybody'd vote for it. We did that once before here a few years back when we had to.

The general mood in the conventional plant looks very different from that of the producer cooperatives. Rather than seeing themselves as a group acting in mutuality to advance their collective interests and happiness, workers in conventional plants perceive their work existence, quite correctly, as one in which they are almost powerless, being used for the advancement and purposes of others, subject to the decisions of higher and more distant authority, and driven by a production process that is relentless. While they do not feel there is much they can do about it, workers in this setting have a fairly sophisticated grasp of the reality of their work situation and their overall place in the order of things. Note the following comments, none of which are atypical of the interviews in general:

[Asked about wages]

The cost of lumber is just out of this world. And compared to wages and the cost of lumber, somebody's making a pile of jack, and it sure as hell ain't the worker [laughter]. . . . They're a big company, they're going to make every dime they can . . . and by the same token, I'm a union man, I'm going to make every penny I can get out of them. . . . I want everything I can get.

The drama of surplus extraction can take bizarre forms as the following story suggests.

TABLE 8.4

To WHAT EXTENT DO YOU FEEL RESPONSIBLE
FOR THE SUCCESS OF THE WHOLE PLANT?
(IN PERCENTAGES)

	Producer cooperatives	Conventional firm
Hardly at all	5.6	16.9
Somewhat	39.6	49.3
Very much	54.99	33.8
	N = 268	N = 142

(Chi square significance = .001)

Oh, there's always pressure . . . well, especially on our job, we're on the glue line making up the panels. There's more pressure in that department than any other one. [I: Really?] Yah, because they figure that's where they make or break, you know. And there was . . . at the last contract now, they were supposed to come up with some increment pay for the guys in that department. But the union's kind of against that too because years ago, about, well, before I even got there, it must have been . . . probably about 1940. They did away with all the piece work, see. And the union don't want to get that back in, which is probably a good thing because you more or less get a cutthroat attitude, you know. Well, a few years, oh, about five or six, oh, probably a little more than that, about ten years ago, they started posting this . . . scoreboard up there, you know, and they post the footage of each spreader, you know, during the day. Now, that's. . . . The union went and complained. They should have made them take it down right away, is what happened. But they let it ride, and they put it up during the time that we were out on strike, see. And when the guys came back off of strike, we'd been off about three months, so the guys weren't ready to go out for some little thing like that because, you know, they'd been out so long and they fell behind in their bills and everything. But if the union had put enough pressure on them I think they could have got that taken out of there. But it works for them. You know, it's just a normal thing, they go in there and they see what the other crew got, and some guys now they just, they go down every night and check that scoreboard, see how they did against the other. So, they're working against one another. Well, they benefited the company.

A sense of the general situation they find themselves in is suggested by the following rather bitter remarks:

[Interviewer: Do you feel the plant is fairly secure here?]

Well, it's been there a long time. But, let's face it, times are changing and the building it is old, but the thing is, like I said, the day that plant's not making a profit, the next day we'll be out, as simple as that. As long as we're making a profit, that place will be there. They don't give a fuck about us. . . . The property the mill sits on . . . they've been offered $40 million for the property, 'cause it'll make an excellent marina, the way it situates. . . . If they weren't making a profit there, we wouldn't be there. . . . Well, they'd come in tomorrow and say, hey, you guys are all through, 'cause they don't give. . . . They give a shit less about 300 people.

In response to one question that asked why the company did not fix obvious dangerous conditions, one worker pointed out the financial advantages of paying compensation for injuries in its stead:

Oh, yes they'll pay. They're legally obligated. They have to pay us, but the pay is . . . you starve to death, you know. You just couldn't live on it. So unless it's really a serious disabling injury, why you're better off to work if you can because you don't get anything from them. It runs about $100 a week at the most. And hell a man can't live on $100 a week nowadays.

[Interviewer: So it's a lot cheaper for them to pay people that way than to fix the problem?]

Sure. Sure it is.

What has ultimately developed in this not-atypical plant, given its organization and power arrangements, is a deadening of the spirit, a sense of defeat, hopelessness, and abjectness among the work force. As one worker put it,

I mean they're kind of gung-ho when they get there, at least the ones I've seen, you know, they'll want to get in and try, you know. And just over the years, it's just taking its toll on them. The job loses its challenge and they lose their initiative and they just go and put their time in. And that's precisely the way they would phrase it you know. "I'm just putting my time in, I got eight hours to put in and that's it." No more, no less.

The general mood of these two alternative types of work settings could not be more sharply contrasting. To people who find themselves in conventional, hierarchically structured work environments, the work experience is not humanly rewarding or enhancing. This seems to be a product of an all-too-familiar combination of repetitious and monotonous labor (the manufacture of plywood being very much an assembly line, semiskilled operation) and the structural position of powerlessness, one in which workers are part of the raw material that is manipulated, channeled, and directed by an only partly visible managerial hierarchy.[6] Workers in such settings conceive of themselves, quite explicitly, as objects rather than subjects of the production process, and come to approach the entire situation, quite correctly, since they are responding to an objective situation of subordination, as one of a simple exchange of labor for wages.[7] Work, done without a great deal of enthusiasm, is conceived of as intrinsically meaningless, yet necessary for the income that contributes to a decent life away from the workplace.

As I have shown, this is most certainly not the case with respect to workers in the plywood cooperatives. In these plants, worker-owners come to see themselves, in large part, as the managers of their own fates, as ultimately the ones responsible for the success or failure of their enterprise, as, in short, subjects rather than objects. Retaining a strong commitment to financial rewards and concerned about the safety and return on their investment, it is not surprising that conflict occasionally comes to the surface or that interpersonal tension and squabbling are not rare occurrences. Nevertheless, one comes away from interviews with shareholders with a strong impression of the largely positive, enhancing, and even enjoyable experience people gain in this alternative work setting. This does not mean that the work is not often dull and deadening—after all, the plywood cooperatives are engaged in exactly the same technical production process as are the conventional firms—but the fact is that the experience of both ownership and self-governance, in all of its varied aspects, strongly compensates for the negative aspects of the work. Coming to the cooperatives for almost purely monetary reasons, people come away from the cooperative experience with greatly broadened appreciations and sensibilities not generally available to American workers.

PARTICIPATION IN POLICYMAKING

In the above pages, using primarily the words of the people who work in the very situation they are talking about, I have tried to convey a general sense of the collective mood of both plywood cooperatives and conventional plywood mills. What is almost immediately apparent is the tremendous contrast between them, a contrast that becomes even more impressive when one notes their almost absolutely identical technical process, division of labor, size, and work force demographic composition. What this suggests, in my view, is that these differences in collective mood between the plants are reasonably traceable to differences in the organization of power and authority within them, one set characterized by self-governance, the other by hierarchical authority, and superordinate-subordinate relations. Up to this point, however, I have remained fairly general, and it is worth looking at these governing processes in more detail, to observe and explicate the particular processes and interactions that are involved in this self-governing experience and to contrast them with what generally goes on in American industry.

While the firms are closely linked and interrelated in practice, it makes analytic sense to divide a consideration of these internal plant processes into two categories, or rather, levels of decision making within the plant: that of general enterprise policy formation, and that of job-plant floor decision making. While in actual practice the one cannot be sharply separated from the other, the kinds of decisions to be made, the range of implications of those decisions, the number of coworkers directly involved, the types of information required, and the necessary implementation of machinery do contrast sharply for each level of decision making and are worth careful and intense scrutiny in their own right.

SHOP-FLOOR GOVERNANCE

In some respects, the actual day-to-day governance of the work process does not demonstrate a great degree of variation between the plywood cooperatives and the conventional firms. This is especially the case with respect to the pace and manner by which either raw logs (or in several factories, sheets of veneer) are transformed into finished plywood panels. The similarities can be traced to the simple fact that the technical processes, the composition of the machinery, the optimal level of operation of that machinery, and the division of labor are virtually identical in all of the plywood plants, cooperative and commercial. Unless one were especially knowledgeable and blessed with a discerning eye, one could not easily tell the difference in the actual production process between cooperatives and conventional firms. To all outward appearances, they are the same. Given the fact that most of the technical processes of plywood production are repetitious and machine paced, with only semiskilled labor required, one finds many similar reactions to and complaints about the actual work between the two types of firms.

> You're doing something that's basically kind of unpleasant in the first place. You're really not too enthused about it, and it's a repetition kind of thing. . . . Most jobs are monotony and repetition once you get the hang of it [conventional plant].

> It's coming constantly. . . . It's always coming [conventional plant].

But he got up there and it was so automated [a saw] he couldn't handle it. . . . You sit there and the machine's going. . . . It was driving him nuts. . . . It goes so fast [production]. . . . You got to keep going fast all the time [cooperative].

It's different than it used to be. It used to be a slow work pace, and you had some time to do things and think a little bit. Today, it's just like you're always up against something to be done, that has to be done [cooperative].

The rhythm of the machinery imposes a kind of sameness to the actual work found in both kinds of plants. The work itself, tied as it is to a fairly inflexible technical procedure, has not been formally redesigned in the cooperatives so as to allow for greater choice, greater self-governance if you will, with respect to the work task and how it is performed. Indeed, what is so intriguing about this issue is that not a single respondent in our cooperative sample spontaneously mentioned that such an issue had ever become a matter of discussion among shareholders. Although general enterprise policy is made by them, it has apparently never occurred to shareholders that matters of choice and self-governance might be extended to the job itself. Rather, as far as I have been able to determine, members of cooperatives have assumed that the technical production and work processes are fixed, that worker-owners must of necessity adjust themselves to the requirements of those processes, and that boring yet fast-paced work must be compensated for by higher financial remuneration and the satisfactions derived from participation in general enterprise policy-making.

And yet, while the plywood cooperatives demonstrate no significant deviation from conventional plants in their willingness to allow for greater self-governance in the most important shop-floor matters, namely, the technical performance of the work task itself, one should not exaggerate this powerlessness. Many significant differences do exist between the plants in virtually all of those matters that surround the technical work process, all of which point to some degree of self-governance in the co-ops. I refer here to the informal social arrangements by which work is performed, those arrangements attached to job rotation and assignments, and propensity for innovation, and most importantly, the nature of supervision. I will look at these matters in more detail.

At the simplest level, as one might expect within firms where workers own and are responsible for the entire enterprise, there is a much greater tendency for cooperation on production problems among shareholders than there is among workers in a conventional plant.

Indeed, there is a very strong tendency in a conventional plant to stick to one's assigned job, to not meddle in what is considered the business of other workers or the responsibility of some other production unit in the plant. The boundaries of work responsibility are clearly drawn, and while workers in conventional plants are willing to put in hard work on their assigned tasks, they are not likely to move beyond those boundaries, to act in ways that will enhance the productivity of the entire process. In the cooperatives, the job boundaries, while existent, are less rigid and more permeable when, in the opinion of the people actually involved in production, the situation demands it.

> If the people grading off the end of the dryer do not use reasonable prudence and they start mixing the grades too much, I get hold of somebody and I say, now look, this came over to me as face stock and it wouldn't even make decent back. What the hell's goin' on here?

> [Interviewer: That wouldn't happen if it were a regular mill?]

> That wouldn't happen [In a regular mill]. . . . he has absolutely no money invested in the product that's being manufactured. . . . He's selling nothing but his time. Any knowledge he has on the side, he is not committed or he is not required to share that.

> It took me a little while to get used to this because where I worked before . . . there was a union and you did your job and you didn't go out and do something else. Here you get in and do anything to help. . . . I see somebody needs help, why you just go help them.

> I also tend to . . . look around and make sure things are working right a little more than . . . if I didn't have anything invested in the company. . . . I would probably never say anything when I saw something wrong. . . . I don't know. It gives you a feeling of responsibility . . . that's pretty much shared by the rest of the shareholders, you know, the same feeling.

This natural and spontaneous cooperation in the production process extends to matters related to the informal rotation and sharing of jobs, something that is notable for its absence in the conventional plant where jobs are assigned through precise and formal agreements made between management and the union, and where once assigned, these jobs are not generally altered by informal and alternative arrangements among workers. Once assigned a job, such workers tend to stick to them until such time as they apply for some other position. While job assignments are made in a similar fashion in the plywood cooperatives (a bidding system based almost exclusively on seniority), there

is a greater tendency, when the occasion arises, to share and rotate jobs.

> I'm on a three-man crew that edge glues stock . . . and we rotate positions.
> I have insisted on this. We have a feeder and a jointer and an off bearer.
> And we each one of the three rotate.

> Well, if you're on the dry belt, that machine never stops. You know there
> are machines that just don't stop. And that's one of them. And you don't
> just walk off and let the wood go. . . . You holler at somebody, "Come
> here and give me a quickie." And he comes over there and takes your
> place, and you go.

> They used to have a policy where when the guys went hunting, you could
> trade around. . . . Hell, you can pretty much take off when you want.
> You can always get somebody to cover for you.

While some of these same informal job assignment processes may
occasionally take place in the conventional plants as well, they were
never spontaneously mentioned by any workers during the interviews.
What this suggests in my view is that, while it may happen on occasion,
it is not a regular occurrence, nor is it done with the sense of freedom
enjoyed by the shareholders.

Given both the commitment to the success of the overall enterprise
and the relative freedom to constitute informal work arrangements in
them (that is, within the boundaries set by the technical process), it
is not surprising to learn that shareholders in cooperatives are much
more likely to suggest and to initiate various innovations in work
procedures.

> [Everybody] should do the job his own way, and he'll do it better than if
> he's forced to do it a certain way. . . . The same with . . . patching a
> panel. We've had some, a couple of them, very good panel patchers here,
> they made their own equipment, they made their own glue pots.

The place where the greatest differences are noted between producer
cooperatives and conventional plants in terms of shop-floor governance, however, is in the area of supervision. Again, this should not
be surprising in view of the fact that supervision is precisely the meeting
point, in capitalist society, between the owners of enterprises and the
work force which produces surplus value. It is through the supervisory
hierarchy that the desires of the owners (or managers acting in their
stead) are transmitted to those persons who perform the actual production of commodities. Besides the technology of production itself,
that is, of the machinery and its requirements, the control of production in conventional factories is communicated through persons

(supervisors and foremen) who represent capital, and is exercised upon those who are wage laborers. The goal of this hierarchical network remains that of checking the spontaneous and informal networks of independent action found among workers and of imposing order upon the human portion of the production process so as to harness its abilities and energies to the purposes of the owners and managers of the enterprise (Braverman 1974; Marglin 1974). The historic political problem internal to the enterprise, therefore, has been the struggle over the control of the work force, and how to get it to work willingly, energetically, and smoothly for the purposes of capital. One must surely see reforms and reorganization efforts such as Taylorism, scientific management, humanistic supervision, personnel management, and the like, in this light (Braverman 1974; Greenberg 1975). The continued existence of this opposition of purposes between capital and labor, the inherent political struggle within the walls of the plant, is demonstrated by the ubiquitous presence of an elaborate supervisory machinery in most industrial enterprises. One can see these relationships reflected in the interviews with workers in the conventional plywood plants.

The fact that is most striking is the vast difference in the number of supervisors and foremen found in conventional plants as compared with the plywood cooperatives. While the latter were quite easily able to manage production with no more than two per shift, and often with only one, the former often requires six or seven. Such a disparity is not uncommon. I discovered in one mill that had recently been converted from a worker-owned to a conventional, privately owned firm that the very first action taken by the new management team was to quadruple the number of line supervisors and foremen. In the words of the general manager of this mill who had also been manager of the mill prior to its conversion,

We need more foremen because, in the old days, the shareholders supervised themselves. . . . They cared for the machinery, kept their areas picked up, helped break up production bottlenecks all by themselves. That's not true anymore. We've got to pretty much keep on them all of the time.

This theme of close supervision and intense control was also a recurrent theme in our interviews with workers in the conventional plants.

I mean you're under pressure all the time . . . because the minute that thing is shut down . . . if something goes wrong, they're over there finding out what's wrong.

They're never completely satisfied.

I think one of the things I notice most about supervisors is their silence. . . . You're looking at your work, he's looking at you and your work,
and he doesn't say a word. He walks away finally. . . . You don't know
whether he's thinking about something else and he just happens to be
standing there, or if he's thinking about your work and doesn't wish to
comment on it. Or if he's thinking about your work with a frown on his
face, you know, he's had a frown, it's intended for you and he just doesn't
feel like saying, you know, and that what's even worse than one supervisor
standing in silence, it's two supervisors standing in silence, who then walk
away and talk together and you never hear what it was about. They do a
lot of their planning when they're on the floor walking around and you,
then, you can get paranoid I think.

Almost identical words were used by another coworker.

On day shift you never know when they're going to pop through there. . . .
They might stand there and watch you for awhile and they'll move on.
Very seldom that they'll ever speak to any of us. . . . [When they're
watching you] you kind of tense up and wonder, geez, am I doing this
right, am I doing that right? Then they'll come through there with three
or four guys all dressed up in suits and you don't know who they are. The
other day there was some of the bigwigs in there. . . . Nobody knew who
they were. . . . They walk by there, and they might stand there for five
minutes and just be talking back and forth amongst themselves, and they're
watching every move you're making. You know this, you know. God, I
hope I'm doing it the right way. After they walk away you just kind of
relax. He don't say much anyway. He's going to the foreman and say
something. When they have their executive meeting, that's when that
all comes out. They'll tell them what they think the guys are doing wrong.
And you better tell them, get them on a straight road, you know. They
do it in a friendly way, like I say. They're . . . the manager himself never
says anything. He goes to your foreman and tells him; he lays it on the
line to him and then he comes down there and lays it out to us guys.

In such a hierarchical system of supervision, workers are treated
not as autonomous, rational, and responsible people, but as persons
to be watched, carefully managed, and compelled to work. A recurrent
theme among workers in our interviews was this tendency to be treated
by the supervisory system as children, a relationship they greatly resent.

They like to treat you like a kid going to school. They like you . . . how
will I say it? They act like they're a little better than you are.

[Interviewer: Why wouldn't you like to be a foreman?]

I've never had the practice at telling people what to do. . . . So I don't know if that's the direction I'd want. I'm good at telling little kids what to do, but not adults. Sometimes they treat the adults like little kids down at the mill.

Being wage earners and not owners of capital, workers in conventional enterprises are forced, on pain of losing their jobs, to listen to foremen and supervisors even when they have little confidence in them, or even if they know a better way to accomplish a certain task. Supervision may be the object of grumbling and complaints in the lunchroom or at the dinner table, but it is to be obeyed, not always enthusiastically to be sure, at the point of production.

Well, like I said, every guy grades the way he thinks, and I grade the way I think it should be graded. But if the foreman insists he wants it that way, there's not much you can do. You have to do it the way he tells you to do it. And there's no two foremen that'll come by and tell you the same thing. But what is really frustrating sometimes . . . I'm supposed to have the authority to tell my crews what to do and my helper what to do. And then sometimes due to this foreman business, I got . . . there's two or three that come in there and try to be boss. Well, they'll tell somebody something, somebody else something else and all of a sudden my crews will say, well, what are we supposed to be doing? Well, I already told you what to do. Yah, well so-and-so said so-and-so. And it really irritates that they don't go down through . . . if they don't go down through . . . if they want to change to tell me and let me tell my guys, you know. Because if they think that I'm telling them stuff that's wrong or confusing to them, then they're going to lose respect for me. And a couple times I've been . . . made a couple of these frantic changes that the foreman's told me to do. I have to tell my spreader crew and then the press crew 'cause after they're glued together they go over in the press to get pressed down. And so I'm telling about six or seven guys what to do and I just no sooner tell them one thing and they want to change something else, so I do that.

I'm not bragging, but I know my job . . . and yet they'll bring a foreman in . . . like we call a ninety-day wonder in the army. He don't know nothing, and yet we have to carry him and then he gets all the glory . . . and it does gall us. It galls me! They don't need near the supervisors they got . . . half of them don't know their tail from a piece of wood.

The contrast with the producer cooperatives could not be more marked. In the first place, since there are significantly fewer of them, supervisors are not on the backs of the production workers, but are forced to be concerned with broader, plant-wide issues having to do with the flow of materials and machine usage. In the second place, even when there is some direct contact between them, the nature of the relationship between workers and supervisors stands in marked contrast to that in the conventional mill. This should not be much of a surprise, for being worker-owners rather than wage laborers, shareholders are ultimately responsible for the fates of their own supervisors. While supervisors do have the formal power to fire and to discipline shareholders (subject to appeal to the board of directors), this power is rarely exercised. In firms where the supervisors are hired nonshareholders, this is the case because continuation of employment depends entirely on the sufferance of the shareholders taken as a whole, expressed either through the board or the general membership meeting. In those firms where the supervisors are themselves shareholders, they must continue to coexist over the long haul with the other shareholders. Thus the fact that the shareholder is an owner and not a wage laborer transforms the function of supervision from that of exercising control in the name of distant capital and management to that of coordinating the production. Note the response pattern, for instance, to a question that asked, Does your foreman act more as a coordinator or more as a boss? (table 8.5).

This relationship might have been even stronger with some refinement of the question, since workers in the conventional plants were prone to interpret the item in light of their perception that the real bosses were the plant manager, the personnel director and, most centrally, the parent corporation, with the supervisor being, in the words of one worker, "nothing but lackeys."

The words shareholders use to describe these relationships are even more compelling, especially when placed in relationship to the observations of workers in the conventional plant set out above. In contrast to the latter's view that supervision was close, intense, and omnipresent, shareholders give a much more benign and pleasant characterization of supervision.

[Inteviewer: What is supervision like in this mill?]

Pretty loose really. . . . It's probably the most unsupervised place I've ever worked . . . myself, I have little or no supervision . . . on this shift there's only one foreman.

They're there to help us. They're there to make our job easier. They're not there as bosses. . . . They're just hired help. [If he wants us to do something], he says, would you please? Would you mind?

TABLE 8.5

DOES YOUR FOREMAN ACT MORE AS A
COORDINATOR OR MORE AS A BOSS?
(PERCENTAGE RESPONDING)

	Plywood cooperatives	Conventional firms
Coordinator	66%	49%
Boss	20	36
Neither	8	7
Not sure	5	9
	N = 277	N = 152

(Chi square significance = .001)

My job down there is real good because, the bosses, nobody bugs you. They know you're going to work. Now . . . if I was working there and you'd walk in, I wouldn't hesitate stopping and talking to you . . . and if a boss went by he'd never say anything. . . . They know I was going to go right back and hit the ball and try to catch up what little time I lost.

A handful of shareholders, all with experience in conventional mills, are somewhat bothered by this style of supervision.

[Supervision] is not quite as good as it should be . . . too much laxity and letting people do what they want to, and then you fool around.

This is hardly a complaint that is likely to be voiced in a conventional mill.

Beside this general looseness and distance of supervision, a state of affairs that allows a great deal of free space for individual initiative and informal cooperation among production workers, there is also a marked contrast between cooperative and conventional mills in the style of interaction between supervisor and worker. In the conventional plant, communication is hierarchical and one-way, with orders coming from the top, and compliance (whether willing or unwilling, enthusiastic or begrudging) coming from the bottom. In the producer cooperatives, communication is two-way, open, and relatively freewheeling, characteristic of communications between relative equals.

But like I say, you have got to realize that you're in a whole different ball game. Your foreman is still entitled to respect and adherence to and things like that. . . . And if I have an idea that I feel should be instituted or should be called to his attention, instead of like at Boeing where you just . . . you didn't tell them what they should do except through the usual channels of a suggestion system which I've cashed in on many, many times in those fourteen years. But at the co-op, I go and see the boss, and I say, now look, these are things that I think should be done and there's reason for it and here's the reason and I think that it'd be profitable to get to it. Whereas at a private company, you just don't do this.

Some guys get abusive [with the foreman] because they know they aren't going to be fired.

If the plywood isn't made up right, we call him over and tell him. Then he's got to do something about it.

How free do I feel to make suggestions? Just as free as I would to be talking to you. No hesitation at all.

For those who had experienced supervision in conventional factories, relative freedom on the line helps compensate for the problems, aggravations, and tensions connected to the job.

You know as far as the job goes, it's better than in any other mill. You know, if they were going to do the same work . . . 'cause just because the fact that there's a foreman standing there and you can thumb your nose at him if you want to.

How is it possible, then, to operate a mill in which upward of 150 men work on a shift without close supervision? How does this complex production processing, using a variety of woods and glues, and manufacturing a wide range of grades of finished panel, get coordinated? The answer is startlingly obvious, one that crops up in every one of our interviews in one form or another, yet so divergent from normal industrial organization assumptions that it gives pause. The shareholders individually manage themselves and one another. On one hand, filled with a sense of responsibility for the enterprise as a whole, they work in a manner that is sufficiently diligent and responsible as to require little outside supervision. On the other hand, where coordination becomes necessary, or where some members are not contributing in a way considered appropriate by other members, groups of shareholders will tend to act as collective supervisors on the job. These multiple and interrelated themes were perhaps the most often articulated views in our conversations with them. The following gives a sampling of these views.

And if somebody . . . is goofing off, you can holler over there and tell him, "Let's get going here." You know, frankly, we're all watching each other so that nobody else is goofing off too much.

And I also tend to look around and make sure things are working right a little bit more than . . . if I didn't have anything invested in the company.

If the shareholder sees another one who's not involved . . . and screwing around, well, all the shareholders would frown at it. And if it gets bad enough, they can make it tough enough for the guy to fall out.

[Interviewer: What would happen if you made a bad mistake on the job?]

I think I'd probably feel like hell just for general principles. But I think the other shareholders would probably rub it in, you know. The superintendent would come over and let you know . . . and then that's all you'd hear out of him, the one time, you know. But the rest, they can rub it in for weeks. They wouldn't hold it against you, but they'd tease the shit out of you. We got guys make mistakes around here lots of times, you know. Everybody makes mistakes. They razz them. Nobody really gets . . . you know, you just robbed me of a dollar. Nobody gets irritated. You don't find that feeling.

THE SHOP FLOOR AND DEMOCRATIC GOVERNANCE

The attention that the plywood cooperatives have attracted in recent years has been focused primarily on their self-governing character, on matters of general enterprise policy. Most of the interest has been drawn to the processes whereby a large group of worker-shareholders democratically formulates company policy through discussions in general meetings, election of a responsible and responsive board of directors composed of working shareholders, and the hiring of a general manager and a continuous monitoring of his performance. Little or no attention has been devoted, however, to decisional processes on the work line at the point of production. What I hope to have demonstrated in the above pages is the degree to which mechanisms, practices, and relationships characteristic of self-governance have indeed invaded this area in the producer cooperatives, an area hithertofore considered appropriate mainly to authoritarian forms, whether harsh or benign.

One can not carry this too far, as I have already suggested. In the plywood cooperatives, total and complete self-governance at the point of production is strictly delimited by the tyranny, if you will, of the technical, machine process itself. And yet, in the spaces and interstices of that technical, machine process, the work process is largely self-governing in the direct democratic sense. The work is organized in such a way that considerable space is available for individual initiative, informal work cooperation, and self-management, with supervision generally in the background as a nonthreatening and assistance-giving institution. On the job, shareholders are active, informed participants in those informal decisional processes by which work is organized and executed.

ENTERPRISE-LEVEL DECISION MAKING

Let me now turn to a consideration of enterprise-level policymaking in the plywood cooperatives. What is of immediate interest is the degree to which the formal and informal mechanisms are of a complex, mixed type, incorporating elements from both the direct and representative democratic models. Or to put it another way, I shall show how representative institutions are set within a direct democratic milieu, and how those institutions are shaped by the milieu.

Before examining these issues in detail, it would probably be of some use to review the formal instruments of policymaking. Recall that enterprise policy on all matters is lodged, in a formal sense, in the general meeting of shareholders. At these meetings, discussions take place pertaining to raw material purchases, plant modernization and expansion, wages, division of the surplus, vacations, health insurance, managerial and supervisory staff performance, sales, relations with government agencies, and product mix and quality, and at one time or another, policy is determined with respect to these matters. Moreover, elections are held at these meetings to fill positions on the board of directors, a group charged with conducting the general business of the enterprise in the period between regular and special meetings of the shareholders. The hired general manager is responsible for the everyday business of the enterprise, subject to the direction of the board and of the general membership meeting.

The first thing that one would want to know about these procedures is the degree to which shareholders are, in practice as opposed to theory, actually informed, interested, and involved in the mechanism by which general policy is formulated. When I began to talk with shareholders about this issue, the first thing that became evident in almost every interview was the impressively widespread availability of information necessary to develop informed judgment, and the rather high level of continuous discussion about this information and about the policy decisions for which it was appropriate. Information is available in the cooperatives in a number of forms. All of the enterprises, for instance, publish the minutes of board meetings and make them readily available, either by putting copies in the lunchroom or posting them on bulletin boards. Furthermore, any shareholder is free to go to the general manager or the treasurer in the office and ask to see whatever documents or data he so desires, a right that is often, in fact, practiced.

Oh, yah, the guys are always talking back and forth, this and that, you know . . . discussing other things and whatnot and how they think and where they might be pissed off or have you heard this or heard that, you know. Rumors fly fast, you know. And if I'm really interested, if I find something that, a rumor going around that I want to clear up, I'll come straight into the office. I'll talk to the secretary. He'll tell you, he'll clear it right up for you. If there's something I really want to know or find out how things are going on with some particular thing like, oh, these _____ claims we got or on a couple of lawsuits or something, how things are going, whatnot, then I'll go on in and talk to the manager, you know. And express my views on some things. But I like to keep informed.

Since only a small percentage of shareholders make it a regular practice to examine the books, to read all of the minutes, or to interrogate the manager, information flow is vital and is maximized by the fact that board members continue to hold their regular jobs in the mill and are continually, often to distraction, required to discuss policy matters with the shareholders working with them.

Well, when I worked with George . . . he was always real active in what was going on in the company . . . he was on the board a lot . . . and I used to always get all the information from him.

Well, we post the minutes all the time; the minutes have to be posted. . . . If they are interested, they're up on that, and then they ask a lot of questions and want to know, after we've had a board meeting, the first thing you get when you come in is. . . . You either get hell for something you've done, or they want to know what you did, or so on and so forth, the ones that are interested . . . why, the ones that want to know, they want to know certain things. Like I say, sometimes, they jump us the first thing we come in and they want to know why we did this or why we done that. And I don't know how they learn about it so fast; sometimes I think they learn about it before the day's over in the board meeting.

This availability of information contrasts sharply, of course, with the situation in conventional mills where decisions are made by distant persons of authority, with virtually no sharing of information with workers. Decisions are made, and workers in such settings must simply adapt to them. As one of these workers described the situation when he was asked why a certain policy had been implemented in his plant:

I really don't know. Sometime . . . they merged with a couple of other companies . . . we just had to change our name . . . maybe they're taking their orders from the other one we merged with.

What is also immediately evident to an outsider studying the cooperatives is the degree to which matters of company policy are part of the normal, everyday discussion in the plant among the shareholders.

When I asked our shareholder respondents about the level of activity of policy discussion that exists in the mill, I found the following quite impressive figures:

TABLE 8.6

PERCENTAGE RESPONDING "ALWAYS" OR "VERY OFTEN"
TO THE FOLLOWING ITEMS (N = 280)

Item	Percentage
Do you talk about decisions of the board of directors with other share-holders in the plant?	69.5
Among the people you know well in the plant, is there much discussion of company policies that have to do with in-plant, production policies, and working conditions?	71.9
Among the people you know well in the plant, is there much discussion of company policies that have to do with finance, sales, and investment policies?	64.4

The only remotely comparable situation found in the conventional plant was the high level of discussion during periods when active contract negotiations between the union and corporation were in progress. Fully 78 percent of the workers claimed to discuss the union contract with their coworkers during this period. Significantly, only 18 percent of such workers reported discussing union affairs when it was not a contract negotiation period. Either standing by itself or in comparison with other workers, then, the level of involvement and discussion by cooperative shareholders is quite impressive and, I might venture to add, unprecedented.

As for the shareholder meetings, the interviews suggest that no particular single description serves to characterize the prevalent mood. Some meetings are generally routine, with the manager and other officers reading reports and responding to questions. At other times, especially when a major investment policy suggestion has been made by the board, or when business has not been consistent with expectations, or when the performance of the general manager is under attack, discussions can be lively and intense. What is known for sure about them, however, is first, that attendance is very high (92 percent of our sample reported regular attendance), something that is encouraged by paying shareholders a day's wage for attending, and second, that involvement in discussions at the meetings are, comparatively speaking, quite significant. Thirty-one percent of our shareholder sample reported that they "often" or "always" participated in discussions at these sessions.

In many respects, the key institution of democratic life in the plywood cooperative is the board of directors, an elected representative institution that is more actively engaged in making policy, formulating alternatives, and monitoring the performance of the hired management team than is the general shareholder meeting. What needs to be known with respect to such a representative institution (as I stated earlier in this chapter) is the degree to which the board is responsive and responsible to its constituency, and, conversely, the degree to which it evolves into a distant institution of quasi-permanent, professional politicians formulating policy not consistent with the wishes and desires of the membership.

Most significantly, with respect to this issue, while only a minority of the shareholders has actually served on it, the board of directors of the plywood cooperatives are universally characterized by regular and significant membership turnover. As far as I have been able to determine, no tight-knit group of people regularly dominates these positions and imposes its views on the remainder of the membership. This turnover can probably be attributed to two key factors: first, the active participation of the shareholders in elections for board positions, and second, the significant degree to which being a board member involves certain disadvantages. Let us look at each of these points in turn.

One can observe the active participation of the shareholders from any number of vantage points. I have already pointed out, for instance, the relatively high degree of information held by the shareholders relative to company policy, the degree to which they demonstrate a continuing interest in the activities of the board, and the level of continuous discussion that goes on in the mill about these matters. Another way to gain a sense of the level of participation is to note that 31.5 percent of all shareholders reported to interviewers that they had, at one time or another, actively run for a board position, and that 17.5 percent of all shareholders had, in fact, been elected and had served. In comparison with these figures, only 10.2 percent of workers in the conventional plants report having ever run for union office, while only 7.6 percent have served in such positions. Or one might take note of the interest shareholders take in elections to board positions.

> Oh yah, they're pretty active campaigns. . . . We're having an annual meeting . . . in March, so it's starting in now. You can see that. Some guys run every year for twenty years and never get elected. . . . They don't give up. That's good too.

Finally, we might take note of the relatively high turnover rates in board membership each year, a tendency that became so marked in one plant that the membership was forced to place controls on the turnover process so as to gain some greater stability in operations.

> There used to be, you see . . . each year we elected all nine members on the board. Now we don't do that. We elect only three and the people serve for three years. . . . You can't have a company . . . each year elect nine new people. . . . You never get nowhere. . . . It takes a while to learn what it's all about.

> This is another thing that's wrong with this company. There's no continuity of boards.

> Interviewer: What happened after that board policy led to financial losses?

> The membership dumped everybody. Everybody but a couple of people.

> Interviewer: Do the younger, newer shareholders get to serve on the board?

> When I first got here, they were real strong about getting young guys on the board . . . and we got two or three on the board of directors and they were doing a good job.

With the exception of such psychic rewards as prestige, status, and a sense of involvement, membership on the board does not have an attractive package of rewards and perquisites. Indeed, with the exception of a company-paid lunch on the day of a board meeting, members receive no additional compensation or reward for the long hours they devote to enterprise business, a fact that probably helps explain why more people do not run for the board and why turnover is so high.

> Interviewer: You've never thought about running for the Board?

> No, I'd rather not. I've been nominated but . . . for one thing, there isn't any additional pay in it. . . . You get your day's pay same as if you was tending dryer.

> Interviewer: Why did you decide to serve only one term?

> I had that one year and I really didn't like it too well. You get involved in all the business of the company. You have to make all the decisions. There's no extra pay for it. There's not even extra thanks for it, hardly.

It is readily apparent, then, that the board of directors does not become dominated by a professional political class since turnover is relatively high and the rewards of office holding are not only small but, in some cases, negative in their effects. Service on the board is sometimes seen as more of a burden than a position of comfort and largesse, a distraction from other, more rewarding activity, and not inherently attractive. That so many different people serve at one time or another is unquestionably a tribute to the vitality of democratic life in the cooperatives.

It is also apparent that the board does not become a distant and separate institution because of the inescapable fact that board members continue to hold jobs in the mill during their tenure and are accessible to the shareholders. I might add that such access is not simply theoretical but is a fact of everyday life in the mill.

> If I have a gripe? Well, I generally go over and talk to the president of the board. Most people do . . . and you can find out what the scoop is most of the time.

> If somebody's got a gripe, they come to me; I like to hear them. And I tell them what I think and I say, by golly . . .let's go after so-and-so, he's on the board and sometimes we'll go together and ask. . . . We'll get the answer and the guy's happy.

> If you got something that you want to find out, you go to a board member, "What about this?" Explain what you think should be done and he'll let you take it to the board.

> But most of the action comes from them talking to a board member and telling him different things. . . . They work in all different places [in the mill].

Sometimes the relative ease of access causes problems for board members. It is evident from the interviews that service on the board requires not only a sense of dedication but a thick skin as well.

> I've been on the board thirteen years, so I sure get hell once in a while. . . . They all jump on me. . . . We've had quite a few guys who couldn't take it and had to resign. . . . For years . . . I was the only member of the board to eat in the lunchroom. Yah, the rest of them would hide out in their car or have a nook and corner where they'd be all by themselves, 'cause they . . . didn't want to take the guff.

From all of the above indications, it is probably safe to conclude that the board does not succumb to the problems of rigidity, distance, and professionalization so common to representative institutions. The tendency for shareholders to actively participate in and be well informed about aspects of the business of the board of directors serves as a powerful guard against such developments. Can the same conclusion be made about the general manager, a position that seems

even more prone to the ossification tendencies in representative institutions? The potential for ossification and professionalization is strong.
First, with the exception of one plywood cooperative, the manager is
always a nonshareholder, and is thus a person with a set of interests
and perspectives that may be at odds with the membership. Second,
the manager does not have a production job in the plant and is,
therefore, not as immediately accessible to the shareholders as are
members of the board. Finally, the manager is hired because of his
presumed expertise in matters of business, and therefore is a holder
of a set of skills that is apart from the direct experience of most of
the shareholders.

Most of the shareholders, in fact, are prepared to give the manager
a relatively wide latitude in conducting the business of the enterprise.

> When you hire a man and you pay him $35,000 to $40,000 a year, you
> figure he's supposed to know what he's doing and you're going to listen
> to him.

> We don't try to interfere with the manager . . . 'cause he wouldn't be no
> good to us. . . . If we had to tell him, interfere with him all the time,
> why hell, we just as well get rid of him and try to run it ourselves.

Nevertheless, while shareholders generally give the manager a free
hand, what keeps the position from becoming too distant, too independent, and too out-of-tune with the membership is the simple fact
that the occupant of the position is a hired hand and is universally
so defined. This structural relationship is critical, for it leaves the
shareholders psychologically free to approach the manager about any
business matter whatsoever, as well as to both criticize him and to fire
him when the company is not performing as the members believe it
should.

> We own it lock, stock, and barrel. . . . I'm not working for that turkey
> in the office; he's working for me. And when I go into that office and
> want some information, I demand it and get it!

While few of the respondents put matters so vehemently, this sense
that the general manager is a hired person, without tenure, and subject
to the desires of the shareholders is powerful and pervasive, but most
importantly, regularly acted upon. Average tenure for cooperative
managers, in fact, is quite low.

> But we hire the manager . . . running the mill is up to him. If we don't
> like it [the way he's running it], we can his butt.

This does not mean that managers do not often prevail on some issues close to their training and expertise. Nor does it mean that managers in some cooperatives are not more persuasive than managers in others, either by dint of their own personalities or by the particular configuration of shareholders on the board. It does mean, however, that expertise has its limits in terms of political power within the plant. Much like a baseball manager, he is often the first to go when the team is not performing in the manner that the owners deem appropriate.

Taking into consideration all of these materials relating to the politics of enterprise-level decision making, it appears that the shareholding membership is in overall control of the policy of the producer cooperatives. Whether it is manifested in the general membership meeting, in the relationship of the shareholders to the board, or in the relationship of the manager to the membership and the board of directors, it is obvious that the general direction of activity in these enterprises is lodged, in fact as well as in theory, in the hands of the shareholders taken as a whole. To the extent that its work force controls the enterprise, the producer cooperatives in plywood stand in vivid contrast to the remainder of American industry.

SOME CAVEATS ON COOPERATIVE AND CONVENTIONAL FIRMS

One of the ways I have attempted to highlight the unique aspects of the cooperatives has been to compare their politics and modes of governance with those of firms considered normal, a task I have attempted to pursue by making continual references to the internal life of a conventional plywood company. In that comparison, I believe that the contrast between the democratic cooperatives and the authoritarian, conventional firm stands out in bold relief. I would not want to leave the impression, however, that workers in conventional firms are completely without resources in their struggle to carve out a sphere of decision making. Certainly, there are means by which this can be done. While it has nothing to do with the internal life of these enterprises, workers are completely free to quit and to offer their labor power elsewhere. Furthermore, workers have found that passive compliance—working within the boundaries of rules and expectations but with little enthusiasm and no extra, unpaid effort—is often a method for creating free space. It is not unknown, moreover, for workers in such settings to informally regulate the pace of the production line, to set production quotas, and the like. In extreme circumstances, finally, it is a fact that workers sometimes sabotage the production process to regain some control over their labor.

In the plant I examined, all of the above methods have made their appearance at one point or another through the years. Nevertheless, the most powerful instrument available to workers in the conventional enterprises remains the labor union. As the only collectively organized expression of the labor force, it represents a potentially powerful instrument of worker participation in enterprise governance.

Much like labor unions throughout all of American industry (Aronowitz 1973), however, the union in the conventional plywood plant I studied acts not as an instrument of governance, an institution able to impose the wishes and desires of the work force upon the enterprise, but as an organization for self-defense against the continual impositions of management.

> Without unions we'd be working for peanuts. . . . If it wasn't for the union, we wouldn't have a damn thing.

> Our higher-ups there . . . don't care two cents for the workers, you know. They'd give us as little as possible . . . if it wasn't for the union.

While this self-defense role is vital and inescapable in a context where labor and capital stand opposed, by so confining its activities to this narrow arena, it leaves the work force without an effective voice in those processes of governance by which the policies of the entire enterprise are formulated and executed.

In the description of the plywood cooperatives, moreover, and in the comparisons of these enterprises with conventional ones, I by no means wish to leave the impression that the cooperatives are totally harmonious institutions, without tensions, problems, and irritations. In fact, the cooperatives suffer from a set of significant problems, some of which relate to their market position, some to the health of the plywood industry in general, and some to their internal political life. In this paper, I am only concerned with the last set, problems, I would argue, that seem to be irretrievably linked to active, participatory democracy. One often-heard theme in these interviews, for instance, was the complaint that too many people were active in the governance of the cooperatives.

> There's too many chiefs and not enough Indians in this place. Everybody thinks they're boss. . . . Everybody stands around and tells everybody else what to do. . . . You know, if you're part owner, then you think you're shit out of sand.

Another complaint is that cooperatives are torn by constant arguing and bickering.

But we get to arguing, fighting, and quarreling, and we lose production.

We get to arguing among ourselves, then we don't do nothing. I think that's a bad thing.

Finally, I even ran across several shareholders who complained that too many people were involved in running the cooperative who were without the competency and intelligence to do so.

We don't have the brains. . . . We don't have the business brains, I'll put it that way.

But each one of those directors feels that they're important although they . . . don't have the ability to do the job. And they want to put their two cents in and 90 percent of the time they're wrong. They've had no education.

I think a lot of the guys are well meaning, but I think there's a great amount of incompetency. I mean, when you go into a plywood mill, you don't find the more educated group of people.

These are very real problems and not to be taken lightly. They suggest that even a relatively successful and functioning democratic work environment is not devoid of problems and tensions but, in fact, generates its own unique ones. Nevertheless, I would submit that these problems remain problems that attest to the very vitality of these enterprises as fully democratic institutions, as environments in which amateurs are actively and intensely involved in running an important part of their lives, and doing so quite successfully.

PLYWOOD COOPERATIVES AS CASE STUDIES

In this paper, I have focused attention almost exclusively on one set of producer cooperatives located in the Pacific Northwest plywood industry. Reliance on this sample does not mean, however, that nothing can be said about firms of sizes that fall outside the range of this sample. What one can do, and indeed has been done in the body of this chapter, is to make reasonable extrapolations based not only upon available empirical materials but also on the existing organizational literature. I have pointed out in various places, for instance, how the governance of plywood cooperatives differs from the small handicraft and service cooperatives, based on a reading of the internal dynamics of face-to-face groups.

I might point out in passing that if one goes in the other direction, that is, toward a consideration of large-scale self-governing enterprises, one finds that many of the problems previously considered endemic to self-managed firms are relatively absent in the plywood cooperatives I have examined. Much of the literature on self-managed enterprises in Yugoslavia, for instance, suggests that these firms are often plagued with problems of false and symbolic participation, the gradual formation of a dominant ruling faction, indiscipline at the point of production, and a growing distance between managerial-technical experts and the rank and file (Adizes 1971; Horvat 1976a; Vanek 1975b). While the plywood cooperatives have serious problems of their own, as I have pointed out, they do not seem to be prone to those that plague the largest self-managed firms described in the literature. Thus, while perhaps not suitable for the technical processes in other industries, their middle-range size enables them to avoid the important shortcomings of the largest and smallest of the self-governing enterprises. They are sufficiently large to escape the informal, often troubling intensity characteristic of face-to-face groups, while at the same time, sufficiently small to avoid the rigidification of status and technical differentiations within the plant. Ordinary worker-owners, the board, and the hired technical stratum are sufficiently accessible to one another in a direct sense that these tend not to develop.

It is important to add, in closing, that the good fortune of the plywood cooperatives in their ability to avoid most of the problems of large-scale self-managed enterprises may be partially attributed to the relatively compressed and constricted skill range found in the plywood industry. The mood of camaraderie and spontaneous cooperation, as well as the avoidance of the formation of a rigid stratum of technical experts, may be as traceable to the narrowly constricted range of skills as to the fact of moderate size. It is conceivable that in industries characterized by a complex division of labor and hierarchy of skills, that producer cooperatives even of moderate size might find themselves confronted with many of the problems found in the Yugoslav examples. Unfortunately, because of the absence of suitable research cases, the question will have to remain unanswered for the time being.

PRODUCER COOPERATIVES AND
DEMOCRATIC THEORY

Having considered the above caveats related to the plywood cooperatives as case studies, let me now turn to the issue raised at the very beginning of this analysis—namely, the consideration of producer cooperatives in the light of democratic theory. What can be learned from this examination of the plywood cooperatives that will allow one to speak to some of the central concerns of democratic theory? What can be drawn from democratic theory that will shed some light on the internal dynamics of the cooperatives?

It should be recalled that I posited the existence of two distinct and opposed conceptions of democratic governance. The first and oldest form is generally known as direct or participatory democracy and stresses the direct, participatory experience of ordinary people in their own governance and the capacity of that experience to act as an educative medium for the molding of interested, active, informed, and rational citizens. The second form is generally termed representative democracy and stresses how problems of size and limited time, as well as the limited capacities of ordinary citizens, make it reasonable to create a class of individuals, selected through open and universal elections, to act as intermediaries for a mass population unable to rule itself in a direct fashion.

These conceptualizations of democratic governance are characterized by opposed notions of the most appropriate form of governance, the evaluation and expectations of the capacities of ordinary people, and the values to be served by the act of government. Consequently and quite correctly, they have always been seen as competing democratic forms, quite incompatible with each other. What this analysis of the plywood cooperatives amply demonstrates, however, is not only that these historically competing forms can in certain cases coexist but, to put matters even more strongly, can also mutually reinforce the most positive qualities of the other model and soften the most negative ones. In a sense, each of the democratic models, as they exist within the producer cooperatives, covers for and fills the problematic spaces of the other. Let us briefly look at the ways in which this is the case.

The producer cooperatives are without question examples of direct democratic institutions in which the rank and file is decisive in the decisions that give direction to overall enterprise policy and in the development of those informal arrangements by which the social processes of production are carried out in the workplace. I have shown the variety of contexts in which these policy decisions are formulated by the shareholders, ranging from the annual or semiannual meeting to the complex processes of self-supervision and mutual supervision at the point of production. It is true, however, that such arrangements are not sufficient to manage enterprises as large and as complex as those found in plywood, and that representative institutions of varying types are required. Most shareholders find, for instance, that the time available to them for matters of formal governance is extremely limited, most centrally because of the very long hours devoted to matters of production. Almost universally in the plywood industry, shareholders work ten-hour days and six-day weeks. Once one adds the time requirements of family obligations, recreation, and the like, the time available for frequent and extensive meetings is not abundant. For these reasons, a representative institution like the elected board of directors is a very useful device for easing the burdens imposed by limited time. Furthermore, while the plywood cooperatives are notable for their constricted skill range, there remain activities that require a certain amount of expertise (mostly relating to business affairs—raw material acquisitions, relations with government agencies, product sales, taxes, etc.) which the shareholders, in general, do not have, and which they are willing to lodge in the hands of a hired (or elected, if you will) general manager.

Representative institutions thus cover or help compensate for some of the problems endemic to direct democracy. However, what makes the coexistence of these two democratic forms not only possible but also attractive is the pervasive participatory democratic milieu and behavior in the cooperatives, which helps prevent the development of those tendencies in representative democracy that have made it problematic in other contexts. Almost all of these problematic tendencies are related, in one way or another, to the distance and lack of communication between a professional political class intensely engaged in governance and a largely uninformed, irrational, and apathetic mass population. While the plywood cooperatives utilize representative institutions, these problematic tendencies do not develop.

One might trace this happy state of affairs to the intensely participatory milieu of these firms, a milieu derived from a complex combination of worker ownership of the enterprise, its human scale, and its formal locus of final decisional power in the general membership, all of which serve to minimize the distance between representatives and the represented. We have seen, for instance, both the existence of a high degree of turnover on the elected board and the degree to which board members remain accessible, often painfully so, to the shareholders who work next to them in the mill. We have also seen the easy flow of information and the frequency of policy discussion among the shareholders, factors that contribute to a well-informed and reasonably rational membership able to hold its own both against the board and the general manager. While representative democracy almost always moves toward rigid stratification, the fact that representative institutions are embedded within a rich participatory environment in the plywood cooperatives allows representative institutions to make their positive contribution without decreasing the reality of self-governance.

If this examination of the governance of producer cooperatives reveals anything about some of the central issues in democratic theory, then, it is that under certain conditions direct and representative democracy can not only exist together but can also serve to enrich each other. It is also reasonable to suggest, to go somewhat further, that some combination of these two forms is probably necessary in any sizable work institution that is seriously committed to self-governance.

Finally, it is worth stressing that the confident expectations about the capacities of ordinary people articulated by the theorists of participatory democracy are largely met in the cases of the plywood cooperatives. I have discovered that perfectly ordinary working people are capable of becoming informed, of reaching reasoned judgments, and of acting cooperatively, and in so doing, of demonstrating the capacity to successfully run fairly complex productive organizations. This, I would submit, is no small finding in a day and age when much of the social science literature and many political practitioners are pointing to the problems of mass participation in governance and of the need to reassert the prerogatives of strong leadership among political elites (Crozier et al. 1975).

NOTES

This paper was prepared for the National Institute of Mental Health Research Project on Producer Cooperatives: Urban Work and Mental Health of the Center for Economic Studies, Palo Alto, California. The empirical work for this paper was supported by the National Science Foundation, grant no. SOC 76–11897 and by the staff and facilities of the Institute of Behavioral Science, University of Colorado. I would like to thank Thad Tecza for his assistance at every stage in this research.

1. The classic treatise on representative government is that of John Stuart Mill. See Mill 1910.

2. There is another model of democratic politics that is not, however, relevant to the present discussion, namely, pluralism. See the discussion of this model by Greenberg (1983:chap. 2).

3. The following discussion is based not only upon published work on the plywood cooperatives already cited but on extensive fieldwork (on-site inspection and interviews) by the author and his research assistant in six worker-owned firms over a period of six months.

4. The pronoun *he* is used because of the virtual absence of women as shareholders. I found only eight in the entire sample.

5. The analysis in this paper is based on data generated by a three-stage process. (1) Interviews with general managers, cooperative officials, and union officers (in the case of the conventional plant), as well as direct observation of the production process in six worker-owned firms, one privately owned unionized firm, and one privately

owned nonunion firm (January 1977). (2) In-depth interviews with twenty-three shareholders from two worker-owned firms, and twelve workers from a privately owned unionized plywood company. The interviews ranged from one and a half to three hours in length, and were all tape recorded. Interviews with shareholders were held either in their homes or in quiet rooms within the plant, free from outside interruption. All interviews with workers from the privately owned firm were held in their homes (January to April 1977). (3) A mail questionnaire sent to working (production) shareholders in four worker-owned plants, and to production-line employees in a large privately owned unionized plant. The questionnaire, only a minor part of which is used in the present paper, is part of a research project whose objective is to examine the relationship between participation in workplace decision making and the possible development of class consciousness. The return rate on the mail questionnaire was 63 percent and resulted in a sample of production workers for data analysis purposes comprised of 280 worker-shareholders and 157 employees from a privately owned firm.

6. For introductions to the vast topic of alienation as formulated by Marx, see Avineri 1971; Fromm 1961; Ollman 1971.

7. For the analyses of the evolution of modern forms of industrial work, see Blauner 1964; Braverman 1974; Landes 1969; Marglin 1974; Nelson 1975; Smith 1937; E. P. Thompson 1964.

PART V

Special Issues for Worker Cooperatives

Precisely because of their cooperative status in a capitalist society, economy, and culture, worker cooperatives face a variety of special issues that do not normally confront traditional firms. This section explores several of these issues, both internal and external to cooperatives.

In the first essay, Zelda Gamson and Henry Levin examine several internal obstacles to survival faced by democratic workplaces. After pointing out the problems created by the tenuous economic conditions in which most cooperatives are formed, they utilize a broad comparative perspective to focus on three particular problems seemingly endemic to cooperatives. First, they look at the lack of common cultural norms among participants in cooperatives. This stems not only from the dearth of any early cooperative socialization in the larger society but also from the great diversity of personal motives that draw workers to organizations antithetical to the larger society. Second, they discuss how the lack of experience in democratic decision making in our society affects those who try to build cooperative workplaces. In particular, they examine here the tangled and troublesome issue of exercising legitimate authority in cooperative situations, a problem on which many countercultural cooperatives have foundered. Finally, they focus on the practical but crucial problem of the inappropriate mixture of skills that troubles many cooperatives owing both to recruitment patterns and to flat pay structures. Throughout the essay, Gamson and Levin discuss concrete ways to overcome these obstacles.

In the second essay, Henry Levin examines the troubles faced by worker cooperatives and worker-owned firms in gaining access to financial capital and how these difficulties might be addressed through Employee Stock Ownership Plans (ESOPs). ESOPs are a mechanism for capital expansion of a firm through the transfer of stock to the employees of the firm with favorable tax benefits for both the firm and employees. They are, therefore, potential devices for workers to acquire firms from their employers and to turn them into worker cooperatives. This, however, was not their original purpose. ESOPs originated as a populist scheme to "make every worker a capitalist" by giving him or her a stake in the firms, although not offering voting rights in the management of stock. Moreover, the actual formation of most ESOPs seems to be more attributable to management's desire to raise capital for the firm at a low cost. Still, recently there has been greater use of ESOPs to gain worker ownership—though not worker control—of several firms. If ESOPs are to be used as a mechanism for creating worker cooperatives, Levin argues that there must be an orderly and systematic way to transfer the overall governance of a plant to the workers. This is crucial since without an orderly transfer, lenders will be scared off. Though to date labor unions have been ambivalent about ESOPs and their potential uses, they can clearly play a major role in this process.

Finally, David Ellerman addresses the complicated question of the appropriate legal structure for worker cooperatives. This is a theoretical essay which tries to lay out, on the basis of our accumulated knowledge, the ideal structure for cooperative enterprises. Drawing on the Mondragon experience, Ellerman argues that the essential distinction between a capitalist corporation and a worker cooperative is how their membership rights are constituted. A capitalist firm is based on transferable property rights, that is, ownership of stock; a worker cooperative is based on nontransferable personal rights, that is, working for a company. In this sense, an employee-owned firm is a capitalist corporation because its membership rights are marketable; if cooperative firms are successful, as the plywood cooperatives have been, over time they tend to undermine continued employee ownership. The rising value of the stock will limit the ability of new workers to purchase the membership shares of retiring workers. As a result, outside investors may be the only possible alternative. By the same token, ESOPs, one mechanism for achieving employee ownership, are also suspect. In Ellerman's view, the legal structure of a cooperative must be based on nontransferable personal rights; it must at the same time develop mechanisms to allow workers to invest in their firms without eventual economic penalty. Ellerman suggests such a mechanism, namely a system of internal capital accounts for each worker which represent his accumulated net investment in the firm and a corresponding, but separate, system of membership certificates which are attached to the functional role of working in the firm. Ellerman argues forcefully that worker cooperatives, since they are based on personal rights, are not strictly speaking owned by workers. Cooperatives are rather the legal embodiment of the workers themselves; a cooperative is, therefore, not a piece of property but a democratic social institution.

9

Obstacles to the Survival of Democratic Workplaces

ZELDA F. GAMSON
AND
HENRY M. LEVIN

INTRODUCTION

It is a major anachronism of American society that democracy is defined as relevant only in the political sphere of life. The relative freedom of the political arena stands in sharp contrast to the authoritarian principles governing the American workplace. Clearly, a strong case can be made for bringing greater democracy into the workplace in order to create a citizenry that participates in all of the major areas affecting its daily circumstances and its future. In fact, it has been argued that political democracy must necessarily be seriously constrained in effectiveness in the absence of economic or workplace democracy (Mason 1982; Pateman 1970).

Partially as a response to deteriorating economic conditions as well as to a search for new political directions, there appears to be a rising interest in workplace democracy. Community groups and workers are increasingly considering and consummating the purchase of firms that are threatening to cease operations in order to protect the jobs of employees as well as the economic life of their communities (see Zwerdling 1978, and chapter 10 by Levin, this volume). Other small businesses have been started by groups of workers in order to create work organizations grounded in collective ownership and democratic principles of participation. Perhaps the prototype of this type of democratic workplace is that of the worker cooperative. The worker cooperative is a firm that is both owned and managed by its workers. In the smaller cooperatives, democratic operation is based on direct participation of workers in all important decisions, while in the larger ones the direct participation on the shop floor is accompanied by representative forms of governance in the delegation of major decisions to worker-elected managers or boards of directors (Bernstein 1976b).

But, before considering this recent upsurge in workplace democracy as a vanguard of a larger social movement, one should be aware that there exists a major basis for skepticism. Throughout their history, many worker-controlled enterprises have been short-lived phenomena. They have been cyclical in their appearance and demise, and they have not been significant overall factors in the United States economy (Jones 1977; Shirom 1972). It is unusual to find examples of democratic workplaces that are more than a decade old. Although one of the plywood cooperatives of the Pacific Northwest is sixty years old, this is atypical. A recent survey of small worker cooperatives in the United States found that almost all were less than ten years old, and the median tenure was about 5.8 years (Jackall and Crain, chap. 5, this volume). Historically, the same pattern has been evident in every periodic cycle in which democratic enterprises were established (see chap. 3 by Jones, this volume). Indeed, one must look to other nations to find significant numbers of democratic economic entities with greater longevity (e.g., cooperatives in France and the kibbutz in Israel).

THE SHORT LIVES OF DEMOCRATIC WORKPLACES

There exist two major reasons for the short lives of many democratic workplaces. First, the circumstances under which they are typically established are ones of economic marginality; therefore, such businesses experience high rates of failure. Second, the internal requirements for sustaining democratic processes often conflict with the rigors of functioning in a competitive market environment. Normally, it is the first of these reasons on which the greatest emphasis is placed, but in this paper we will suggest that even when the economic foundation of cooperative firms is sound there may arise serious challenges to the internal functioning and reproduction of the democratic enterprise.

The causes of economic frailty derive directly from the circumstances under which democratic enterprises typically arise, that is, the preservation of existing firms and jobs as well as the initiation of new, small businesses. When a community or a group of workers joins together to purchase a firm and operate it according to democratic principles, the firm is almost always in dire economic straits. In fact, community or employee purchase is often a last-ditch effort to stem economic failure and closure. In such circumstances, the optimistic alternative to massive unemployment and economic dislocation is an unbridled enthusiasm that collective action of the existing work force of the firm can overcome these severe hindrances (Zwerdling 1978).

In contrast, the establishment of many new democratic enterprises is less a response to threatened unemployment than to deeply felt personal and political convictions that are in conflict with more conventional forms of work organization. Such initiators may see cooperative and democratic forms of enterprise as a preferable alternative to the controlling structures of corporate and bureaucratic forms of work life. In these respects they are likely to be committed to greater development of their human and social talents as well as to a higher measure of social equality than they believe is possible in a more traditional workplace. Further, they may see democratically controlled enterprises as the fundamental building blocks of a broader movement toward a more democratic and egalitarian society. But, these convictions are not usually accompanied by access to the substantial capital and markets required to form and sustain a larger firm, so that these newer democratic enterprises tend to be concentrated among the typically fragile areas of business in which it is possible to start a small firm with little capital.

This means that these businesses are established in the most competitive and risky product and service domains of the U.S. economy. They are initiated in those areas that require relatively little capital investment and experience, and they are forced to compete with the many other small businesses that have been established in these relatively accessible portions of the marketplace. But, wherever it is easy to start a business, failure rates tend to be high. As with all small businesses, even those that are democratically operated may lack adequate capital to sustain them until the break-even point is reached. In fact, their unconventional form of organization may make it even more difficult for these firms to obtain loans through conventional financial channels. Market potential and profitability may be considerably lower than projections, and a lack of experience may also take its toll.

Further, even if the business becomes profitable, the relative ease of entering the market serves to attract new competitors who vie for clientele. It is not surprising to find that the goods and services that are produced by these businesses are heavily concentrated among restaurants, food stores, bookstores, printing shops, repair services, and other areas characterized by high failure rates (Jackall and Crain, chap.

5, this volume). It should also be noted that these businesses reflect the types of goods and services consistent with the values of their members, such as natural food, production and sale of political and feminist literature, alternative energy forms, social services, and so on. Thus the very circumstances of such small businesses, whether organized as conventional or democratically operated firms, contribute to high rates of instability and low longevity.

Any firm that cannot solve its economic problems—in a simple sense, obtaining revenues that are equal to or greater than costs—will be unable to survive. In this sense, producer cooperatives and other democratically managed firms are not unique, but share a dilemma with other types of enterprises. However, the very conditions that lead to the formation of democratic or cooperative workplaces tend to overlap with circumstances leading to greater economic marginality than in the cases of the more conventional firm.

There is a second reason for the relatively short longevity of the democratic enterprise. Democratically managed firms must not only survive economically in the marketplace but they must also survive as democratic organizations. This means that there must be effective mechanisms for promoting democratic decision making and participation as well as appropriate behaviors by co-workers that contribute to this end. If a democratically managed firm tends to be characterized by an inability to make decisions, by widespread and unproductive conflict among co-workers, and/or by a work force with inappropriate skills for the task of carrying out the operations of the firm, the firm will have a short life. Regardless of the intrinsic viability of the enterprise as an economic entity, it will not survive as a democratically operated entity unless it is able to reproduce the conditions required for sustaining its organizational form.

The purpose of this paper is to address three organizational obstacles to the reproduction and effective functioning of democratically managed workplaces which our experiences have convinced us have been endemic to such enterprises in the United States.[1] These three obstacles are: (1) the lack of a common culture or social contract in which there is a widely accepted set of values and processes that guide behavior; (2) the lack of democratic norms for decision making; and (3) an inappropriate mixture of skills for the needs of the enterprise. The importance of addressing these obstacles lies both in their crucial role in the success or failure of the democratic firm as well as in the relatively high incidence of these problems in cooperative firms. We shall attempt to explain, for each of these, the nature of the obstacle and the reason that it seems to be endemic to democratically and/or cooperatively run enterprises. We will also suggest some particular approaches to overcoming such obstacles, with a rather heavy emphasis on both educational and technical assistance strategies.

LACK OF A COMMON CULTURE

For any social organization or collectivity to function and survive, there must exist a common set of norms, values, and expectations about organizational functions and operations that are accepted by all or most of the members of that organization. These may take the form of accepted traditions, laws, rules, procedures, or guidelines for the organization, which serve as the glue that integrates individual participants into the overall functioning of the organization. This sort of common culture can be both implicit and explicit. Thus in a capitalist firm, most employees accept the notion that workers, managers, and capitalist owners have different rights and obligations. For example, workers are hired as wage labor with certain work obligations that are set out by their superiors on behalf of the profit motive for capitalist owners. These work obligations must be performed by the individual, if he or she is to retain employment and receive wage payments. Further, the precise nature and organization of work and definition of each work role, the relation of the workers to other workers in production as well as to the firm, the method of performing the work and the tools available to do so are the prerogatives of the capitalist owners and their managers.

This common culture of the workplace also assumes that workers compete as individuals with other workers for wages and promotion; that the place of workers in the hierarchy of the firm determines their degree of relative autonomy; that the interpersonal relations among workers are matter-of-fact relations designed to facilitate control and productivity rather than based upon traditional social relations such as those of family or kinship; that the main rewards for work activity are extrinsic ones such as wages, salaries, vacations, pensions, and promotions to higher status rather than the rewards of a high degree of control over one's work activities and of the ability to express one's human and creative potential on the job.

To a very large degree, these premises are accepted implicitly by most workers, so that they are rarely questioned. That is, they are reinforced by the norms, values, and expectations of workers as part of the common culture of the workplace. Thus, the capitalist firm can function on the premise that most of these matters are uncontestable, and that it is only issues such as the level of wages and salaries, fairness in promotion policies, the amount of work effort required by supervisors, and so on, that will be the potential subjects for contention. Although in recent years some aspects of this common culture have begun to deteriorate, at least in particular instances, this overall characterization of the common culture and the organizational practices of capitalist firms and government agencies that support it can be found in the vast majority of workplaces across the United States.

Why is it that workers in diverse occupations, regions, and economic sectors can be expected to share a culture of the workplace so generalizable that typical workplace orientation and behavior by employees can be assumed? To a large extent the answer is found in the schools (Bowles and Gintis 1976; Carnoy and Levin 1976a; Dreeben 1968), or, more precisely, in the schooling experience. In their study of six societies, Inkeles and Smith (1974) found that schooling seems to be the main contributor to the development of those personality traits that are fundamental requisites for factory work. In fact, schools tend to be impersonal, bureaucratic, and hierarchical, like the typical workplace. Course grades and promotion in the school are similar to wages and salaries and job advancement in the workplace. Expulsion or academic failure have their counterparts in job loss and unemployment. In both the workplace and the school, the activity of the student (workers) is determined by factors external to them, such as the curriculum (production activity), the organization of instruction (production), and the instructional materials (tools) that will be used. Supervision and evaluation are carried out by teachers (work supervisors) whose authority derives solely from their superior positions in the organizational hierarchy. These supervisors control the content of the work activity as well as the rewards and sanctions, and successful students learn quickly to accept the norms of the organization.

It is not surprising to find that by the time young people are conditioned by at least ten to twelve years of this regimen, they have learned to accept its legitimacy and internalize its norms or, at the very least, to conform to its requirements. This common culture is further reinforced by experiences in the workplace which rather consistently buttress these norms in supporting existing work relations. Of course, the media and the family also tend to portray this work culture as normal and acceptable, if not inevitable, because of its pervasiveness in the workplace.

The new democratic workplace is likely to be characterized by more of a yearning for a common culture than by the actual existence of such a culture. In fact, the ties that typically bind together members of this type of organization are based either on the need to ensure organizational survival, as in the case of worker takeovers of failing businesses, or on the common aversion to the culture of the traditional workplace with its strong elements of control and authoritarianism (Blauner 1964). To the degree that there is a common set of values, they represent a rejection of the conventional norms of hierarchy and control and an abstract acceptance of what is perceived as their opposite: equality, democracy, and freedom of expression.

However, one should not confuse what are typically abstract and romantic views, no matter how strongly they are held, with what is a common culture of shared beliefs and understandings about appropriate behavior for members of democratic work organizations. Such shared beliefs can arise only out of an intense, common set of experiences that derive from the cultural context in which these experiences take place. Indeed, it is this factor that has determined the common culture of existing workplaces, in that the totality of experiences in the home, school, community, and workplace have led to a shared set of norms. In fact, in those historical cases where democracy in the workplace has succeeded, members have built their own democratic organizations around their common experiences and values. For example, from the Scandinavian immigrants and various religious groups who founded cooperatives in the United States, to the Eastern European Jews who initiated the kibbutzim in Palestine, to the Basques who created the industrial cooperatives of Mondragon, there has been a common experience and culture on which the democratic values and sense of destiny have rested. Further, in all of these cases the cooperative endeavors were workplace manifestations of larger movements for solidarity and survival.

This common background has not been true for most of the groups that have initiated democratic workplaces in the United States. For a while, it was thought that the shared generational experience of young people during the 1960s and early 1970s would provide a common culture (Flacks 1971). The experiences generated by opposing the war in Southeast Asia (as well as all the other upheavals associated with those protests) were viewed as at least a catalyst that would provide a new set of values for the "greening of America" (Reich 1970). When new democratic organizations were formed, however, the dominant culture was typically replaced by a set of romantic notions based on rejection of conventional norms rather than a shared vision of appropriate behavior. This normlessness often created paralysis, even in the face of obvious dangers to survival.

For example, the common rejection of hierarchy and control often brought persons with rather different needs into the cooperative or democratic entity. One of the principles of these organizations tended to be openness toward new members who preached similar values. Individuals who rejected personal or collective responsibilities were thus joined with those with a strong sense of social and personal responsibility and integrity. The former would often reject conventional demands on their energies or behavior, including getting to work on time, doing work of high quality, economizing on the use of organizational resources, and so on. In some cases, there were "rip-offs" in the form of massive telephone bills to friends across the country; stealing or giving away the resources of the organization (e.g., free meals and supplies) to friends; or outright extortion. Although most of the members of the organization would see these acts as antisocial and destructive, the lack of a clearly acceptable code of behavior meant that formal action would have to be taken to expel such persons from the organization and to recoup losses. However, few wished to be accused of being on a "power trip" which in the negative milieu of rejection of the establishment meant that any member opposing the acts of another member was being antidemocratic and attempting to control the organization. Unfortunately, the fact that many of the democratic workplaces of the late 1960s and early 1970s were unwilling to expel members who were obviously engaged in destructive behavior meant that some were destroyed.

Another general ethos often associated with the rejection of conventional work structures is a peculiar form of anarchy in which it is assumed that an organization should make no demands on its members. Rather, it is assumed—at least tacitly—that individual voluntarism alone should replace the structure and discipline of the typical work bureaucracy. Pushed to its extreme, this view paralyzes an enterprise to the point that workers cannot engage in collective efforts. Using the term *the tyranny of structurelessness*, Joreen (1973) described some of the pathologies that arose from the resistance to structure in the early years of the women's liberation movement. Fear of power and a reluctance to exercise authority led to a variety of troubles which sometimes undermined the very existence of the organization. Under such conditions, rumormongers, narcissists, and petty thieves flourished in countercultural cooperatives and collectives. The tendency was to refrain from doing anything until it was often too late or to address these problems with such ambivalence that a destructive factionalism was generated among members. Graphic examples of these problems are found throughout the democratic workplace movement.

Without some consensus about the positive values of the enterprise and fairly explicit ways of dealing with destructive members, cooperative enterprises either die out or sell out. The landscape of alternative organizations is strewn with collectives that could not work collectively and with "hip" businesses manipulated by clever entrepreneurs (Kreiger 1979; Case and Taylor 1979). This is not only true of enterprises that started out devoted to democratic values and social and political change but also of democratic enterprises formed for strictly pragmatic reasons. In both cases, a vacuum left by the absence of a culture of democratic work has left these enterprises vulnerable to outsiders representing different interests.

It is fairly obvious that the development of a common culture is a necessary condition for survival of the democratic workplace. Unless a set of norms can be established about the relations of workers to one another and to the enterprise as well as about the acceptable and desirable range of behavior of workers, it will not be possible to work collectively and to survive economically. Even the most basic decisions regarding the organization of production, the structure of rewards, the choice of products, and pricing and investment decisions require a common set of values for democratic participation to succeed. Further, the fine detail of daily operations and worker interaction require that, to a large degree, all members accept these norms.

We argued earlier that a common culture must necessarily arise out of a common set of experiences. From these shared experiences there tend to evolve norms for social interactions that come to be accepted as appropriate values and behavior for a social entity. The problem is that the types of democratic experiences that might create these shared understandings are typically absent in the major institutions that mold the social values, attitudes, and behavior of most Americans. Accordingly, the common culture must be largely created within the democratic workplace itself, a rather heavy burden considering that it may take all of the energy of the members just to meet the demands for economic survival. Nevertheless, there are at least two major strategies that might be pursued in developing a common culture: first, the development of a formal code of social statutes and second, a special emphasis on the recruitment and training of workers.

FORMAL CODE OF SOCIAL STATUTES

Probably the most important foundation for creating a common culture is the initiation of a written code of social statutes that describe both the rights and obligations of workers in the democratic work setting, as well as the methods by which the decisions will be made. The importance of this foundation is less in its permanence than in the process of transforming vague principles of democracy and equality into a concrete code of behavior. By going through this process, the organization must confront virtually all of the issues that will be an integral part of its common culture.

In fact, the original Rochdale principles enabled the Rochdale weavers to formalize their relationship as a worker cooperative and to establish a set of values and expectations about their participation. Such a code does not have to endure forever in its entirety. Indeed, a part of establishing a common culture is to periodically revise social statutes as necessary. It is this continuing interaction between the social code and social practice that creates the common experiences and the evaluation of those experiences that form the basis for shared values, attitudes, behaviors, and expectations.

What issues should a formal set of statutes address? There are a number of excellent sources that provide a discussion of these requirements. For example, Vanek (1977*b*) has provided a "basic folder" in which he distinguishes between the needs of self-managed firms and those of other businesses, as well as setting out suggestions for a constitution, available legal forms, ways of initiating the firm, guidelines for finances, and relations with the local community. Strongforce, a group in Washington, D.C., devoted to promoting self-management, published practical manuals on implementing the principles of democratic organizations (Strongforce 1977). The Industrial Cooperative Association (ICA) in Somerville, Massachusetts, has developed a number of documents for such purposes, with special attention to legal and governance details (for an example of this, see chap. 11 by David Ellerman). The most elaborate social statutes are probably those of the Basque Cooperatives in Mondragon, Spain, where more than twenty years of development has created a code that covers virtually all important areas of behavior.

The particular areas that ought to be addressed are virtually all of those that are necessary to characterize the nature of the enterprise and its relation to its workers and clientele. Clearly, these should include a description of the purpose and nature of the firm, including the types of products and services that it will provide; the basis for membership and the rights of members; the obligations of members to the enterprise; the criteria for making decisions on matters such as the organization of work, the basis for remuneration, the distribution of any surplus, and the pricing policies; the relationship to other democratic workplaces and the larger community; and the organizational and financial principles that will be employed. The initial steps in formulating these principles will require the members to address the question of what are their shared values and to create an initial process for resolving differences among them. The undertaking of this process, in itself, will go far to provide a set of common experiences for establishing the common culture necessary for survival. However, it is also important that workers be amenable to altering these codes over time as the needs of the organization change. Thus the formal social code should be seen as both a framework for functioning as a democratic organization as well as the catalyst for creating a common culture.

RECRUITMENT AND TRAINING OF WORKERS

One way in which a common culture can be emphasized is through the recruitment and training of new members to the democratic work organization. By selecting new members who are in agreement with the formal code of social statutes, it is possible to reduce the vagaries of trial and error that are often involved in finding appropriate co-workers. Countercultural enterprises have generally drawn their members through friendship networks (see Gamson et al. 1978; Rothschild-Whitt 1979; and chap. 5 by Jackall and Crain, this volume). Recruitment has been informal and inexplicit, and serious problems have resulted. When the values of these enterprises have not been clarified in concrete terms, the criteria for selecting members have been difficult to specify, leaving mutual affinity as the dominant factor. In some cases this has meant that workers have been selected on very superficial grounds, such as the length of their hair, their style of clothes, or the attractiveness of their rhetoric.

Unfortunately, an organization using such an inexplicit selection process often ends up with persons whose only common value is negativism toward the traditional workplace, rather than a positive commitment to create and sustain a positive alternative. When demands are made upon such persons, they often become divisive, using their well-honed destructive energies to undermine the organization. Virtually all democratic organizations have had experience with these types of people. To a large degree, the recruitment of new members along the lines established by the social code can eliminate such applicants from the outset. In fact, it can be argued that an active recruitment program should take place outside of friendship networks, to attract a broader range of persons.

Formal attention to the training mechanism is also likely to be important. Exposing new members to discussions of the social code and its application can introduce them rather quickly to the expected behavior that characterizes the organization. It is true that this training requires time and organizational resources that are usually in short supply in fledgling democratic workplaces. Yet, such efforts may actually increase the total capacity of the organization by reducing the conflicts that typically erupt when members do not share a common set of values.

Like any group, democratic workplaces develop informal ways of encouraging conformity to group norms—but again, these are often not very explicit. Inculcating and maintaining certain standards of behavior, therefore, is accomplished indirectly, through a variety of subtle means. In a collectively managed bar, for example, workers who did not conform were subjected to the treatment that all small, cohesive groups mete out:

> If people are unable to do their job or consistently use drugs or alcohol, they are pressured into conforming or leaving. The pressure is exerted in subtle ways. If someone is hired and does not do the job, he or she is given feedback immediately, usually by someone who is close to the person. Then if the behavior continues, there is a great deal of discussion and

consternation behind the person's back. Except in extreme cases, as with stealing, the time-lag between recognizing poor performance and acting on it may be months. (Sisson 1978:166)

As time passed, this bar and similar enterprises became more self-conscious about recruitment and training. In an Ann Arbor food cooperative, a formal hiring system evolved in its fourth year. One of the purposes of the new system was to move hiring decisions away from the paid coordinators—who tended to select people they already knew—and into the hands of community people and co-op members. For the first time, a job description was spelled out. This did not happen without some conflict, however: several applicants who were turned down under the new hiring procedures expressed dismay because they felt they deserved to be hired by virtue of the work they had put in at the co-op as volunteers. The new system held, though, and led to a formal training program for new volunteers. Such devices do not guarantee the formation of a common culture but, with the passage of time and the development of a stable work force, they can help in legitimating practices consistent with democracy in the workplace and in weeding out those that are inconsistent (Gamson 1979).

None of these devices can substitute for an organic connection with a culture that infuses larger meaning into the workplace, whether a religious culture, like that of the Bruderhof (Zablocki 1971) or Koinonia, whose economic enterprises are a part of a devout communal life; a nationalist culture, as with the Mondragon cooperatives and the Israeli kibbutz; or a self-conscious working class culture, as in Yugoslavia. We do see some hopeful signs, however, in the growing appeal of small towns and neighborhood associations, particularly among young adults, which are described regularly in publications such as *Communities, In These Times, Workplace Democracy,* and *Working Papers for a New Society.* But it is too early to know whether they will last long enough to form common cultures. Based on some shared generational experiences among young people who came of age in the 1960s, they may have a profound impact on the cities and college towns—Madison, Minneapolis, Boston, Berkeley, Ann Arbor, Seattle, Eugene, New Haven—where large numbers of them have settled (Training for Urban Alternatives 1979).

LACK OF DEMOCRATIC NORMS FOR DECISION MAKING

In addition to the general lack of a common culture among the workers in democratic workplaces, there is a specific lack of democratic norms and a dearth of experiences in decision making. Because of the favorable imagery of democracy in the political realm, democracy in the workplace has an appealing halo. As we have seen, most people, however have had only limited experience with democratic organizations. Major agencies such as families, churches, and schools, as well as workplaces, tend to be organized along hierarchical and, often, authoritarian lines. Even those political institutions that are based upon democratic precepts tend to practice representative rather than participative democracy—that is, with chosen or elected representatives making the decisions.

To the degree that people have participated in democratic situations, that participation has tended to be episodic rather than pervasive and marginal rather than central to their lives. Most typically these experiences are found in voluntary organizations and among ad hoc civic groups. Even people who have participated regularly in non-economic, democratic organizations such as town meetings report a good deal of ambivalence about democratic norms, especially those that involve broad participation (Mansbridge 1973). As a consequence, those who have become involved in democratic workplaces have often lacked the skills and knowledge necessary for effective democratic participation, which in turn contributes to the demise of the enterprise or encourages the development of a more hierarchical structure (Case and Taylor 1979).

There are at least four problems in democratic decision making that appear frequently enough to constitute common issues. These are: (1) the legitimate exercise of authority; (2) obtaining accountability from members; (3) the productive use of conflict; and (4) the productive use of meetings.

LEGITIMATE EXERCISE OF AUTHORITY

However much one might question hierarchical forms of organizational control, they often have the virtues of clarity and familiarity. They may not be efficient—indeed, the efficiency of hierarchical forms of authority has been exaggerated—and they may not be accepted without some resentment by those who are constrained by them. But they are usually relatively clear, at least, about who has responsibility for what. Democratic work organizations can rarely make this claim. Part of the problem lies in the confusion between responsibility and authority. In democratic organizations, the effort to minimize differences in power and influence often leads to resistance in giving legitimate authority to a particular position or individual.

One way of dealing with this issue is to vest authority in the work group as a whole, not only to set policy but also to execute group decisions. We have seen instances where pure participatory democracy has worked well, but this is limited to small enterprises with a stable work force. A worker-managed bar in Ann Arbor began in the late

1960s under a traditional manager system. But inequities in scheduling (if the manager liked you, you got scheduled well; if she didn't, you ended up working Sunday afternoon) led to a rebellion among the workers, who designed a collective work organization that won approval from the owners. After several years of experimentation, the system at the bar was institutionalized; subgroups of workers—waiters and waitresses, bartenders, cooks—govern the day-to-day scheduling and organization of work. The work force as a whole (some thirty-five people) makes decisions about hiring and firing, the disposition of the profits which workers share with the owners, and other issues of policy (Sisson 1978).

Pure participatory democracy has not worked well in larger, less stable enterprises. When turnover is high, decisions made by one set of workers are often subject to criticism and reformulation by another set. Since there are few structures and procedures to channel the influence of new members, they can have a profound effect on the way the organization operates. One of the other consequences of the lack of structure is the unequal distribution of influence, which tends to favor the most articulate, best educated workers (Mansbridge 1979).

Another way of minimizing authority differences in democratic workplaces is to rotate tasks among workers. The kibbutz provides a good example of a democratic system with a clearly defined structure of work rotation: all members take turns doing onerous tasks, such as kitchen duty, and jobs in the various production and service branches are rotated regularly among the workers in them. Collective workplaces in this country are likely to rotate jobs, but this is done informally. In the bar and a food co-op in Ann Arbor, for example, workers switch jobs periodically when enough workers agree that they are ready to try something else.

But rotation, even in the kibbutz, has its limits. When jobs require scarce professional and technical skills, only certain people can perform them. Law collectives, countercultural newspapers, therapy groups, and health cooperatives founded in the 1960s and early 1970s found they could not freely rotate jobs between professionals and nonprofessionals because of the limited technical competence of nonprofessionals and because of lingering resistance among professionals (Rothschild-Whitt 1976; Case and Taylor 1979). Rotation works best among jobs whose skill requirements are relatively similar.

Large enterprises generally turn to some version of formal management, either by selecting managers from among the workers or by hiring an outside manager. The kibbutzim rotate management of each of the work branches among a small group of people who receive special training in kibbutz management, while the plywood cooperatives hire a manager from outside. In both cases, the members have ultimate authority over the manager. In democratic workplaces, there is a tendency to minimize the importance of administration and management. We do not know why this is so—perhaps because information about the organization seems to be widely available, and because administrative tasks that would be limited to a few managers in a traditional firm are spread among more people, or perhaps because of closer connections between planning and production—but it does place greater burdens on managers. Because their work is seen as somehow not legitimate, managers in a democratic workplace must justify themselves to workers considerably more than managers in a nondemocratic firm. While we do not have any hard data, we suspect that turnover among managers is higher in democratic enterprises than in traditional ones; there are some indications that job stress among kibbutz managers is high (Yuchtman 1972). Adizes's close study of the operation of two Yugoslav firms under the worker council system (1971) documents the frustration of managers. He quotes one executive who put it this way: "I don't tell workers how to work on a machine because they know how to do it. Why should they tell me what price to set for a product? They don't know markets. They don't know the state of competition." Adizes notes that Yugoslav executives, "weary of slamming tables and delivering tirades," would become increasingly withdrawn and apathetic at meetings (Adizes 1971).

Managers in democratically organized workplaces complain that they have responsibility without authority. The other side of the complaint is that workers have the unusual opportunity to pick their leaders and to hold them accountable.

Whatever the precise form of the problem in different democratic work settings, the issue of the legitimate exercise of authority is often a serious one. Exactly how to resolve it depends on the nature of the organization, its size and functions, the backgrounds and orientations of its members, and the experience of the members in working together. Typically, the challenge is one that will ultimately yield to a concerted trial-and-error approach. A particular alternative is chosen by the members in the spirit that it will be given a chance to work. Based on the results, it will be retained intact, modified, or abandoned in place of another strategy. The best alternative will be discovered through this rather positive approach to ascertaining the minimal authority structures consistent with both democratic decision making and effective organizational functioning.

OBTAINING ACCOUNTABILITY FROM MEMBERS

A related problem in a democratic work organization is that of obtaining accountability from members. Most of the evidence we have seen indicates that democratic workplaces are more productive than conventional ones because of the collective commitment engendered by worker control and/or ownership (Blumberg 1968; Jones and Svejnar 1982). From our own observations of democratic workplaces, it is clear that most workers put a good deal of effort into their enterprises, both in performing production tasks and in participating in governance and administration. It is also clear, however, that individual workers differ in the amount and quality of the work they do. While this occurs in other types of enterprises, it seems to have particularly deleterious consequences for morale and productivity in democratic organizations. In a situation where no one is boss, how do workers hold one another accountable? If responsibility is vested in the group as a whole, how can any particular individual feel responsible?

In the Yugoslav firms he examined, Adizes (1971) found that workers quickly learn what they can be held responsible for and what they can get away with; penalties for transgressions are not clear-cut and managers are powerless to discipline workers. Small work groups are notoriously resistant to firing their own members and will often rely on some superordinate authority or on the fates to do the dirty work. In the Ann Arbor bar, for instance, the workers asked one of the owners—whom they criticized harshly on most occasions—to fire a worker who was stealing rather than face doing it themselves (Sisson 1978).

People who have worked in democratic organizations for any length of time become aware of the unconscious traps workers fall into (Wyckoff 1976; Steiner et al. 1975). A typical trap is the emergence of an informal "straw boss" who becomes exasperated with fellow workers who take on the characteristics of irresponsible children. There was a dramatic example of this pattern at the food co-op in Ann Arbor:

> She [a veteran coordinator] went around discovering problem after problem, all caused by negligence. The refrigerator was set on 52 instead of 32, meaning that food will rot more quickly. The scale was set too high so that when people measured food for bags they were giving too much for the customer's money.
>
> She began yelling at him (a novice coordinator). She called up one of the other coordinators to complain, waking her. She talked about the refrigerator mistake costing them business and shoppers' respect. They moved away from the desk to a place farther back in the store. He continued, "You pushed me . . . I feel real uncomfortable with that." She responded, "You make *me* feel uncomfortable. We should share the work. You've sat around for two days and we're paying for it." He said, "You play boss." (Gamson 1979)

It is not enough to urge avoidance of such unconscious work roles; their frequency indicates deficiencies in the operation of democratic work organizations that must be addressed in some other way. Otherwise, they lead to scenes like the one at the co-op. In the more mature Yugoslav system, the elected committee of workers deals with disciplinary matters. Foremen and workers can initiate complaints to the company's legal counsel, who then calls the disciplinary committee together. The committee hears the workers' side and then decides if a disciplinary action is needed. Adizes (1971) claims that his review of disciplinary cases over a period of three years in two firms indicates that the "committee seems to 'put on the hat of justice and impartiality' during the hearings. Likewise, the idea that the committee members are workers and thus should side with workers does not occur, because unless the members of the organization are disciplined, all workers will lose income as a result of the income distribution system."

In the long run, most of the individual accountability problem is resolved by the development of a common culture. Even so, provisions must be established for particularly serious and persistent violations of the social code (Bernstein 1976b:chap. 8). However, in the early periods of development of democratic workplaces, this problem is likely to be more severe as norms tend to be more ambiguous. This factor underlines once again the need for a formal set of statutes that provide a clear picture of the responsibilities of and expectations for each member so that new workers can be informed concretely about their roles. The period of trial and error in dealing with issues of individual accountability should be considered a normal phase of development for the democratic workplace.

PRODUCTIVE USE OF CONFLICT

Overt conflict is proscribed from the typical capitalist workplace by the highly detailed division of labor and sharp delineations of hierarchical supervision and responsibility. There are latent feelings of resentment and inner conflict among individual workers in such a context, but they are rarely displayed openly. Rather, there is a substantial resignation to the allocation of tasks, the nature of work activities, pay and promotion policies, and other decisions of the firm. Even in the upper echelons of these firms, where decisions are generally made, open conflict is suppressed (see Jackall 1983).

In contrast, conflict is a central feature of democratic decision making, since democratic forms of participation are designed to allow the routine expression of different interests and values. The question that faces democratic workplaces is how to treat such conflict as a normal part of the decision-making process by using it in a productive way to explore and select among alternatives.

Both Jackall (chap. 6, this volume) and Mansbridge (1973), close observers of a variety of democratic organizations, conclude that conflict seems unusually high. Yet, at the same time, these authors and several others (Gamson et al. 1978; Reinharz 1983) observe that there are often attempts to suppress such conflict. There are at least two reasons for this. First, the intimate and peerlike relations that develop among co-workers in a democratic workplace may seem threatened when conflicts arise. Given the negative aura that surrounds disagreement or conflict in the larger society, there is an emotional bias against open expression of conflict; it is thought to smack of uncooperative behavior and to undermine the warm relations among colleagues. Second, the seeming lack of conflict in bureaucratic workplaces makes the open expression of conflict among the warm and collegial co-workers of the democratic workplace seem a poignant failure.

Unfortunately, such views and the tendency toward suppression of conflict are incompatible with democratic decision making. As long as freedom of expression is encouraged, conflicting points of view will also manifest themselves. Eventually, the suppression of disagreements will build up pressure in the group until a major conflict erupts. Often this conflict will take on a highly personal and destructive form or waste energies by making much ado about an apparently unimportant issue which has only symbolic significance. If these eruptions are frequent and emotional, they take their toll on the organization. Some workers resign, others withdraw much of their involvement, and the cycle begins anew.

Thus the goal of a democratic organization should not be to suppress conflict, but to welcome it and use it productively. Freedom of expression is a value that should be widely embraced, for it enables an airing of alternatives that would otherwise not be considered. The more deeply involved the members are, the more likely they will wish to express and discuss the problems and the potential solutions of the organization. It is therefore necessary to create a format in which conflict and its resolutions are expected and can be addressed systematically. To a large degree this necessarily must be done at regular meetings of the membership.

PRODUCTIVE USE OF MEETINGS

Closely allied with the productive use of conflict is the productive use of meetings held by the worker-members of democratic workplaces. Meetings among the membership represent the prime arena for addressing the problems faced by the organization. Accordingly, they are a major focus for group decision making and for the airing and resolution of conflicts among members. Unfortunately, however, cooperative members often lack experience in using meetings in this way, and thus their meetings often exacerbate the conflicts, take inordinate amounts of time away from other productive activities, and fail to resolve important issues. In part, these shortcomings are the result of poor planning and naive leadership.

While a portion of every meeting should permit open discussion of anything that is on the participants' minds, this period should not preclude the planning of an agenda. All members should be invited to submit items for that agenda, with at least a brief description of the issue, alternatives, and recommendations. Recurring problems should be placed on the agenda by those convening the meetings. The fact that individuals will be asked to come forward with agenda items and analyses will mean better preparation for meetings and will encourage informal discussions prior to the meeting which will often point the way toward resolutions.

The meeting facilitator should take the responsibility of ensuring that the meeting is completed in a reasonable period of time and that all members are encouraged to participate. This role is often a difficult one to fill because of the reluctance of co-workers in a democratic organization to be viewed as on a "power-trip." However, by rotating the job of facilitating meetings and by setting out a particular format, it is possible to make the facilitator responsible for keeping the meeting on track.

Observations of democratic organizations have often indicated that meetings are not productive because: (a) too much of the agenda reflects personal conflicts among particular workers rather than organizational issues; (b) much of the debate represents an airy discourse on abstract political or social issues rather than a practical discussion of problems faced by the organization; and (c) an excessive amount of time is often devoted to a dull discussion of the pressing details of daily life. By the over-reliance on meetings and ineffective use of them, democratic workplaces engender timidity ("I can't do that unless I check with the group"), mistrust ("You can't do that if you didn't check with the group"), and cynicism ("All we do is have meetings"). It is no wonder that people in democratic workplaces complain about being burned out and yearn for a chance just do to their work without the burden of an endless round of meetings.

How can meetings be used more productively? First, a planned agenda, a reasonable time limit for addressing it, and an appropriate style of facilitation are important. Second, personal conflicts that emerge in meetings should be discussed privately by the conflicting parties outside of the organizational meeting. A different meeting can be arranged with the principals if they cannot resolve their differences. Third, the small details of daily organizational life ought to be addressed on a daily basis among those who are affected by the decisions, and short reports of their resolution may be made at the regular meetings of the members.

In addition, there are a number of sources that can be drawn upon for assistance in conducting democratic meetings and decision making. The Movement for a New Society, and the presently inactive New School for Democratic Management have worked out a variety of techniques for encouraging the legitimate exercise of authority, evaluating performance, confronting disagreement, and working out consensus. These techniques are a fascinating amalgam of Quaker meeting techniques, group dynamics, and sound business practices. There is a growing network of consultants around the country servicing alternative work organizations, some of whom have expertise in this area (Reinharz 1983; National Center for Employee Ownership 1983).

The Movement for a New Society, for example, makes the following suggestions for facilitating meetings:

1. Bring out opinions. Encourage the expression of various viewpoints—the more important the decision, the more important it is to have all pertinent information (facts, feelings, and opinions).

   Call attention to strong disagreements. When handled forthrightly, differences of opinion yield creative solutions.

   Ask people to speak for themselves and to be specific.
2. Help everyone to participate.
3. Keep the role of facilitator neutral.
4. Keep the discussion relevant. Point out to the group when discussion is drifting off the topic or becoming trivial. Cut off discussion when repetition occurs or when people become weary.
5. Keep track of time.
6. Encourage individuals to pursue on their own, projects or ideas in which they have a strong interest but which do not concern the group (Coover et al. 1978).

LACK OF APPROPRIATE SKILLS

The final obstacle to the survival of democratic work organizations that we wish to address seems far more mundane than the first two discussed above. This is the lack of appropriate skills represented among the work force of many worker cooperatives and other types of democratic workplaces. Unfortunately, it is often these mundane issues that cause democratic workplaces to founder.

As we have already argued, members of democratic work organizations largely come together to either prevent the closure of a firm or to create a new work entity based on democratic principles. It is only by coincidence that such enterprises find themselves with exactly the right combination of persons trained and experienced in the varieties of activities that they must conduct. The relative equality of pay and loss of hierarchical authority that characterize democratic organizations will often result in substantially lower salaries and less status for educated workers than they would be likely to find in traditional organizations. While some workers will be so committed to the democratic ideal that they will readily forgo higher salaries and prestige, others will simply choose to work in conventional organizations where their skills and talents will command greater rewards. Some worker cooperatives will become so proficient that economic sacrifices will not be required, and in other cases, workers may actually see larger benefits than in the traditional firms (see Jackall, chap. 6, this volume).

Of course, many conventional small businesses face this problem as well, in that they cannot afford to hire planners, administrators, publicists, and accountants and still produce their product or service. This surely is a contributing element to failure rates among these businesses (Hosmer, Cooper, and Vesper 1977; Stein 1979). In the case of democratic workplaces, however, the problem is even more pervasive, for two reasons. First, the relative equality of pay and status even in larger democratic businesses may make it difficult for them to attract people with the best training and experience. This is especially true for financial and administrative personnel and for those with high-level technical skills. Second, members of democratic workplaces tend not to recognize the need for skilled people. The members of a democratic organization may believe that because conventional firms justify skill differences as an important criterion for ranking people in the work hierarchy, such distinctions should not be used in a democratic firm. Some may believe that the concept of a skilled person is not intrinsically meaningful, on the assumption that any highly motivated person assigned to a particular role can learn that role rather quickly. Thus members sometimes suspect that the perceived need for skilled persons is not a real need, but only a tendency to mimic capitalist enterprises.

There is a particular tendency to minimize the importance of management in democratic workplaces, primarily because of the association of administrative roles with bureaucracy, capitalist enterprise, and hierarchy. Even when the necessity of planning and management is accepted, it is often done so ambivalently. For example, at the food co-op in Ann Arbor everyone acknowledged the need for better business practices and coordination. When a new coordinator was hired to handle bookkeeping, however, he was neither selected for previous bookkeeping experience nor trained to acquire bookkeeping skills. In fact, the new coordinator was supposed to be trained by the previous coordinator, who it turns out had learned bookkeeping on his own. In any event, the previous coordinator was too busy doing other things and had little time to teach the new one. So for several months, no one knew the financial status of the co-op, and the new coordinator was unsure about how to handle the situation.

Because it operated at an economic margin, the co-op—like most small businesses—had little time for planning, let alone for training; the daily tasks shaped the way the coordinators used their time. Since no one coordinator was at the co-op all the time, all of them did many of the same things. Their time perspective, therefore, was very tele-scoped—they had little time for planning, anticipating problems, or training. Even the task everyone considered to be one of the most important—organizing and training volunteers—was not accom-plished well. A vicious circle operated: it took time to train people to take on jobs that would ease the burden on the coordinators, but since the press of daily jobs prevented the coordinators from investing time in training and planning, they did most of the work themselves (Gamson 1979).

There are a number of solutions to this problem, all of which have both strengths and weaknesses. The approach that is least consistent with the promotion of democratic values is to hire long-term consul-tants or employees on terms different from those for other workers. For example, if the firm can afford it, it can go into the marketplace, find someone with the necessary skills, and offer to pay an appropriate salary or fee on a regular employer-employee basis. As we mentioned earlier, one increasingly finds consultants with specialized skills in accounting, organizational development, training and education, computers, and law, available to work with democratic firms at some-what reduced rates. However, these consultants or employees are ob-viously not full participants in the democratic process of the firm.

Another possibility is to concentrate on recruiting new members with the necessary skills. Even so, it may be necessary to offer a somewhat higher wage than is normally paid for most positions, though even then the new employee might still be expected to sustain a substantial personal, financial sacrifice. For example, in one worker cooperative that we studied in 1978, the highest level administrator was making about $18,000 a year, while department heads were re-ceiving about $11,000 to 12,000 and other workers about $7,000 to 9,000. A salary of $18,000 for the top administrative position of a firm with annual revenues of over $3.5 million is modest; indeed, it was only about one-third of the going remuneration for such a post at the time.

A possibility that is most consistent with the principles of demo-cratic workplaces is to train existing workers for the skills that are needed. This solution has substantial promise, but it also has limi-tations. For example, there are some positions for which internal training is not adequate. The obvious examples are those of lawyers and certain types of health personnel as well as accountants with expertise beyond the bookkeeping level. In most cases, however, these types of needs can be met through short-term consulting arrangements. The second limitation is that democratic workplaces typically lack the resources to train existing workers to fill job areas where skills are lacking. Indeed, it is this lack of skills in the enterprise that has created the problem. In these cases the chosen trainees will likely have to obtain formal instruction at local colleges or universities or other training organizations.

Fortunately, there are an increasing number of organizations that can assist in fulfilling the training requirements. These have included, among others, the New School for Democratic Management in San Francisco, which has provided training sessions around the country for cooperatives and self-managed firms. Courses offered included training for financial management, marketing, democratic practices, legal issues, and so on. At the present time, the New School is inactive but the North American Student Cooperative Organization runs training programs for people in cooperative workplaces. At a more advanced level, the doctoral program in Social Economy and Social Policy at Boston College develops expertise in worker self-management, co-determination, land trusts, community development corporations, consumer councils, and other areas related to democratic work organizations. Programs on self-managed firms and democratic organizations are also found at Cornell University and at the Five-College Consortium in western Massachusetts (University of Massachusetts at Amherst, Amherst College, Hampshire College, Smith College, and Mount Holyoke).

FUTURE DEVELOPMENTS

In this paper, we have addressed three major categories of obstacles to survival of the democratic workplace. In each case we have suggested the origins of the problem as well as some potential solutions. In this final section we wish to address some general possibilities for improving the knowledge base as well as the democratic functioning of these organizations. In particular, we wish to point out potential developments that could help clarify the functioning of democratic workplaces as well as promote their formation and survival.

There exists a large body of research in social psychology on the effects of group size and individual anonymity with respect to cooperation and problem solving (Jones and Vroom 1964; Lott and Lott 1965; Fox and Guyer 1978; Singer, Brush, and Lublin 1965). This research has hardly been explored in the context of the democratic workplace. For example, research findings have consistently shown that groups are more likely to take risks than individuals acting independently. This literature suggests that individual accountability is increased in smaller groups with shared information. While many collectively organized work groups intuitively understand these principles, the social psychological literature provides a rational basis for organizing groups in ways that maximize risk taking and accountability. Several educational researchers (Cohen 1974; Slavin and Tanner 1979; and Slavin 1983) have been investigating the effects of different cooperative learning strategies on intellectual performance and interpersonal relations. It is clear from this pioneering work that there are many ways to teach cooperation and that these methods often lead both to better individual and group performances and to improved interpersonal relations. Teaching strategies, however, must include tasks that are appropriate for a cooperative structure and construct groups in a way that allows individuals to participate equally (Cohen 1974).

Since the best way to learn democracy at work is to participate in other democratic institutions encouraging cooperation and democratic decision making, schools would be an obvious place to start (Levin 1980). Labor studies programs (Stack and Hutton 1980), adult education schools such as the Highlander Folk School, and certain American colleges, such as Antioch and Berea, have developed ways to teach democracy, primarily by institutionalizing student participation. The distinguishing feature of these schools is the nature of their moral environments (Clark 1970; Grant and Riesman 1978). They all have in common a commitment to humanistic values, a deemphasis on status differences, and organizational mechanisms for including students in decision making. Unfortunately, they represent but a small fraction of schools in the United States, although we suspect that their students have been overly represented in democratic movements for change. The notion of a moral environment is critical for any educational program for democratic work, for it lays down the real conditions for students to experience directly the values and practices of democracy (Dewey 1916). Otherwise, education for democracy degenerates into technique stripped from its cultural and ideological bases (Bernstein 1976a).

An experiment that combined many of the characteristics of these schools in a democratic community setting occurred in New Haven, Connecticut. Using what they called *contextual training*, the Training for Urban Alternatives Project (1979) (with funding from the Center for Studies of Metropolitan Problems of the National Institute of Mental Health) applied the principles that Vanek (1977b) spelled out as necessary to successful education for self-management. Vanek (1977b) has argued that all educational programs for democratic work should be designed according to the following principles: *identity* between the practice of self-management and the nature of educational programs for self-management; *proximity* between the educational activities and the workplace; *subordination* of training in skills to the development of a critical consciousness; *pairing* of co-workers; and *transparency* and *full disclosure*.

There are also other organizations that provide models for the democratic governance of work; most have some training programs. The kibbutz, with job rotation, a differentiated system that combines broad participation in policymaking with implementation by the groups closest to the tasks performed, is a model whose detailed workings have not been examined closely enough by proponents of democratic work. The kibbutzim operate their own primary and secondary school system designed to teach youngsters democratic, egalitarian values and skills. The kibbutzim also run training programs for teachers, administrators, and technicians geared to specific needs, values, and structures of the kibbutz. The Mondragon network of cooperatives in Spain began through the efforts of the graduates of a technical school that had been established in that Basque community. While its curriculum is focused on technical subjects, the school itself is operated according to the same cooperative principles as the other cooperative firms (Ornelas 1982; Gutierrez-Johnson and Whyte 1977; Thomas and Logan 1982:52–59). At the present time there are no democratic workplaces in the United States that have developed educational and training systems as extensive as those of the kibbutz and the cooperatives of Mondragon.

Finally, we would like to emphasize the emergence of various regional and national networks as well as technical advisory groups that can provide services and personnel for democratic workplaces. We have suggested that, to a large degree, the obstacles to survival of these entities are hardly idiosyncratic. Rather, these obstacles are shared by most democratic workplaces, whose internal organization and goals are largely incompatible with the society around them. The network, then, is a means by which democratic workplaces can join together to share resources, ideas, personnel, and training programs. For example, a regional network can provide technical advisory services on matters from marketing and financial management to democratic processes and formulating bylaws. Such a network can also assist in training personnel and in serving as a personnel clearinghouse for workers for democratic organizations. Services can be provided through the network mechanism that would not be affordable or practicable for most individual enterprises. While no regional network that we are aware of has developed its services to this extent, except the Philadelphia Association for Cooperative Enterprise, the potential for doing so exists in the formal and informal networks of cooperatives, nonprofit organizations, and social change groups in college towns and in many major cities in the United States. In addition, at the national level, the Industrial Cooperative Association in Somerville, Massachusetts, the National Center for Employee Ownership in Washington, D.C., the Association for Workplace Democracy, the Center for Community Self-Help in Durham, North Carolina, and the National Consumer Cooperative Bank are responsible for providing financing and technical assistance to cooperative ventures.

To a large degree, we believe that many of the obstacles to the survival of democratic workplaces can be effectively surmounted by major programs of education and technical assistance at both the regional and national levels. For those of us who are committed to the democratic firm, it is important to support the establishment of such programs and the expansion of their services.

NOTE

1. This chapter is based upon information drawn from a variety of sources. Both authors have engaged in extensive fieldwork on worker cooperatives and democratic work organizations. Gamson (see Gamson et al. 1978) studied collectives and cooperatives in Ann Arbor, Michigan, and has extended this work to western Massachusetts. Levin has studied worker cooperatives since 1975, including the producer cooperatives of Mondragon (see chaper 2 of this book), the Meriden Triumph Motorcycle Cooperative in England (Carnoy and Levin 1976b), and worker cooperatives in the San Francisco Bay Area. In the summer of 1978, he devoted considerable time to an intensive study of a cooperative, wholesale book distributor with thirty-five workers and about $3.5 million in sales. In addition to the fieldwork, the authors have relied on interviews with other members of cooperatives and discussions of these subjects at conferences. Finally, they have drawn upon the substantial and expanding literature on the internal dynamics of democratic organizations.

10

ESOPs and the Financing of Worker Cooperatives

HENRY M. LEVIN

INTRODUCTION

One of the major difficulties faced by worker cooperatives and worker-owned firms has been access to financial capital. Without the ability to borrow for purposes of meeting short-term cash flow needs or long-term expansion, these firms have faced substantial difficulties in surviving and competing in the marketplace. In the last decade or so, Employee Stock Ownership Plans (ESOPs) have been proposed as mechanisms for financing corporate expansion while systematically shifting a portion or all of the ownership of a firm to its employees. In general, ESOPs are established as a trust on behalf of the employees of a firm, and a loan from conventional sources is obtained by the ESOP for purchase of corporate stock. The loan is invested in the firm. In exchange, the firm agrees to make annual payments into the trust in amounts sufficient to enable the trust to pay its debt. The firm obtains major borrowing advantages, since the tax laws permit the firm to treat these payments as deductions because of their status as contributions to a qualified employee-deferred compensation trust.

As the principal and interest are paid on the ESOP loan through the tax deductible payments of the firm, the shares of stock become free of the lien and are transferred to individual accounts for each employee according to pay level and length of service. Thus, over time, the employees acquire ownership interest in the firm to the degree that they share in the ESOP. Generally, the employee receives his or her vested shares only at termination of employment or retirement, and employees have full vesting rights after ten years of service.

In summary, ESOPs represent a vehicle for capital expansion of a firm through the transfer of stock in the firm to its employees. Both the firm and the employees receive favorable tax benefits from this transfer, and it has been used in the last decade as a method of expanding worker ownership of firms. In this respect, it can be viewed as a potential device for workers acquiring their firms from employers and operating them as worker or producer cooperatives. In this essay, I wish to explore the potential of ESOPs for serving this role. Before addressing the issues of ESOPs directly, however, it is important to point out the reasons that worker cooperatives have faced difficulties in obtaining access to financial capital.

In addition to the possibility of outright discrimination against worker cooperatives and employee-owned firms, there are two major reasons that such firms have problems in obtaining access to loan capital. First is the issue of leverage or control, and second is the issue of collateral. Financial lenders prefer to have some measure of control over the affairs of their borrowers, in order to assure that the borrower is following prudent practices with regard to its financial condition. In most cases, this is established through a process in which the lender is somewhat involved in the business of the borrower. The most typical case is where firms seek members of the financial community to serve on their boards of directors. In this way, the function of overseeing is served for the financial community by its participation on the board, which provides both inside financial information to potential lenders as well as the assurance that the representatives of the financial community are overseeing the operations of the firm. In the case of small businesses, a personal relation is usually established between the owner and the local banker with whom all financial transactions are made. In this way, it is the personal involvement and knowledge by the banker that maintains access to loan capital for the business.

In contrast, worker cooperatives often govern themselves without outside members on their boards. Further, there is no guarantee of a single owner or officer who always represents the workers, given the democratic management of such firms. As a result, the financial community cannot obtain the leverage over cooperatives seeking to borrow that they can over capitalist firms. This problem is compounded by the fact that cooperatives usually cannot offer their stock as collateral for a loan. All forms of external ownership are usually proscribed by the cooperative agreement, meaning that banks and other financial institutions cannot be treated as potential owners in the event of a loan default. For these reasons, the traditional financial community has been reluctant to provide access to capital for cooperatives, and until recently, the government has not provided loans through its public programs such as those of the Small Business Association (SBA).

Under a federal law passed in 1980, the SBA can provide loans to cooperatives, and the establishment of the National Consumer Cooperative Bank in the late seventies promised to provide another government-related source of capital for worker cooperatives. The budgetary stringencies of the Reagan administration, however, and its new policies for both agencies have raised doubts about whether government loan capital in substantial amounts would be available to cooperatives.

Two other major alternatives for worker-owned and cooperative firms to obtain loans for meeting cash flow or expansion needs have been the model used by the Spanish cooperatives of Mondragon or the ESOPs approach. The Mondragon group of cooperatives has its own banking system that provides loan capital as well as other business consulting services and banking functions to the cooperatives and to households in the region (Oakeshott 1978:chap. 10). Although the Mondragon system is highly successful, this extensive approach is beyond the capability of a single cooperative or a small group of cooperatives. Thus, the ESOPs model appears to be one of the few possibilities, particularly for workers who wish to purchase their own firms to operate them as cooperatives.

ORIGIN OF THE ESOP

The concept of the ESOP is derived from a visionary plan to make all workers into capitalists. Though authored by both a lawyer, Louis Kelso, and a philosopher, Mortimer Adler (Kelso and Adler 1958), the plan is usually credited to Kelso because of his later explications and his active promotion of the approach (Kelso 1967). In *The Capitalist Manifesto*, Kelso and Adler argue that while private ownership of property is an indispensable prerequisite for political freedom, the existing concentration of capital ownership among a small portion of the population could lead to labor unrest and social upheaval. For example, it was estimated that in 1971 the top 1 percent of families in total income owned about half of all corporate stock, and the top 10 percent held more than three-quarters (Blume, Crockett, and Friend 1974:27). Kelso's goal was to distribute capital ownership more widely by making "every worker a capitalist."

It was argued that if all workers shared in capital ownership, there would be benefits such as a second income for workers from dividends as well as a stake in the capitalist system. The mechanism for doing this was the Kelso plan, which has become better known as the ESOP, or Employee Stock Ownership Plan. In order to bring the plan into operation, the firm establishes an employee stock ownership trust (ESOT) on behalf of its employees. The ESOT obtains a loan from a bank or conventional lending source on the basis of a note which is guaranteed by the corporation. In turn, the ESOT uses this money to purchase stock from the corporation. The firm makes annual payments to the ESOT up to a maximum of 15 percent of the qualified annual payroll, or up to 25 percent if combined with a money purchase plan (a pension plan that invests in employer securities and under which employer contributions are credited to separate employee accounts). This amount is tax deductible. In turn, the contributions from the company are used to pay the bank loan, and the amortized shares are usually distributed to the individual accounts of employees in the proportions their salaries bear to the total payroll of participating employees.

Employee stock rights are vested (irrevocably assigned to the employee) upon a specified term of service with the company, although the right to vote the stock may be attendant on its allocation to the individual employee accounts of the ESOP. Alternatively, voting rights may be delayed until the vested stock is distributed to the employees upon retirement, termination, or death. Clearly, this aspect of ESOPs has important implications for worker participation and control of the firm, a matter that will be discussed below. Depending on the features of the particular plan, dividends paid on the stock are held by the ESOP or paid out directly to the individual employee as a second income.

ADVANTAGES OF AN ESOP

Advocates of ESOPs maintain that the approach has advantages for management, employees, and existing stockholders. As Kelso has argued in his various works, the advantages to employees are their shares or stake in ownership of the firms in which they work as well as the second income created by the dividends that are generated by the stock. There are also some tax advantages (U.S. Congress, Joint Economic Committee 1976:35). From the perspective of management, ESOPs provide a source of capital expansion at far lower costs than conventional sources of funds as well as a way of increasing the number of financing options (U.S. Congress, Joint Economic Committee 1976:32–35). From the vantage of existing stockholders, there is not only the low cost of capital that ESOPs generate but also presumably an improved economic performance of the firm because of higher worker productivity generated by the incentives inherent in worker ownership.

However, there are also advantages for employees and existing stockholders. Since much of the employees' retirement benefits will be tied up in ESOP stock, the receipt of retirement benefits will depend upon the company remaining in good financial health. Yet, large numbers of firms fail each year, perhaps 350,000 to 400,000 per year, according to a report of the U.S. Congress Joint Economic Committee (1976:36). This means that not only would workers lose jobs but their pensions would be in jeopardy as well, since creditors have a priority over stockholders in the creditor queue. Even an unfunded pension plan has higher creditor status than the claims of stockholders.

Although the law under which ESOPs are established requires that they "must be for the exclusive benefit of participants or their beneficiaries," most of the promotional literature gives this aspect rather short shrift. Such entrepreneurs as Louis Kelso and others who earn income from arranging the trust (ESOT) and loans to ESOPs emphasize the value to management of using this approach to obtain capital at considerably lower cost through its tax benefits. The tax advantages to the firm result from the fact that it can deduct the full amount of payments made to the ESOP, while for payments on an equivalent loan, the firm can only deduct the interest costs and not the portion used to repay the principal. Since the payments to the ESOP are a way of repaying the loan while being treated as contributions to employee benefits, a major tax advantage is enjoyed by the firm. ESOPs offer other advantages to the firm when compared with other tax-qualified pension plans. For example, ESOPs are not subject to the minimum funding standards or termination insurance of the Employee Retirement Income Security Act (ERISA) as pension plans.

The actual record for ESOPs appears to be one in which it has been used more to the advantage of the firm than its employees. A recent report of the General Accounting Office (GAO) found that ESOPs have often been used by companies with closely held stock to give the company a captive market for its stock at highly inflated prices (Rankin 1980). Among a sample of thirteen closely held companies reviewed by the GAO, all had contributed common stock to their ESOPs at "questionable prices," usually overvaluing the stock, a practice that raises tax benefits and exaggerates employee benefits and stockholdings. One company had overvalued stock contributions by over 600 percent in one year. The GAO also found that workers in these firms were generally not granted voting rights with their stock. The employers appointed trustee committees to vote the stock without provision for participation from the employee-owners.

THE ISSUE OF VOTING RIGHTS

One of the most controversial issues regarding ESOPs is the potential loss of managerial control as employee equity holdings increase. In the past, consultants promoting ESOPs typically emphasized that stock acquired by the ESOP trust would remain under managerial control, since the board of directors of the firm would appoint the trustees to administer the plan and to vote the stock. In fact, most firms that adopted ESOPs prior to 1974 did not pass voting rights on stock owned by employees until the stock was distributed to employees on retirement or termination of service. However, the Trade Act of 1974 and the Tax Reduction Act of 1975 stipulated that firms desiring to capture the financial advantages of the legislation would have to confer voting rights to employees on stock allocated to their accounts under employee trusts.

Although Louis Kelso has consistently argued that ESOPs are an important device for giving workers a stake in the capitalist system, he does not believe that stake should be extended to control of the stock that workers own. His argument seems to be that management is a complex and difficult art, so it would be unreasonable and undesirable to encumber workers with additional responsibilities. Recently, he advocated amendment of the Tax Reduction Act of 1975 to eliminate the requirement for voting stock in opposition to the recommendation of a government study on ESOPs (U.S. Congress, Joint Economic Committee of 1976:1,390). Even if voting rights of stock are protected for employees, the rights may be inconsequential unless employees hold a significant percentage of outstanding stock and have a means to organize their vote to their mutual interest. A particularly strong limitation of recent proposals such as that of the Joint Economic Committee is that voting rights on ESOP stock would extend only to publicly held corporations, excluding many smaller "closely held" ones. Thus, the issue of voting rights of employee stock and worker involvement in decision making for the firm is still highly problematic.

In summary, the concept of ESOPs and their actual implementation may be somewhat at variance with each other. Although the major social arguments for ESOPs are based upon giving workers a stake in their firms and the capitalist system, the actual formation of ESOPs and their promotion seems to be attributable to their advantages in raising capital at lower cost for the firm through using employee pension funds for this purpose. There is a distinct management bias to the forms of the plan and a reluctance to provide full voting rights for employees on the basis of their stock ownership. Given this history, it is important to explore the potential of ESOPs for creating worker-owned firms that might operate as cooperatives.

ESOPS AND WORKER PURCHASES OF FIRMS

ESOPs were not really designed for the instrumental purpose of enabling workers to purchase their firms, and this has not been the predominant approach to their utilization. However, in recent years a deep concern has arisen about how to respond to impending plant closures that would create particularly heavy impacts on the economic base of local communities (Bradley and Gelb 1983; Stern, Wood, and Hammer 1979). In many cases, plant shutdowns are less related to the profitability of operations than they are to the various types of tax and other incentives faced by conglomerates in rationalizing their production, product mix, and plant locations (Bluestone and Harrison 1982). If the plants are economically viable, the question arises as to whether the workers might purchase their own firms through ESOPs or through the option of using vested pension funds and unemployment benefits that would otherwise be paid to the workers who would lose their jobs from plant closures (Whyte and Blasi 1980).

In the last decade, a number of firms have been saved through the use of ESOP-type plans, with some of the most notable being the group of firms surveyed by Whyte and his colleagues (Whyte and Blasi 1980; Whyte et al. 1983) and the South Bend Lathe Company in South Bend, Indiana (Moberg 1980). More recently, this has been the strategy followed by the Rath Packing Company of Waterloo, Iowa, which saved 2,000 jobs (Gunn 1981) and a former plant of Timken Roller Bearing, a division of General Motors Company in Clark, New Jersey. A Fortune 500 firm, Weirton Steel, is in the final stages of worker purchase to avoid closure. This purchase will save about 7,000 jobs and will maintain the eighth largest steel producer in the nation. Ex-employees of several A & P supermarkets that had been closed in the Philadelphia area have been purchased and re-opened as O & O (Owned and Operated) worker-owned markets (Egerton 1983). All of these cases except O & O are predicated on the establishment of an employee trust (ESOT) that is used to purchase the plant through a loan, for which the stock of the firm is placed in the trust and used as collateral. In some of these cases, the loans have been acquired from commercial sources; in other cases, from government sources; and in yet other cases, from the parent company.

The fact that employees purchase the firm through the ESOP mechanism does not mean that they control it. That is, worker ownership in these cases has not necessarily meant worker control. For example, in the case of South Bend Lathe, the president of the company was also the chairman of the board of directors, chairman of the ESOP committee, a director of the bank that served as trustee for the ESOP, and the individual responsible for choosing the board of directors and the ESOP committee. The lack of worker input on important matters as well as the failure of management even to provide rudimentary information of concern to the workers prompted workers to go on strike in 1980 against a firm in which they owned two-thirds of the vested shares (Moberg 1980). When queried on why they went on strike against themselves, their response was that the strike was against management, not against themselves.

This situation illustrates a basic schism between the ESOP mechanism as a financial vehicle for transferring ownership to workers and as a method for transferring control of the workplace to the workers. The two are not synonymous. ESOPs were designed neither to create worker control nor to implement the establishment of worker cooperatives. They can only be used in this way if the basic design of the overall plan is tailored to transfer, in an orderly and systematic manner, the overall governance and management of the plant to workers and their representatives. While such a mechanism is feasible, its design and application are fraught with challenges.

Clearly, one major issue is the ambiguous role of unions when workers acquire ownership of a firm. Historically, unions were established and functioned to represent the concerns of workers in negotiating with the owners of the firm and their managers. Since that role would be obviated by worker acquisition of the firm, the question is whether the union could create a new role in serving as an organizational form for governing a firm in which the workers are the owners. Ellerman (1979a) argues that unions have an important function in serving as a legitimate opposition to management in democratic firms. Such a loyal opposition, he argues, is necessary to make certain that managers respond to other employee-owners.

To the degree that unions view ESOPs that incorporate worker governance as a challenge to their traditional function and survival, their support and participation may be less than enthusiastic. In the past, unions have not seen the control of capital as being central to a strategy for representing the interests of workers. Though union pension funds include an enormous amount of corporate stock in their portfolios, investment strategies and the voting of stock have been relegated to the financial intermediaries such as the banks that maintain the pension funds in trust. Paradoxically, labor has been placed in the position of owning a great deal of corporate America with its pension funds, while not trying to influence the policies of the entities in which it shares ownership (Barber 1982; Carnoy and Shearer 1980:chap. 3). Indeed, in some cases, the pension funds of workers are invested in some of the most antilabor firms in the nation.

Yet, it is important to stress that a number of ESOPs have been established with unions playing a central role in representing the workers in the ESOP negotiations (e.g., Stern, Wood, and Hammer 1979:chap. 3). Thus, it may be more a matter of pragmatics than an insurmountable challenge in ascertaining how unions can be incorporated into the governance mechanism in a productive way (Gregory and Logan 1982). Clearly, the role of unions is an area that will require considerable attention in the case where ESOPs are used for worker purchase and control of the firms in which unions are present.

An even more fundamental issue with respect to the creation of worker cooperatives under an ESOP mechanism is the problem of uncertainty faced by potential lenders. The attractiveness of lending to an ESOP for purchase of the firm will depend critically upon an assessment of the future prospects for the firm. Both the ability to service the debt and the value of the stock used for collateral will depend on the economic performance of the enterprise. There are two aspects of an economic evaluation of the firm pertinent to the lender. The first is whether the business is essentially sound and has strong prospects for becoming and/or maintaining profitability. The second is whether a shift to worker ownership will provide the type of management and operations that will ensure a smooth and efficient operation.

The ability of the workers to make a successful transition to a worker-managed firm is far from certain. Workers will be expected to select and work with managers without either the experience or precedent for worker participation. Although I have suggested that these forms of enterprise seem to promise greater productivity than more conventional firms at maturity, this is not necessarily so during the transition from a traditional organizational form to one based upon worker governance. Particular issues that arise during this transition have been discussed elsewhere in this volume (Gamson and Levin, chap. 9). What is important to this discussion, however, is that the uncertainty of the transition period represents a risk to potential lenders which may discourage their willingness to provide a loan to the ESOP.

The dilemma created by this situation can be seen when one considers that it will be difficult to obtain a loan for the ESOP without providing assurances of stability during the transition to a worker-owned firm. In general, lenders will prefer a safe transition to worker ownership in which traditional forms of management will be utilized with little worker involvement. Not only does this approach preclude democratic management but it may also create frustrations for workers who are told that they are the owners even though their views on policy are neither solicited nor reflected in decisions. On the one hand, it is impressed upon workers that through the ESOP they have become the owners of the firm. On the other hand, their concerns and dissatisfactions are given no systematic and meaningful channels for expression and resolution. It will be obvious that it is the managers and the trustees of the ESOP who have the real power to make the decisions, even though the firm is presumably owned by the workers.

At some stage, workers' frustrations will lead to tension and open conflict with management. Such seems to have been the case at the South Bend Lathe Company, leading to their recent strike (Thurston 1980). It should not be expected that this type of situation will be unique to that firm, given the nature of the origins of the conflicts. Thus, in the long run, there must be a plan to transfer both the ownership and the control of firms to workers rather than just the ownership. The question is how to do this while maximizing the stability of the transition and minimizing the uncertainty.

The most appropriate approach is to design a specific plan that will transfer both ownership and control to the workers through an orderly process composed of a number of transitional steps. Such a plan would need to incorporate two major features. First, there must be an appropriate structure for democratic management in which all the workers can participate in appropriate and productive ways while, at the same time, ensuring a responsive and efficient decision mechanism for the firm. The structure must take into account the unique features of the enterprise, including the nature of the product, its history of previous worker participation or the lack of it, the timing and characteristics of the major decisions, and the opportunities for worker decision making and participation as they are reflected in the particular work areas and demands.

Second, all participants will need to acquire experience in participation. This can be obtained through any combination of shop-floor participation, membership on committees, elected representation on a board, or direct participation in management. Such experiences are crucial to the success of a worker-governed firm, and they must be designed systematically into the transitional model. Under normal circumstances, workers will not have had prior experiences that lend themselves to participation in democratic workplaces (see Gamson and Levin, chap. 9).

In short, a model for organizing worker-owned firms purchased through ESOPs and a method of implementing the model in an orderly fashion are called for. Generally, such a model would be characterized by a transitional approach in which the movement from a traditional firm to a democratically managed one would be set out in reasonable detail. Clear plans would be drawn up for the initial phases of management as well as for the intermediate phases and for the ultimate structure of full worker governance. Training and other requirements for shifting from one phase to a subsequent one would be specified clearly. A timetable for the full transition and its various phases would also be established.

The plan would set out the transitional forms of workers' decision involvement in order to provide them with the experiences for undertaking full responsibility for the operation of the firm. In addition, appropriate forms of information would be developed over this period to provide workers with the type of data they will need for effective participation. By setting out a concrete blueprint for the eventual form of the organization and for the transition period, it is possible to provide the stability and organizational development that are crucial to both lenders and workers alike during the transition, while, at the same time, creating an orderly movement to full worker control in the longer run. The details can also be modified if changes seem appropriate during the transitional period. This plan can benefit from the experience of other firms that have made the transition (Sachs 1981).

A CRITICAL VIEW

On a more sobering note, David Ellerman (1982b) of the Industrial Cooperative Association has questioned the use of ESOPs to form worker cooperatives. He emphasizes that ESOPs were never designed to meet the needs of democratic and worker-controlled firms, and a number of disparities between the needs of such firms and the ESOP structure are evident. Since the stock of the firm will be placed in a trust—whose trustees are usually chosen jointly by the lender and the firm—the trustees will be responsible for voting the stock, for choosing a governing board for the firm, and for other major decisions. Thus, the employee-owners of a worker cooperative must obtain an agreement with the trustees that the stock will be voted only on behalf of decisions reached by the employee-owners. It should be noted that this approach was followed by the (non-ESOP) Meriden Triumph Motorcycle Cooperative in England in placing the stock in trust as collateral for a government loan while arranging for the trustees to vote the stock according to the democratic decisions of the cooperative members (Carnoy and Levin 1976b).

Further, even when stock is vested in individual worker accounts, there is a problem in reconciling such ownership with the needs of a cooperative. Stockholders are entitled to traditional property rights in that the more stock one owns, the more votes one has. But cooperatives are based upon "people rights" in which each member has an equal vote. This suggests that all members would have to agree to a system of control that is divorced from the amount of stock ownership, or to an arrangement in which employee-owners would receive two classes of stock—a single share of voting stock and additional shares of nonvoting stock—to satisfy the conflict between people rights and property rights. The latter arrangement might require legislation.

Finally, the ownership of a cooperative is generally limited to its members and excludes outside stockholders. This means that somehow an arrangement must be made for departing employee-owners to sell back their vested shares to the firm to avoid outside ownership. This can be done by establishing a mandatory requirement that stock owned by a departing member must be purchased by the firm within a stipulated period of time following the member's departure. However, during periods of economic hardship, or when unusually large numbers of members leave within a short period, this requirement may place the firm in great financial jeopardy.

In short, Ellerman asserts that each of these challenges requires elaborate arrangements to forge an ESOP into a cooperative, for the ESOP was never conceived or designed to be used in this way. On both ideological and pragmatic grounds he argues in favor of direct establishment of cooperative firms with conventional financing. Certainly, there can be little disagreement on this point. If it is possible for workers to purchase a firm and obtain financing in a more conventional way, it will be far easier to transform the firm into a worker cooperative. It simply makes eminent sense to establish a cooperative directly rather than to do it through a "bastardized" ESOP. But, of course, that is the problem in the first place, the dearth of financial capital available through traditional channels for the establishment and assistance of worker cooperatives. Where funding is not obtainable, it appears that ESOPs can provide a feasible, although second-best, solution.

11

Workers' Cooperatives:
The Question of Legal Structure

DAVID ELLERMAN

INTRODUCTION: THE SETTING AND THE PROBLEM

What is a workers' cooperative? In a general sense, a workers' cooperative is a firm controlled and operated by the people who work in it.

There are several different types of firms that are called *worker cooperatives* or *worker-owned firms*. In some cases, such as the original Vermont Asbestos Group (VAG), the firm simply has a conventional ownership structure where a majority of the owners are employees. In many of the urban centers and college towns across the country, there are a number of loosely structured, worker-run *collectives* or cooperatives which might be legally organized as partnerships, statutory cooperatives, nonprofit corporations, or for-profit corporations. In the Pacific Northwest, there are eighteen or so workers' cooperatives in the plywood industry, most of which are legally organized under the cooperative statutes of Oregon and Washington. Daniel Zwerdling's survey *Democracy at Work* (1978) is an excellent illustration of the diversity of worker-run businesses in the United States and Europe.

This diversity reflects, in part, the wide variety of origins of worker-controlled businesses. Many are established by young people seeking an alternative to the materialistic and authoritarian structure of ordinary businesses. Others are the result of worker buyouts following plant closings where no conventional buyers could be found. Yet others are set up by retiring business owners who have no interested heirs and/or who want to reward employees for their past efforts.

The diversity in the legal forms of organization reflects the lack of any coherent, widely used legal code for workers' cooperatives. The general cooperative statutes in the various states are applied across the board to consumer, marketing, housing, and workers' cooperatives (see, for example, National Economic Development Law Project 1974). These statutes are oriented primarily toward agricultural marketing cooperatives, with a secondary focus on housing and consumer cooperatives (with barely a mention of worker cooperatives). The statutes tend to be archaic, to be poorly thought out, and to represent a rough compromise of cooperative and conventional corporate attributes.

Workers' cooperatives are sometimes classified as *producers' cooperatives*, but that classification also includes the numerous marketing and processing cooperatives of independent agricultural producers (e.g., Land O' Lakes, Agway, Ocean Spray). The agricultural cooperatives are not worker controlled and indeed are quite conventional from the employees' viewpoint. To the employees who process milk and produce butter, cottage cheese, and other milk products in a dairy cooperative's plant, it may matter little if the absentee owners are simply investors, individual dairy farmers, or agribusiness dairy farms.

The first statute specifically for workers' cooperatives was recently (May 1982) passed in Massachusetts (see Ellerman and Pitegoff 1983; Pitegoff 1982). This statute, drafted by the Industrial Cooperative Association, provides a statutory basis for the Mondragon-type internal-capital-account structure for workers' cooperatives. This paper will outline the legal theory behind this type of legal structure.

Many different legal structures for worker cooperatives have, in effect, been tested—and the time has come for a preliminary appraisal of the various legal structures. Worker-run businesses often face large internal and external difficulties (see Gamson and Levin, chap. 9, this volume) which may threaten their very survival. I will argue along with Jaroslav Vanek (1975a, 1977c) that some legal and financial structures used in worker-run firms have inherent flaws that will, in the course of a generation, almost inevitably lead if not to the outright demise of the company, then to the gradual or sudden degeneration of the firm back to a conventional company. Vanek has aptly termed them "mule firms," since they are sterile hybrids of conventional and cooperative forms that cannot reproduce themselves for another generation. The employee-owned corporations, such as VAG, and to a lesser extent the traditional workers' cooperatives, such as the plywood co-ops, are examples of mulelike firms.

In addition to presenting an analysis of this structural degeneration problem, I will propose a solution. This legal structure for workers' cooperatives can be and is being implemented in the United States today, for example, in the cooperatives assisted by the Industrial Cooperative Association such as the Workers' Owned Sewing Company of Windsor, North Carolina, and the Cedar Works in Ohio.

The best examples of worker cooperatives are, however, not in the United States but in the Basque region of northern Spain, the Mondragon industrial cooperatives (Gutierrez-Johnson and Whyte 1977; Oakeshott 1978; Thomas and Logan 1982; Ellerman 1982c). The first industrial cooperative of the complex was established in the city of Mondragon in the mid-1950s. Today, there is a system of about 85 industrial worker cooperatives with over 18,000 worker-members. The range of industrial products includes refrigerators, stoves, machine tools, and electronic equipment. The complex has its own technical school which offers college-level courses in engineering and other technical subjects for the workers and young people of the region. The Mondragon group also has its own social security system and an advanced research center to stay abreast of recent technical developments (e.g., printed circuits, microprocessors, robotics, CAD/CAM, and solar technology).

At the hub of the complex is an institution, the Caja Laboral Popular (Bank of the People's Labor), which includes a credit union with over 200,000 members, a computer center, and an Empresarial Division (Entrepreneurial Division). The Empresarial Division represents the institutionalization and socialization of entrepreneurship (Ellerman 1982c). It has over 100 staff members who assist worker-groups to systematically launch new cooperatives (about five new co-ops a year under present plans) and who provide technical and managerial assistance to the existing Mondragon cooperatives. With the exception of one ill-fated fishermen's co-op, no Mondragon cooperative has ever failed.

The legal structure I recommend is of the same general type as the legal structure of the Mondragon cooperatives. While one can hardly claim that the phenomenal success of the Mondragon cooperatives is due to their legal structure, the structure has complemented and reinforced, rather than hindered, the other positive factors, such as the solidarity of the Basque nation, the inspiration of the founder, Father Arizmendi, the rare combination of idealism and technical competence present, the industrial tradition of Mondragon, and the comparatively recent development of the market for consumer durables in Spain.

There is such a multiplicity of factors affecting cooperatives that it is always difficult to single out any particular elements as being responsible for any given success or failure. Indeed, any attempt to design a proper legal structure solely by extrapolating from past successes would be underdetermined. Facts are always viewed in the light of theory. The question of legal structure is no exception. In particular, the model legal structure considered here is based on theory and is derived, in its broad contours, from first principles. The application of the legal structure has been much refined in practice and will continue to be honed as more experience accumulates.

CORPORATIONS:
INVESTOR-OWNED OR COOPERATIVE

The principal legal forms of business organization are proprietorships, partnerships, and corporations. The main legal difference between a corporation on the one hand and a partnership or proprietorship (a one-person partnership) on the other hand is that a corporation is a separate legal person from its members, whereas a partnership is not a legal person separate from the partners as individuals. Since the partnership is not a separate legal or artificial person, the business debts of the partnership are ultimately the personal debts of the partners. The partners are said to have *unlimited liability* for the business debts. For this reason, a partnership is an unsuitable legal form for a workers' cooperative.

Since a corporation is a separate legal person, a member or shareholder has no more liability for corporate debts than he or she has for, say, a neighbor's debts. Lawyers call this *limited liability* but, in fact, the shareholders as private individuals have no liability at all for corporate debts.

Just as the liabilities of a corporation are not the personal debts of its members or shareholders, so the assets of the corporation are not the individual property of its shareholders. Instead of directly owning the corporate assets or directly bearing the corporate debts, the shareholders have a certain bundle of rights attached to their corporate shares. These rights consist essentially of the right to control the corporation by voting to elect the board of directors and the right to receive value from the corporation in the form of dividends while the stock is held and in the form of capital gains when the stock is sold at a higher price. The total value that accrues to the shareholders can be analyzed as the sum of the net book value or net worth (assets minus liabilities) of the corporate assets plus the value of the present and future economic profits (see the "book plus profits formula" in chapter 12 of Ellerman 1982a). Hence the bundle of rights attached to conventional shares is:

voting rights + economic profit rights + net book value.

If we define

membership rights = voting rights + economic profit rights,

then we have the following equation:

conventional share rights = membership rights + net book value.

Enough concepts have now been developed so that we may properly characterize both a conventional corporation and a worker cooperative corporation. A corporation is investor-owned or capitalist if the membership rights (defined above) are property rights, that is, rights that are transferable and marketable. In contrast, a corporation is a workers' cooperative (or self-managed firm) if the membership rights are personal rights attached to the functional role of working in the company.

The membership or citizenship rights (e.g., voting rights) in a democratic political community are an analogous example of personal rights. These rights may not be bought or sold, and they are attached to the functional role of residing in a particular community. A workers' cooperative corporation is a democratic work-community, an industrial democracy, which assigns membership rights to the people who work in it, just as a township or municipality is a democratic living-community which assigns the voting rights to the people who live or reside in it.

Personal rights are rights that are assigned to the person of an individual because the individual qualifies for them, for example, by having a certain functional role, such as residing within the city limits of a municipality. Any such right that is assigned to all and only those who have the qualifying role cannot be treated as a property right, that is, as a salable right. If it were, the buyer might not have the qualifying role, and if the would-be buyer did have the qualifying role, then he or she would not need to buy the right. Hence personal rights and property rights are fundamentally different types of rights.

One acid test to distinguish between personal and property rights is the inheritability test. When membership rights are personal rights assigned to a functional role, the rights are extinguished when a person ceases to play that role. When a person dies, the voting rights he or she may have had as a citizen, a co-op member, or a union member are not transferable to the person's estate or heirs (since those were personal rights). However, if the person was a shareholder in an investor-owned corporation, the shares, as pieces of property, would be inherited by the person's heirs.

Many of the different characteristics of investor-owned corporations and worker cooperative firms result from the fact that the membership rights are transferable property rights in the one case and personal rights attached to the functional role of working in the firm in the other case. For example, when the voting rights are assigned to a functional role, then a person either has that role or not and, thus, either is a member and has the vote or not. There is no possibility of being a "multiple-member" and casting multiple votes. Hence the one-person/one-vote principle is followed in a political or industrial democracy. However, when the membership rights are marketable property rights, then anyone with sufficient wealth can buy many shares, be a multiple-member, and cast many votes. Thus the multiple voting in an investor-owned corporation, in violation of the one-person/one-vote rule, is a result of the membership rights being marketable commodities.

The workers' cooperative differs from the conventional, investor-owned corporation not simply by reallocating the traditional bundle of ownership rights but by restructuring the bundle so that the membership rights become personal rights assigned to the worker's role.

EMPLOYEE-OWNED CORPORATIONS

This understanding of the structural differences between investor-owned and self-managed firms can now be used to analyze an employee-owned corporation—which is often confused with a workers' cooperative or self-managed firm. An *employee-owned corporation* is an investor-owned corporation (that is, the membership rights are marketable property rights) where most of the membership rights are the property of the people who also work in the company, the employees. Sometimes the employees directly own the shares (e.g., the original Vermont Asbestos Group) and sometimes the shares are held in a trust, an Employee Stock Ownership Plan (ESOP), with the employees as the beneficial owners (e.g., the South Bend Lathe Company). In either case, the employees have membership rights solely because they directly or indirectly own the shares, not because they have the functional role of working in the company. This fundamental structural difference between an employee-owned corporation and a workers' cooperative corporation reflects a difference in the basic principles behind the two legal structures, and it has practical consequences.

First, consider the practical consequences of the investor-owned legal structure of a corporation that is directly employee-owned. Since the employees' voting rights are based on share ownership, the one person/one vote principle is, in general, violated. The managers and wealthier employees usually buy more shares and get that many more votes. For example, in the original Vermont Asbestos Group some employees owned no shares, most owned a few, and at least one white collar employee owned one hundred shares. Employees holding one or two shares are somewhat less than enthusiastic to participate in membership meetings when fifty to one hundred of them can be outvoted by one employee owning one hundred shares.

The profit distribution is equally lopsided. Profits are distributed as dividends or retained in the company, in which case they might accrue to the shareholder in the form of capital gains (appreciated share price). The dividends are distributed on a per-share basis, so the dividend distribution follows the allocation of shares. When retained profit appreciates the share price, a "rising tide lifts all the ships," so the distribution of capital gains also follows the historical distribution of shares. Hence, those who could afford to buy more shares in the first place will get the lion's share of the fruits of the enterprise. The inequality in voting rights and the inequity in the profit distribution tend to create disaffection and disillusionment among the less well-off employees, as they see the power and wealth gravitating toward a small group within the company (usually the managers).

The long-term problem with employee-owned corporations is that they embody degenerative tendencies, so they don't remain employee-owned for very long. If the company fails as a business, there is no long term. If the company succeeds as a business, the shares will appreciate in value, sometimes quite dramatically. The managers and older employees will eventually want to realize their capital gains by selling their highly appreciated holdings. If the company is to remain employee-owned, then the new employees entering the firm will have to buy the shares of departing employees. But it is virtually impossible for new workers to buy the large holdings of retiring employees. Hence those shares would tend to be sold to outsiders. As time passes, the normal turnover in the company makes it less and less employee-owned. The employees' disaffection may well have a direct detrimental effect on the business. Eventually an individual, a group, or a corporation may make a takeover bid. The disaffected employees, having witnessed the gradual erosion of employee ownership in their company, would probably jump at the chance to at least get some cash out of the matter. Like a mule, the firm cannot reproduce itself across generations. The conventional treatment of membership rights as marketable property rights in an employee-owned corporation is somewhat like a time bomb that will eventually lead to the demise of the employee ownership of the company.

This process of aging and deterioration in a mulelike employee-owned corporation will normally take place within a generation (fifteen to twenty years), that is, by the time the original founding group retires. In the case of Vermont Asbestos Group, favorable external events led to sharp asbestos price increases shortly after the employees had formed the company and purchased the assets from the GAF conglomerate in 1975. There was a 100 percent dividend the first year, and the retained profits were sufficient over three years to increase the book value of the shares from $50 to around $1,800 per share. These superprofits seemed to act as a hot house to accelerate the process of aging and deterioration. Instead of taking a generation, the process took only three years. Several manufacturing and venture capital firms were prepared to make offers, but the disaffected workers preferred to sell enough of their shares to a local businessman until he could handpick a new board of directors and install himself as the president and chairman of the board.

There have been a number of recent examples of partial and indirect employee ownership through Employee Stock Ownership Plans (ESOPs). The present form of the ESOP was established by the Employee Retirement Income Security Act (ERISA) of 1974 (see, for example, Stern and Comstock 1978). As in a pension plan, the corporate contributions to an ESOP are exempt (as deferred labor compensation) from the corporate income tax. But, unlike an ordinary pension plan, an ESOP invests in the employer's stock, which makes an ESOP into a new vehicle for employee ownership but a risky substitute for a pension plan.

The principal novelty lies in the "leveraged" ESOP, wherein the ESOP gets a bank loan that is guaranteed by the corporation. The ESOP uses the money to buy stock from the corporation, and then the stock serves as collateral for the loan. The company's periodic cash contributions to the ESOP are funneled through to pay off the bank loan. A tax break is captured because the company contributions count as deferred labor compensation, so the company pays back both the principal and interest on the loan with earnings that are deductible from taxable corporate income. Usually only the interest can be deducted as an expense. As the loan is paid off, the shares become vested in the employees' names. The employees do not acquire direct ownership of their shares until they terminate their employment with the company or retire. The value of the employees' shares is in large part counterbalanced by the diluted value or foregone gain on the part of existing shareholders.

The chief architect of this plan was a corporate lawyer, Louis Kelso, who has coauthored books entitled *The Capitalist Manifesto* and *How to Turn Eighty Million Workers into Capitalists on Borrowed Money*. The conservative but populist aspects of the plan appealed to Senator Russell Long, who pushed the ESOP legislation through Congress. ESOPs are usually established by corporate managers or owners who are interested in the tax benefits, and who are not particularly interested in transferring any power or control to the employees. The shares must be distributed in proportion to pay, so the distribution of votes and profits is as skewed as the wage and salary differentials within the company.

It is difficult to predict the long-run prospects for ESOPs since they have not, as yet, been around for a generation and since the legislation is still evolving. If desired, it does seem possible to structure some democratic attributes into an ESOP or, at least, an ESOP containing 100 percent of the shares. One-person/one-vote might be attained by having a two-tiered voting structure (require the trustees to vote the shares in accordance with the members' one-person/one-vote decision) or possibly by using voting and nonvoting shares. By allocating shares to workers in accordance with labor compensation, the ESOP structure does move toward transforming the membership rights from property rights into personal rights assigned to the functional role of working in the firm. In these ways an ESOP can be restructured in the direction of a worker cooperative corporation.

This discussion of investor-owned corporations which are directly or indirectly employee-owned serves to outline the practical problems in these firms and to differentiate employee-owned firms (including ESOPs without co-op attributes) from workers' cooperatives. There is some confusion between these two types of firms since, in both cases, the workers are the "owners." For many purposes, it may not be important to emphasize the distinctions. But, aside from the principles involved, it is of practical importance to understand the difference when observers jump to the conclusion that "worker ownership doesn't work" after observing the perfectly predictable degeneration of employee-owned corporations back into conventional, investor-owned firms. An employee-owned corporation is the counterfeit of a workers' cooperative.

THE NORMATIVE PRINCIPLES EMBODIED
IN WORKERS' COOPERATIVES

The structure of a workers' cooperative or self-managed firm is sometimes recommended on the pragmatic grounds that it provides for workers' control without the suicidal tendencies implicit in conventional employee ownership. However, there are also normative principles involved, and a thorough appreciation of the structure of a workers' cooperative requires an understanding of these principles. I noted previously that a workers' cooperative was a corporation where the membership rights (voting plus profit rights) are personal rights assigned to the functional role of working in the company, rather than commodities or marketable property rights. I shall examine separately the two principles behind this treatment of the voting rights and the profits rights.

The first normative principle, the assignment of the voting rights to the workers, is based on the *democratic theory of government:* all and only the people who are to be governed by a government should have the vote in electing that government. This principle of democracy or self-government is built into the structure of an organization by attaching the voting rights to elect the government or management to the functional role of being governed or managed by the organization. In short, self-government means that the ultimate right and power to govern must be assigned to the functional role of being governed.

There are many outside interests that might be affected by the activities of the firm. The outside parties (e.g., consumers, capital suppliers, and local residents) should have effective indirect or negative control rights to veto or otherwise constrain the activities of the firm in order to protect their own legitimate interests. Positions on the board of directors will not effectively protect outside interests since two or more interest groups cannot each have a majority or controlling position on the board.

The question of assigning the voting rights to elect the board is the question of who should have the direct or positive control rights to ultimately make the policies and decisions of the firm. The democratic principle of government assigns those direct control rights to the people who fall under the command, authority, and jurisdiction of the firm's management, that is, to the governed. The consumers, the suppliers of capital or other material inputs, and the local residents are not managed by and do not take orders from the managers of the firm. Only the people who work in the company, the workers, have that functional role. Hence the application of the democratic principle of self-government to a corporation entails that the voting rights should be assigned to the functional role of working in the company.

The second normative principle is the *labor theory of property* applied to the production process. The labor principle states that people should have the rights to the (positive and negative) fruits of their labor. The products or outputs of a firm are the positive fruits of the labor jointly performed by all the people working in the firm. The used-up nonlabor inputs, such as the consumed raw materials and intermediate goods and the expended services of the machines, buildings and land, represent the negative fruits of labor. From the legal viewpoint, it is the corporation itself as a legal entity that owns the produced outputs and is liable for the used-up nonlabor inputs. Since the labor theory of property states that the workers should jointly appropriate the positive fruits (the produced outputs) and be jointly liable for the negative fruits (the used-up nonlabor inputs) of their combined labor, the labor theory implies that the workers should *be* the corporation, that is, the workers should be the legal members of the corporation.

In terms of market value, the net value of the positive and negative fruits of the labor jointly performed by the workers is the revenues minus the nonlabor costs, which equals what is usually called the *wages* plus the *profits*. Since the wages and salaries already accrue to the workers, the labor theory implies that the rights to the remaining value of the fruits of their labor, namely, the rights to the profits, should be assigned to the workers.

Hence the democratic principle of self-government and the labor theory of property imply that, in a corporation, the voting rights and the rights to the revenues net of nonlabor costs (wages plus profits) should be assigned to the functional role of working in the company. Since the wages already go to the workers, a corporation can be tranformed into a workers' cooperative by changing the membership rights (voting rights plus profit rights) from salable property rights into personal rights attached to the workers' role.

In contrast to the case of an employee-owned corporation, the worker-members of a workers' cooperative are, in the generic sense, neither employees nor owners. The worker-members are not employees because they do not sell their labor; they sell the fruits of their labor. Instead of being employees of a workers' cooperative corporation, the workers *are* the corporation; it is their legal embodiment. The workers, in their corporate body, own the positive fruits of their labor (the produced outputs) and are liable for the negative fruits of their labor (the used-up nonlabor inputs). Instead of selling their labor for a wage or salary, the worker-members are selling their outputs in return for the revenues and are paying the costs of the nonlabor inputs. The labor income of the worker-members is not the market value of their labor as a commodity but is the net market value of the positive and negative fruits of their labor (revenues minus nonlabor costs).

The worker-members are also not owners because the membership rights are not property rights. Any right attached to a person's functional role cannot also be treated as a marketable property right. Like the citizenship rights in a political democracy, the membership rights in an industrial democracy are attached to the functional role of being governed or managed, so they are personal rights that cannot be bought or sold. The rights are held, not owned. The workers are members, not owners. Workers' cooperatives have worker-members, not employee-owners. Unlike a conventional corporation, a workers' cooperative is not a piece of property. It is not privately owned, it is not publicly owned, and it is not even "socially owned"—since it is not a piece of property to be owned at all. It is a democratic social institution.

RESTRUCTURING A CORPORATION AS
A WORKERS' COOPERATIVE

The definition of a workers' cooperative or self-managed corporation given above (i.e., the assignment of the membership rights to the workers' role) is a conceptual and generic definition. Aside from the new Massachusetts worker cooperative statute and mirror statutes passed in Maine and being considered in other states (see Ellerman and Pitegoff 1983; Pitegoff 1982), there are no United States statutes at present, cooperative or otherwise, designed to implement this definition of a workers' cooperative. In fact, the old cooperative statutes are rather archaic and poorly designed. Without an appropriate statute, a cooperative as defined herein can still be realized by starting with a stock business corporation or a statutory cooperative corporation, and then reworking the articles of incorporation and bylaws to internally restructure the company so that it will function as a genuine workers' cooperative (e.g., the Industrial Cooperative Association Model Bylaws for a Worker Cooperative 1980).

The basic idea of the restructuring is to split apart the conventional bundle of rights attached to corporate shares so that the membership rights can then be treated as personal rights assigned to the functional role of working in the corporation. The conventional bundle of rights attached to corporate shares can be analyzed in two parts: (1) the membership rights (voting rights plus profit rights), and (2) the rights to the net book value or net worth of the corporate assets. The strategy is to have the membership rights attached to the shares and to create a new corporate structure—the system of *internal capital accounts*—to take over the function of carrying the net worth. With that net worth value removed from the shares, the shares can be treated just as carriers of the membership rights, that is, as *membership certificates*, attached to the functional role of working in the firm.

One of the flaws in traditional statutory workers' cooperatives (e.g., the plywood co-ops) is that the co-op shares continue to carry the net book value, so they cannot be used as membership certificates. To give each newly qualified and accepted member a traditional co-op share as a membership certificate would be to make an unwarranted gift of a proportionate part of the net worth to each new member. Thus a new worker is required to buy at least one share to become a member, and this gets to be prohibitively expensive (e.g., $60,000 or more in some plywood cooperatives). Moreover, membership should be designed in such a way that the person qualifies for membership by working in the firm and does not have to buy membership (even though, as specified below, there are financial obligations of membership).

The solution is to split off the net worth or net book value from the shares using a system of internal capital accounts, one account for each member recording that member's share of the net worth. When a person leaves the firm or retires, the balance in his or her account is paid out by the firm over a period of years. A new worker does not have to individually pay off a retiring worker—as would be the case if a new worker had to buy a share with the accumulated value from a retiring member. With the rights to the portions of net worth recorded in internal capital accounts, the shares can then be treated as nontransferable membership certificates issued to new members and collected from exiting members. The new member would not be getting a portion of net worth, since the balance in the new member's account would start at zero.

Rights usually come together with obligations. For example, one does not have to buy the rights of union membership or the rights of political citizenship, but there are union dues and government taxes. In a workers' cooperative, one similarly does not buy membership but there would be a fixed membership investment required of each new. member as a financial obligation of membership. That paid-in membership fee would be recorded in the new member's account. At the end of each fiscal year, interest would be added to the account, and the member's share of the retained positive or negative surplus computed after interest on the accounts) would be added to or subtracted from the account's balance. Each member's share of the surplus would be proportional to his or her labor as measured by the hours worked or by his or her pay.

Usually there would also be a *collective account* that is unindividuated in the sense that it never has to be paid back to anyone during the lifetime of the corporation. By having a certain portion of the net worth that never has to be turned over or revolved as the membership turns over, the cooperative is helping to insure that it could eventually pay off the individual accounts. Hence the allocation to the collective account is a form of self-insurance. The individual and collective accounts are adjusted each year to reflect the retained net income, paid-in membership fees, and paid-off accounts so that the sum of the account balances always equals the net worth.

With this internal restructuring, based on the internal capital accounts and the share membership certificates, a corporation would legally function as a genuine workers' cooperative. It might be noted that this internal restructuring does not change the external legal categories. For example, while the worker-members do not function as employees or owners as explained above, they nevertheless would still be legally classified as both employees and owners because at present there are no other legal pigeonholes available.[1]

AN ANALYSIS OF ALTERNATIVE
LEGAL STRUCTURES

The traditional statutory workers' cooperatives in the United States (e.g., the plywood co-ops) do not detach the net book value from the co-op's shares (i.e., no internal capital accounts, no separation of personal and property rights). The new workers often cannot afford to buy the shares of retiring members, so in order to fill the jobs, new workers tend to be hired as nonmembers. And, if permitted, retiring members might have to sell their shares to outsiders. Sometimes, as the founding members approach retirement with no prospective market for their individual shares, they band together and sell control of the company to a conventional firm in order to capitalize their shares. Indeed, some of the plywood co-ops were sold, while most of those that remain as cooperative have a significant number of nonmember employees. The flawed structure of traditional statutory worker co-ops gives them suicidal or mulelike tendencies not unlike those exhibited by the employee-owned corporations.

The common ownership firms of Great Britain and the Yugoslavian self-managed firms do, in effect, treat the membership rights as personal rights assigned to the functional role of working in the firm. But they do so at the price of eliminating the members' property rights to the net worth, the reinvested fruits of their past labor. It is as if there were no individual internal accounts and only the collective account. Thus the net income or profit rights assigned to the workers are incomplete, since the workers lose any claim on the retained net income. It becomes "common property" or "social property." Misplaced idealism and Marxist ideology notwithstanding, there really is no good reason why the workers should be forced to forfeit the value of the fruits of their labor simply because they reinvest it in the company. This destroys the incentive to invest by retention of earnings as opposed to borrowing. Instead of retaining earnings, it would be rational for the workers to distribute all earnings, deposit a portion in a savings account, and then have the bank loan the money back to the firm.

Some economists (e.g., Furubotn and Pejovich 1970, 1974) have detailed numerous distortions that arise from the treatment of the net worth as social property. However, instead of recognizing the known solution to the problem, they present the problem as an inherent characteristic of self-management. I previously noted how the firm could have access to the earnings without the workers losing their claim, by routing the earnings through external savings accounts. That is impractical, but the practical solution is to move the savings accounts into the firm itself. That is the conceptual origin of the idea of the internal capital accounts. Moreover, that is the solution worked out and field-tested by the Mondragon cooperatives over the last two decades.

The key to cooperative restructuring is to unbundle the traditional bundle of ownership rights by separating and partitioning the membership rights (evidenced by co-op membership shares) from the net book value rights (recorded in the new internal capital accounts). Jaroslav Vanek has particularly emphasized that all capital financing should be separate from or external to the co-op membership rights (e.g., Vanek 1977c). The unfortunate use of the word *external* might lead one to think that Vanek is calling for co-ops with complete outside financing, that is, with 100 percent leveraged financing. However, Vanek has explicitly recognized the appropriateness of internal financing using "redeemable savings deposits of members" (1977c:186) such as the Mondragon internal capital accounts. Then all capital financing, from outsiders or members, is "external" to the membership rights so that those rights can be assigned to labor, and yet the members can eventually recoup their reinvested earnings.

The use of a proper legal structure, with a set of internal accounts to split the net worth due each member off from the membership shares, is certainly no guarantee of economic success or longevity. But such a structure seems to be a necessary condition for avoiding the self-destructive forces embodied in employee-owned corporations and traditional statutory workers' cooperatives. A proper legal structure is not just important for negative or preventive reasons. The avoidance of the structural degenerative tendencies creates the preconditions for the development of a humane work environment and the growth of internal democracy.

The importance of partitioning the conventional bundle of share rights into the membership rights and the net worth rights cannot be overemphasized. The partition is of such fundamental importance because it allows the membership rights to be transformed from property rights into personal rights (attached to the workers' role), which means that the company itself is transformed from a piece of property to a democratic social institution.[2]

SUMMARY

The theoretical analysis for the various types of legal structures for worker-owned firms can now be summarized according to the treatment of the conventional bundle of ownership rights.

Conventional Capitalist Corporation

(A) Voting rights,   Owned by the
(B1) economic profit rights, and ⟶ shareholders (property
(B2) net book value rights.   rights).

Employee-Owned Corporation

(A) Voting rights,   Owned by the
(B1) economic profit rights, and ⟶ employee-shareholders
(B2) net book value rights.   (property rights).

Traditional Worker Cooperative

(A) Voting rights and   ⟶ Partially treated as
(B1) economic profit rights.   personal rights held by
                                                      workers who own one
(B2) Net book value.   ownership share
                                                      (property rights).

Yugoslav-type Self-Managed Firm

(A) Voting rights,   ⟶ Membership rights held
(B1) Economic profit rights.   by the workers
                                                      (personal rights).

(B2) Net book value rights. ⟶ Social property.

Mondragon-type Worker Cooperative

(A) Voting rights,   ⟶ Membership rights held
(B1) economic profit rights.   by the workers
                                                      (personal rights).

(B2) Net book value rights. ⟶ Internal capital accounts
                                                      (property rights).

Employee-owned corporations are based on the conventional structure wherein the membership rights are property rights—albeit owned by the employees—so such a company is still a piece of property, a (temporarily) employee-owned piece of property. Industrial democracy cannot develop inside a piece of property. Most "employee-owned" companies do not even attempt to develop an internal democratic structure.

The traditional worker co-ops moved part way toward the treatment of the membership rights as personal rights by allowing shareholders only one vote regardless of the number of shares held and by distributing certain net income ("patronage dividends") in accordance with labor rather than by reference to the capital invested in shares. But since the net worth is not partitioned off from the shares by a system of internal accounts, the shares continue to function as carriers of net worth. Thus a worker who could not afford to individually pay off the accumulated net worth due a retiring member by buying a share would not receive the membership rights to vote and to receive a portion of the net earnings. The traditional worker co-ops, instead of making the complete transformation, represent something of a confused and sterile crossbreed between an investor-owned piece of property and a cooperative social institution.

The system of Mondragon-type internal accounts takes the function of carrying the net worth away from the shares so that the membership rights, evidenced by the shares, can be fully transformed into personal rights assigned to the workers' functional role. The net worth due to each worker-member, representing the reinvested fruits of their labor, is not thereby sacrificed since it remains a property right evidenced by the balance in the member's internal account.[3] In this manner, a proper legal structure will transform a company from a piece of property into a social institution wherein people will receive the fruits of their labor and have democratic control over their working lives.

NOTES

1. From the present external legal viewpoint, the internally restructured corporation, with share membership certificates and internal capital accounts, would be viewed as a whole set of stock purchase and sale agreements geared to employment in the corporation. After the probationary period, an employee must purchase one and only one share at a preset price (the membership fee) to obtain permanent employment in the firm. The agreement stipulates that the share is nontransferable during the tenure of employment. Upon termination of employment, there is a mandatory sale (a "mandatory call") of the share back to the corporation for a formula price. The formula price is the balance in the shareholder's internal capital account. The price is paid partly in cash and partly in subordinate notes to be paid off over a period of years. This is the external view of the structural transformation which would be described internally or generically as transforming the membership rights from the property rights into personal rights attached to the functional role of working in the firm, while maintaining the worker-members' property rights to their capital reinvested in the firm. The external can only be brought in line with the internal viewpoint by the creation of new statutes and new legal institutions. For the present, the new must be built within the shell of the old.

2. The theme that capitalism treats some nongovernmental social institutions as private property has also been developed by Karl Polanyi (1944) and Carole Pateman

(1975). Indeed, since the development of political democracy in the Western countries, the "public/private" distinction has served to quarantine the democratic germ in the sphere of political government, keeping it from spreading to other social institutions such as business firms. Thus some people argue that big corporations should be democratized because they are really "public," as if the concept of self-determination were only applicable to the public domain. And others defend the corporation against the encroachment of democratic ideals by asserting that it is a "private" firm, as if that were a relevant defense. Even socialists (or perhaps one should say, *especially* socialists) think in terms of the public/private distinction. Instead of rejecting the identification of social or public with the government, and extending direct self-management to the nongovernmental institutions of society, traditional socialism (e.g., Marxist socialism) maintains the equation that *social* equals *governmental* and extends the reach of the government to the formerly nongovernmental institutions of society.

3. Since the balance in each member's account represents a property right, the question of its transferability arises. For example, prior to the termination of membership, could a member be issued subordinate debentures, representing part of the account's balance, which were transferable? The answer could be yes only if enough was left in the member's account to cover future debits. If most or all of the account's balance was turned into a debt note which was then sold by the member to some other party, there may not be enough balance left in the account to cover the losses charged to the member. After such losses, the account would show a negative balance, and any member who leaves with his or her account showing a negative balance would be transferring those losses to his or her coworkers. To prevent that eventuality, a sufficient balance should always be maintained in a member's account to cover future debits. Indeed, one reason for the membership fee is to provide a beginning positive balance in a new member's account which will function as a damage deposit to cover future losses. Thus if a cooperative does not allow most or all of an account's balance to be capitalized as a transferable note, it is not because the balance is not a property right, but because the cooperative has a lien on a part of that property to cover any future debits.

PART VI

Conclusion

12

The Prospects for Worker Cooperatives
in the United States

ROBERT JACKALL
AND
HENRY M. LEVIN

In the last century, the main historical trend in the West has been toward the increased centralization of both economic and political power. In the United States, for instance, every major sphere of the economy is now dominated by oligopolies. The scope and range of decision making by highly concentrated elites has increased exponentially; today decisions made in corporate offices in New York or Detroit or in government bureaus in Washington reverberate in every corner of the land. The bureaucratization of the society, particularly in its occupational structure, has been one of the main features of this centralization; virtually every occupation in the United States—from physician to assembly-line worker—is now specialized, standardized, certified, arranged in a hierarchy, and bureaucratized in other ways.

One can hardly exaggerate the impact that these processes of centralization and bureaucratization have had on our entire social landscape. These processes have transformed our demographic patterns, refashioned our class structure, altered our communities, and shaped the very tone and tempo of our society. Unlike a century ago, we are today an urban people, largely propertyless (in the productive sense), and dependent on big organizations—in short, a society of employees coordinated by bureaucratic elites and experts of every sort. At the ideological level, of course, all of these developments—and the entire social fabric woven on this warp—come to assume a taken-for-granted status, an aura of inevitability; it becomes difficult for most people to conceive of other ways of arranging the world, even when, as in our society, the social costs of the pattern begin to mount.

Worker cooperatives stand as anomalies to these main historical trends. In a society where productive wealth is increasingly centralized, cooperatives work toward decentralized ownership; in a thoroughly bureaucratic social order, marked by the fragmentation of skill, expertise, and work process, cooperatives try to develop holistic approaches to work; in a society where decision making with enormous social impact is in the hands of comparatively few people, cooperatives strive to institute a genuine democracy. What are the real prospects for worker cooperatives in a bureaucratic, capitalist society?

HISTORICAL CONTINUITIES

The place to begin an understanding of these prospects is in the remarkable historical resilience of the worker cooperative movement. Since at least 1790, as chapter 3 by Derek Jones points out, there have been hundreds of documented cases of worker cooperatives in America. This suggests that cooperatives are recurring, transitional responses to deeply rooted, persistent problems in our social structure and in its whole historical drift. There seem to be three principal sets of reasons for the continued and persistent emergence of cooperatives: periods of unemployment as a result of poor economic conditions; periods of rapid technological change which occasion a similar social dislocation; and periods of social upheaval which call into question conventional world views about the nature and proper structure of work. In our view, all of these will continue to be important reasons for the emergence of worker cooperatives, although to different degrees and in quite different ways.

THE EFFECTS OF ECONOMIC CONDITIONS

Worker cooperatives have regularly been seen by workers as one response to hard times. As Derek Jones and Donald Schneider demonstrate in chapter 4, during the massive unemployment of the Great Depression, workers formed hundreds of self-help cooperatives initially to provide food and clothing for themselves and ultimately to trade labor for produce with farmers and to trade food for their goods with one another. Cooperatives have also been vehicles for maintaining employment in situations when capitalist firms close or for stabilizing employment in industries subject to wide economic fluctuations. When workers face massive unemployment with few alternatives for other work (this seems particularly true in rural areas and in small towns), they have often adopted cooperative solutions, either by purchasing the workplace or by creating their own alternative firms.

The plywood cooperatives of the Pacific Northwest (see chapter 8 by Edward Greenberg) are the best examples of this response to unemployment in America. The plywood industry is sensitive to the swings of the business cycle because most of its output is sold to the cyclically sensitive construction industry. As a result, cycles of prosperity and bankruptcy and of hiring and layoffs are very common. In response to this continual economic insecurity, workers created more than thirty producer cooperatives over the last sixty years, and about half of these still survive. In some cases, workers formed the firms because they were convinced that they could provide greater job security for themselves by owning and managing their own enterprises; in other cases, workers purchased firms that were near bankruptcy because of poor market conditions. In virtually all cases, however, the principal motivating force seemed to be to increase employment security.

There is little doubt that for the foreseeable future, economic conditions will be poor with relatively high rates of unemployment. High and rising costs of energy and other natural resources run counter to technologies that have been based on assumptions of cheap, unlimited energy. Further, the government is unable to stimulate economic growth through traditional fiscal and monetary policies because of the ever-present danger of triggering inflation through various shortages, bottlenecks in production, and administered price increases by the oligopolies that dominate most industries. Finally, the low wages and the high profitability of production in many third world countries will continue to provide major inducements to invest outside the United States. There is every reason to expect, then, that economic growth will be slow, particularly in contrast to the earlier post-World War II period.

In addition, certain regions of the country will face particularly difficult employment problems as a result of firms shifting their production to other areas of the country (to the Sunbelt in particular) and to those areas of the world that promise lower labor costs and fewer restrictions on production, such as regulations on worker health and safety and environmental pollution. While employment security will, therefore, be a serious issue for the country as a whole, it will be particularly grave for workers in older cities and in traditional manufacturing regions. In these areas it is conceivable that entire plants and industries will be shut down with devastating effects both on the workers who are directly affected and on those who service workers and their industries.

Given this rather grim but entirely likely scenario and given, at the same time, the history of worker cooperatives, there will probably be an increase in the number of cooperatives established in response to unemployment. In particular, there are likely to be more worker purchases of firms that are still viable but are sold off by parent enterprises because other corporate alternatives are more profitable. The use of Employee Stock Ownership Plans (see chap. 10 by Henry Levin) will become an increasingly important mechanism for workers to acquire ownership of enterprises and thus protect employment. This is especially true in firms with 500 or fewer employees, but it is also possible in much larger firms as illustrated by Weirton Steel, Rath Packing Company, and Hyatt Clark Industries.

Briefly, then, the whole history of the cooperative movement suggests that we will see recurring, largely spontaneous cooperative attempts to combat the persistent and growing unemployment in our society. This will happen even in the absence of sustained policy interventions or of systematized efforts by the cooperative movement itself to insure the initiation and survival of cooperatives.

THE EFFECTS OF TECHNOLOGICAL CHANGE

In the nineteenth century, the formation of worker cooperatives was stimulated not only by the overall impact of the economy on employment security but also by the employment dislocation effects of technological change. The replacement of artisan practices in the workshop with machine processes in the factory was especially important. In some cases, workers responded by destroying the machinery that threatened to displace them, the strategy of the Luddites. But in other cases, artisans—coopers, bakers, shoemakers, foundry workers, cigar makers, and others—joined together in cooperative workshops to attempt to compete with the factories. In most instances, their cooperative efforts were short-lived because they were unable to produce goods as cheaply as the factory system.

Today, the pace of technological change in some occupational areas is almost as profound as it was with the introduction of the factory system. For instance, the development of the silicon chip and the microprocessor is transforming virtually all jobs in the area of office work and information processing; in fact, these developments may result in a level of automation in many areas that is almost unimaginable today. However, it is very unlikely that these technological changes will produce a cooperative response similar to those of many nineteenth-century artisans. While disemployed shoemakers could start cooperative workshops to make shoes with artisan methods, that sort of strategy is unavailable for office workers. Today not only does the adoption of new capital-intensive technology by established firms eliminate some jobs and exploit less-skilled and cheaper labor in other jobs—which was also true when the factory system was initiated—but these same firms also usually maintain strong market advantages because of their size.

Today's technological change will not, therefore, have a major direct impact on the formation of worker cooperatives. However, it may have an important indirect effect. The automating developments presently underway—despite the great hopes invested in high tech by politicians, the press, and much of the public—consistently work to reduce the skill requirements needed in manufacturing and office work; in the future, they will standardize, indeed trivialize, many people's work even more than is currently the case (Levin and Rumberger 1983). Over time, particularly during periods of social unrest, this phenomenon may well produce large numbers of men and women seeking greater challenges and involvement in their workplaces than conventional firms can offer. One possible outlet could be the increased formation of small cooperative enterprises.

THE EFFECTS OF SOCIAL UPHEAVAL

The third important historical reason for the development of worker cooperatives was the period of great social, political, and cultural upheaval in the 1960s and early 1970s. Several long-term historical trends and several persistent and new issues coincided to bring about that upheaval. First, the economy was expanding rapidly; this provided young people, in particular, with a sense of long-term security and a concomitant willingness to experiment with alternatives to normal career paths. Second, the educational system also expanded rapidly in the post-World War II period, putting larger numbers of young people together than ever before into what were essentially youth ghettoes. This phenomenon created social experimentation and rapid changes of life-style on a widespread scale. Third, in the midst of postwar affluence, the unresolved and persistent problems of gross inequality in America—particularly among American blacks, but also among other minority and ethnic groups, poor Southern whites, migrant workers, and women—were forced by young organizers to the forefront of the national consciousness. This stirred deep sentiments of moral outrage, on the one hand, and produced well-grounded criticisms of the whole social structure on the other. Fourth, American foreign policy adventures produced the debacle of Vietnam, an issue which brought together virtually all the other themes of the period. The tumultuous demonstrations around civil rights, Vietnam, and all the social issues that came to be seen as related, progressively attenuated the legitimacy of our entire social, cultural, and political order.

One particular focus of this process of delegitimation was the very lifeblood of the new middle class—that is, bureaucratic work and the stable careers that are the enduring promises of the big organization. Young men and women came to see the routinization, the fragmentation, the very stolidity of the bureaucratic world as both the cause and the symbol of the serious institutional deficiencies that prevented the society from resolving the great issues that threatened to tear it apart. In this context, communal or collective work became for many young people not just a way to make a living but also a means to alter the entire social order. As the chapters in Part III point out, many of the small worker cooperatives started during that period are still flourishing.

Although the 1960s were unique in some ways, the period was also of a piece with the whole history of youthful social and cultural revolts against the culture of industrial capitalism in this century. Greenwich Village Bohemia, the Flaming Youth of the 1920s, the youthful Communists of the 1930s, and the Beatniks of the 1950s were all forerunners of the cultural and political radicals of the 1960s. There is every reason to believe that this historical pattern of youthful revolt will surface again, despite changing economic conditions. One of the most important factors in that revolt is likely to be, in fact, the clash of overeducated youth with a declining, stagnant, and increasingly bureaucratized economy which is simply unable to utilize youth's skill and educational levels or their creative potentials. This clash would call all the traditional promises of the American system into serious question and could generate, once again, a search for alternate work, even if only for periods of people's lives (Levin 1981). Small cooperative enterprises could once again be the beneficiaries of such a pattern.

We noted earlier that the historical resilience of cooperatives suggests that they are recurring transitional responses to deeply rooted problems in our social structure. Indeed, one of the most interesting characteristics of cooperatives is that they provide a window on some of these problems—the nagging, cyclical unemployment generated by our system; the sporadic social disruption produced by technological change; and the long-term disaffection of our youth. The relatively short life of cooperatives—in comparison with the "eternal" corporations—has to be seen in this light. Cooperatives spring up to meet needs generated by problems in the social structure; many, though by no means all, do not outlive their founders. The social structure moves on, problems are patched up, legitimacy is reestablished—until the next crisis and the reassertion of the same or similar problems. When this happens, new cooperatives burgeon and flourish at least for a time, counterposing to the dominant bureaucratic forms of legitimacy the possibility of welding society through "participatory milieux." In this sense, cooperatives represent not only the antithesis of what our society has become but, somewhat ironically, embodiments of its most long-lived and best tradition—its democracy. The worker cooperative form seems to be now a permanent, if irregular, part of our heritage. The intriguing issue, and the final one we wish to address here, is how the cooperative movement can solidify its own institutional base and make its social contributions a more regular feature of our society.

BUILDING COOPERATIVE INSTITUTIONS

There are very persuasive reasons for building cooperative institutions. As suggested throughout this book, cooperatives represent a method of saving existing jobs and of creating new ones at a lower investment cost per job than alternative courses offer. They are very productive enterprises, often more so than comparable noncooperative firms. Moreover, they involve workers deeply in the decision making of the firm; and in doing so, they not only address the important issue of the quality of working life for cooperators themselves but also provide models of the possibilities of workplace democracy for our whole society. The problem, however, is that our whole social order is geared in a noncooperative direction. Our legal structures, access to capital, education, and the forms of entrepreneurship and management in the United States are all open invitations to the establishment of corporate and other conventional forms of enterprise; as such, they constitute imposing barriers to the formation of cooperatives. Any strategy to fashion a firmer institutional base for the cooperative movement has to address, therefore, at least the following areas: (1) the dissemination of information about cooperatives; (2) the creation of legal vehicles for the formation and continuance of cooperatives; (3) the education and training of cooperative workers; (4) the financing arrangements for cooperatives; and (5) technical assistance for cooperative groups.

INFORMATION

The great majority of American citizens know nothing about worker cooperatives. This includes people for whom cooperatives are very pertinent—for example, workers facing a plant closure, capital-poor individuals who want to open a small business, refugee communities with traditional handicraft skills, and so on. Without some civic literacy about the nature and advantages of cooperatives, their possibilities can never fully be explored. People also need two kinds of specific information. First, they need information about the locations of existing cooperatives and about their products and organizational characteristics. This is helpful not only to those who wish to join such enterprises but also for potential patrons. *The Bay Area Directory of Collectives* (Collective Directory 1977), for instance, is an attractive and usable brochure about the countercultural service and craft collectives in the San Francisco area, which was financed and produced by local collectivists themselves. Second, some specific practical information is needed to explain the mechanics of establishing cooperatives or worker ownership. The State of California, for instance, has prepared a guide for workers facing plant closure to assist them in evaluating the possibility of a worker buyout (Parzen et al. 1982). A number of other groups, discussed later in this chapter, have also prepared a range of materials on worker cooperatives and worker-owned firms.

Ultimately, of course, widespread citizen awareness of anything in our society depends on the mass media, particularly the electronic media. This raises a serious conundrum for the cooperative movement and its supporters—how does a movement whose central values and goals are at odds with basic tendencies in our society gain access to the most powerful molders of public opinion? The only realistic suggestion that we can offer here is for the cooperative movement and its supporters to try to secure funding from sympathetic public agencies such as the National Consumer Cooperative Bank or perhaps the National Endowment for the Humanities to produce some documentary films about the cooperative movement for use in local public television stations. The talent for such an undertaking is already present in several filmmaking collectives in the cooperative movement; what is needed, in addition to public funds, is a clear sense of the long-term importance of establishing public awareness of cooperative alternatives.

LEGAL ISSUES

Worker cooperatives have been largely neglected in the law, although most of the fifty states have specific provisions for agricultural and marketing cooperatives and many for consumer cooperatives. Clearly, this is a crucial area for cooperative effort; without well-established legal institutions, particularly at the state level, there can be no hope for any long-term stable development of cooperatives. As David Ellerman suggests in chapter 11, worker cooperatives have unique legal needs. These include: the need for special provisions for collective ownership, participative arrangements for social insurance, and the rights of members in the event of dissolution of a cooperative firm. In some cases, these matters must be defined by specific statutes; in other cases, they simply need the creation of appropriate legal forms to fit within existing laws. What all of this calls for is, first, research that establishes the most appropriate laws as well as the most supportive types of organizational arrangements; second, preparation of legislation reflecting that research; and, third, the drafting of model arrangements for forming worker cooperatives to be used by newly forming groups. There are already a few groups supportive of the cooperative movement doing this kind of work, notably the Industrial Cooperative Association in Somerville, Massachusetts; in addition, this seems to be an ideal project for the several law collectives around the country.

EDUCATION AND TRAINING

As Zelda Gamson and Henry Levin point out in their essay (see chapter 9), cooperative enterprises demand worker skills and experiences that are largely unavailable in traditional American schools or in conventional workplaces. Cooperative workers must learn how to make democratic decisions, how to rotate jobs and training possibilities, how to make decisions on a wide range of issues that most workers never encounter—from finance, to products, to technology, and pricing. Practically speaking, since widespread educational reforms are simply beyond the movement (Levin 1983), this means that worker cooperatives must establish their own internal training programs to develop cooperative skills, perspectives, and experiences.

Some external institutions, however, can be very helpful in this regard. Academic supporters of cooperatives can, for instance, be encouraged to study cooperative organizations and their management needs and to disseminate their knowledge through writings, seminars, and public forums. Supporters of cooperatives in the academy, business, and government can be identified and drawn into cooperative training programs to impart specific types of business and administrative knowledge. Some private organizations and foundations—such as the Norman Foundation and Gutfreund Fund in New York and the Philadelphia Foundation and William Penn Foundation in Philadelphia which have been supporters of the cooperative movement—and some public agencies can provide invaluable help.

One unique approach to training has been undertaken in recent years by the New School for Democratic Management in San Francisco. The New School is currently inactive but in the past it provided a curriculum for participants in democratic workplaces that included courses on democratic decision making and problem solving, as well as courses on the financial, managerial, and marketing needs of cooperative organizations. The school also offered seminars on such topics in cities around the country to obviate the need for a trip to the West Coast.

FINANCE

There are few areas more troubling to cooperative enterprises than that of finance because worker cooperatives do not have the same access to capital as conventional firms. Banks are reluctant to lend to cooperatives, in part because of their unconventional nature and their democratic control. The very form of the worker cooperative precludes the participation of members of the financial community on the board of directors: further, lending institutions seem reluctant to extend credit to organizations whose managers are removable by their workers. As a result, the personal and institutional ties so crucial to establishing credit relationships are difficult to forge between financial organizations and cooperatives. In addition, lenders cannot obtain a commitment from cooperatives to use equity of the firm as collateral for loans, since this would be proscribed by the requirements of workers ownership. All of these factors inhibit the ability of worker cooperatives to obtain loans. Until quite recently, in fact, even government programs have not provided loans to cooperatives.

In the last few years, however, there has been some movement in this area. Legislation was passed in 1980 to permit the Small Business Administration to make low-cost loans to employee-owned businesses. The National Consumer Cooperative Bank also now has the authority to loan up to 10 percent of its total capitalization (about $221 million in late 1983) to worker cooperatives as an industry group. It can loan up to 2 percent of its total capitalization to any single cooperative. At this writing, it has loans out to thirteen worker cooperatives, and more are planned. And Employee Stock Option Plans have become a mechanism for initiating worker cooperatives, although there are serious potentials for abuse of ESOP financing by existing management (see chapter 10 by Henry Levin). The most promising alternative is a Mondragon-type of cooperative bank that would serve groups of affiliated cooperatives much as the Caja Laboral Popular serves the Mondragon cooperatives (Thomas and Logan 1982:chap. 4). This type of bank would provide loan capital and financial and business services (Ellerman 1982c) to cooperative enterprises and would draw upon the deposits of the firms as well as the capital accounts of the workers and their savings to provide an expanding source of lending. Clearly, financing is an area where the cooperative movement and particularly its professional supporters can and should make extensive lobbying efforts. The New Systems of Work Participation program at Cornell University has already made substantial efforts on this front through research and congressional testimony on worker ownership.

One of the most ingenious credit mechanisms within the cooperative movement was developed by Hoedads Co-op in Eugene, Oregon (see chap. 7 by Christopher Gunn). In its early years that cooperative required a one-time, returnable $1,000 membership fee of each worker joining the cooperative. The money was pooled, and much of it loaned out to new cooperative ventures at very low interest rates. This financial support contributed to the spawning of a great number of small service and craft collectives in the Washington and Oregon areas. More recently, Hoedads has raised its membership to $2,000 and has had to utilize these funds mostly for its own working capital. However, the cooperative credit mechanism that it developed and practiced for many years deserves closer scrutiny and wider dissemination.

TECHNICAL ASSISTANCE

Finally, one of the most pressing needs of the cooperative movement is for organizations that provide an integrated program of technical assistance to help emerging cooperative groups in implementing all of the factors that we have discussed here. The focus of such organizations would be to provide information on how to form cooperatives, develop appropriate organizational and legal structures, obtain proper financing, and develop internal educational and training programs. Potential models are the National Center for Employee Ownership (NCEO) of Arlington, Virginia, the Industrial Cooperative Association (ICA) of Somerville, Massachusetts, and the Philadelphia Association for Cooperative Enterprise (PACE) of Philadelphia, Pennsylvania.[1]

The National Center for Employee Ownership is a nonprofit membership-based organization dedicated to providing information about and increasing understanding of employee ownership. Founded in 1980, NCEO functions as a clearinghouse on employee ownership. NCEO publishes information on employee ownership, hosts conferences on the subject, provides information to the media, works with companies, unions, and employee groups considering employee ownership, and conducts research on the dynamics and effects of employee ownership.

ICA is a six-year-old nonprofit organization with more than a dozen staff members and regular consultants, including economists, a lawyer and legal interns, business analysts, and community development specialists. ICA provides technical assistance to cooperative groups in four specific areas. First, it gives business, legal, and educational assistance to existing and potential worker cooperatives. Second, it does feasibility analyses for worker groups considering a buyout of an ongoing business. Third, it provides advice to workers faced with ultimatums from their corporations to buy the company or face closure (for example, Weirton Steel in West Virginia). Finally it helps unions develop an understanding of corporate strategies when they are faced with concessionary bargaining demands. The recent and ongoing projects of ICA include: a worker-owned sewing company in Windsor, North Carolina; a weatherization cooperative in Milwaukee; a retail and catalogue clothing store in Northampton, Massachusetts; and a furniture and garment manufacturing company in Cuomo, Puerto Rico. The organization has had significant funding from the federal Fund for the Improvement of Post-Secondary Education, of the Department of Education, for a work-force education project. It has also received ongoing support from several churches, private foundations, and individuals. In addition, the ICA has two staff members working full time in an entrepreneurial capacity to move beyond providing reactive technical assistance for cooperatives facing business problems and toward being able to seize business opportunities for cooperatives. It has established a $1 million risk capital fund (with major funding from the Ford Foundation) to help create cooperative firms. It is working actively with churches, community organizations, governments, and especially labor unions to develop an extensive network of men and women in key institutional sectors committed to cooperatives. Finally, it is engaging vigorously in the national debate on reindustrialization, putting forth the merits of cooperatives to help the ailing economy of the nation.

PACE was incorporated in 1976 and began developing the capacity to assist cooperatives in 1979. It has five regular staff members at present, including two lawyers. PACE also employs, on a per-job basis, technical experts from corporate law firms and from business schools, including the University of Pennsylvania's Wharton School. PACE's principal funding comes from local Philadelphia foundations. Its recent projects include: the O & O supermarket chain (formerly A & P); the Atlas Chain Company, a democratic ESOP in West Pittston, Pennsylvania; the Omega Press in Philadelphia; and Infinity Foods in Pittsburgh. Much of PACE's actual work is quite similar to that of ICA. The principal difference between the two organizations is that ICA sees itself as a national group while PACE orients itself only to a specific region, namely, the Middle Atlantic states. The more local emphasis is important to PACE's staff because they see intensive worker education in anticipation of starting up a worker cooperative or worker-owned business as one of the organization's primary roles. This extremely time-consuming educational process involves not only straight information dissemination but, more particularly, training in democratic decision making. This kind of work, PACE's staff feels, cannot be done from too great a distance.

At the moment, NCEO, ICA, and PACE are in the forefront of organizations of their kind, although others, such as the Center for Community Self-Help in North Carolina, and the Community Service Society in New York City, are springing up in response to the cooperative and employee ownership movement. It is precisely through organizations such as these that professional, academic, and business supporters of the cooperative movement can obtain information and can channel their own energies to building cooperative institutions.

CONCLUSION

Worker cooperatives are now a recurring feature of American society. They represent both a response and a symbolic antithesis to the centralization and bureaucratization that are the hallmarks of our social order. As long as our society continues to generate unemployment, social dislocation, and trivialized work—and these seem endemic to bureaucratic capitalism—some men and women will form cooperatives as transitional, mitigating institutions. This in itself is a valuable and important role because it addresses real human needs in a practical way. Moreover, in so doing, cooperatives lay claim to the enduring democratic heritage of our society and try to make that heritage come alive in the workplace. They offer us as well images of a social order imbued with reason, freedom, and, indeed, hope.

Here we have stressed some ways the cooperative movement itself and its supporters in a variety of social sectors can lay a firmer institutional basis for the formation and survival of worker cooperatives. We certainly do not wish to preclude the desirability of more direct public and quasi-public assistance to this undertaking. Potentially there is a strong role for federal, state, and local governments as well as for private agencies to provide the institutional support for expanded cooperative production. For example, the use of unemployment compensation to assist workers in purchasing firms that would otherwise close makes a great deal of sense (Whyte and Blasi 1980). Moreover, the social benefits from such interventions could be, we think, significant. It would, however, be a mistake to count on such assistance, particularly during the present period of political reaction (late 1983). While worker cooperatives offer solutions to some of the economic and social issues that bedevil our society, they also represent a challenge to some of its basic premises. In the long run, the vision and the nerve to achieve a more cooperative future must come primarily from cooperatives themselves.

NOTE

1. The National Center for Employee Ownership (NCEO), 1611 S. Walter Reed Drive, No. 109, Arlington, Virginia 22204 (703-979-2375), produces a wide range of publications on employee ownership. The NCEO also has a West Coast office at

870 Market Street, Room 657, San Francisco, California 94102 (415-986-8865). The Industrial Cooperative Association (ICA), 249 Elm Street, Somerville, Massachusetts 02144 (617-628-7330) publishes a variety of materials to assist in the formation and operation of worker cooperatives; it also publishes a newsletter for members. The Philadelphia Association for Cooperative Enterprise (PACE), 133 South 18th Street, Philadelphia, Pennsylvania 19103 (215-561-7079) produces different papers on co-operatives and worker ownership as well as a newsletter for members. All of these organizations can be contacted directly for lists of publications.

BIBLIOGRAPHY

Adizes, Ichak. 1971. *Industrial Democracy: Yugoslav Style.* New York: Free Press.

Alchian, Armen, and Harold Demsetz. 1972. "Production, Information Costs, and Economic Organization." *American Economic Review* 62 (December):777–795.

Alvarado-Greenwood, William, et al. 1978. *Organizing Production Cooperatives: A Strategy for Community Economic Development.* Berkeley: National Economic Development and Law Center.

Antoni, Antoine. 1970. *La Coopération Ouvrière de Production.* Paris: Confédération Generale Des Sociétés. Coopératives Ouvrières de Production.

Aronowitz, Stanley. 1973. *False Promises.* New York: McGraw-Hill.

Avineri, Schlomo. 1971. *The Social and Political Thought of Karl Marx.* New York: Cambridge University Press.

Bachrach, Peter. 1967. *The Theory of Democratic Elitism.* Boston: Little-Brown.

Barber, Randy. 1982. "Pension Funds in the United States: Issues of Investment and Control." *Economic and Industrial Democracy* 3 (February):31–72.

Bellas, Carl J. 1972. *Industrial Democracy and the Worker-Owned Firm.* New York: Praeger.

Bemis, Edward W. 1896. "Cooperative Distribution." *U.S. Bulletin of the Department of Labor* 6 (September):610–644. Washington, D.C.: Government Printing Office.

Bensman, Joseph. 1967. *Dollars and Sense.* New York: Macmillan.

Bensman, Joseph, and Bernard Rosenberg. 1960. "The Meaning of Work in Bureaucratic Society." In *Identity and Anxiety,* ed. Maurice Stein, Arthur J. Vidich, and David M. White. New York: Free Press.

Berman, Katrina V. 1967. *Worker-Owned Plywood Companies: An Economic Analysis.* Pullman: Washington State University Press.

Berman, Katrina V., and Matthew D. Berman. 1978. "The Long-Run Analysis of the Labor-Managed Firm: Comment." *American Economic Review* 68 (September):701–705.

Bernstein, Paul. 1974. "Run Your Own Business: Worker-Owned Plywood Firms." *Working Papers* 2 (Summer):24–34.

————. 1976a. "Necessary Elements for Effective Worker Participation in Decision Making." *Journal of Economic Issues* 10 (June):490–522.

————. 1976b. *Workplace Democratization: Its Internal Dynamics.* Kent, Ohio: Kent State University Press.

Blasi, Joseph R., and William F. Whyte. 1981. "Worker Ownership and Public Policy." Paper prepared for the International Conference on Producer Cooperatives, Gilleleje, Denmark, 31 May–June 4.

Blauner, Robert. 1964. *Alienation and Freedom.* Chicago: University of Chicago Press.

Bluestone, Barry, and Bennett Harrison. 1980. "Why Corporations Close Profitable Plants." *Working Papers* 7 (May/June):15–23.

————. 1982. *The Deindustrialization of America.* New York: Basic Books.

Blumberg, Paul. 1968. *Industrial Democracy.* New York: Schocken Books.

Blume, Marshall E., Jean Crockett, and Irwin Friend. 1974. "Stockownership in the United States: Characteristics and Trends." *Survey of Current Business,* November.

Bonin, John P. 1981. "The Theory of the Labor-managed Firm from the Membership's Perspective with Implications for Marshallian Industry Supply." *Journal of Comparative Economics* 5 (December): 337–351.

Bowles, Samuel, and Herbert Gintis. 1976. *Schooling in Capitalist America.* New York: Basic Books.

Bowles, Samuel, David M. Gordon, and Thomas E. Weisskopf. 1983. *Beyond the Wasteland: A Democratic Alternative to Economic Decline.* Garden City, N.Y.: Anchor Press/Doubleday.

Bradley, Keith. 1980. "A Comparative Analysis of Producer Cooperatives: Some Theoretical and Empirical Implications." *British Journal of Industrial Relations* 18 (July):155–168.

Bradley, Keith, and Alan Gelb. 1980. "Worker Cooperatives as Industrial Policy: The Case of the 'Scottish Daily News.' " *Review of Economic Studies* 47:665–678.

————. 1983. *Worker Capitalism: The New Industrial Relations.* Cambridge, Mass.: MIT Press.

Braverman, Harry. 1974. *Labor and Monopoly Capital.* New York: Monthly Review Books.

Burgess, J. Stewart. 1933. "Living on a Surplus." *The Survey* 68 (January):6–8.

Cable, John R., and Felix R. Fitzroy. 1980. "Cooperation and Productivity: Some Evidence from West German Experience." *Kyklos* 33:100–121.

Caja Laboral Popular. 1970–1978. *Memoria.* Mondragon, Guipuzcoa, Spain.

————. Division Empresarial. 1973. "Analisis de Productividad: Indicés Generales." Mondragon, Spain.

California State Relief Administration. 1935. *Annual Report: Division of Self-Help Cooperative Service.* .

————. 1936. *Annual Report: Division of Self-Help Cooperative Service July 1, 1934– June 30, 1935.*

————. 1937. *Annual Report: Division of Self-Help Cooperative Service July 1, 1935– June 30, 1936.* March.

————. 1938. *Self-Help Cooperatives in California.*

Campbell, Alastair, et al. 1977. *Worker-Owners: The Mondragon Achievement.* London: Anglo-German Foundation for the Study of Industrial Society.

Carnoy, Martin, and Henry M. Levin. 1976a. *The Limits of Educational Reform.* New York: David McKay and Co., Inc.

————. 1976b. "Workers' Triumph: The Meriden Experiment." *Working Papers* (Winter):47–56.

Carnoy, Martin, and Derek Shearer. 1980. *Economic Democracy.* White Plains, N.Y.: M. E. Sharpe, Inc.

Carnoy, Martin, Derek Shearer, and Russell Rumberger. 1983 *A New Social Contract: The Economy and Government After Reagan.* New York: Harper and Row.

Case, John, and Rosemary Taylor, eds. 1979. *Co-ops, Communes and Collectives: Experiments in Social Change in the 1960s and 1970s.* New York: Pantheon.

Clark, Burton. 1970. *The Distinctive College: Antioch, Reed, and Swarthmore.* Chicago: Aldine.

Cohen, Elizabeth. 1974. "The Dilemma of Group Work." Stanford University School of Education. Mimeo.

Collective Directory, The. 1977. *The Bay Area Directory of Collectives.* 1499 Potrero, San Francisco, California 94110.

Communities: Journal of Cooperative Living. 1977. (May–June):23–45.

Congressional Record. 1981. 97th Congress, 1st Session. "S 1162—Expanded Ownership Act of 1981." Vol. 12, no. 72 (12 May):S4779–4796.

Conte, Michael. 1982. "Participation and Productivity in U.S. Labor Managed Firms." In *Participatory and Self-Managed Firms: Evaluating Economic Performance.* Ed.

D. C. Jones and J. Svejnar. Lexington, Mass.: Lexington Books.

Conte, Michael, and Arnold Tannenbaum. 1978. "Employee-Owned Companies: Is the Difference Measurable?" *Monthly Labor Review* 101 (July):23–28.

Coover, Virginia, Ellen Deacon, Charles Esser, and Christopher Moore. 1978. *Resource Manual for a Living Revolution.* 2d ed. Philadelphia: New Society Publishers.

Creamer, Daniel. 1954. "Capital and Output Trends in Manufacturing Industries 1880–1941." *Studies in Capital Formation and Financing*, Occasional Paper 41. New York: National Bureau of Economic Research, Inc.

Crozier, Michael, et al. 1975. *The Crisis of Democracy.* New York: New York University Press.

Dahl, Robert. 1970. *After the Revolution.* New Haven: Yale University Press.

Dalton, Melville. 1959. *Men Who Manage.* New York: John Wiley and Sons.

de Grazia, Sebastian. 1964. *Of Time, Work and Leisure.* Garden City: Doubleday-Anchor.

Denison, Edward F. 1979. *Accounting for Slower Economic Growth: The United States in the 1970's.* Washington, D.C.: The Brookings Institution.

Derber, Milton. 1970. *The American Idea of Industrial Democracy.* Urbana: University of Illinois Press.

Dewey, John. 1916. *Democracy and Education.* New York: Macmillan Co.

Dolgoff, Sam. 1974. *The Anarchist Collectives.* New York: New Life Editions.

Dreeben, Robert. 1968. *On What is Learned in School.* Reading, Mass.: Addison Wesley and Co.

Dreze, Jacques H. 1976. "Some Theory of Labour-Management and Participation." *Econometrica* 44:1125–1139.

Egerton, John. 1983. "Workers Take Over the Store." *The New York Times Magazine* (September 11):164f.

Ellerman, David P. 1975. "Capitalism and Workers' Self-Management." In *Self Management*, ed. Jaroslav Vanek. Baltimore: Penguin.

———. 1979a. "The Union as the Legitimate Opposition in an Industrial Democracy." Cambridge, Mass.: Industrial Cooperative Association. December.

———. 1979b. "What is a Workers' Cooperative?" Cambridge, Mass.: Industrial Cooperative Association.

———. 1982a. *Economics, Accounting, and Property Theory.* Lexington, Mass: Lexington Books.

———. 1982b. "Notes on the Co-op/ESOP Debate." Somerville, Mass.: Industrial Cooperative Association. April.

———. 1982c. "The Socialization of Entrepreneurship: The Empresarial Division of the Caja Laboral Popular." Somerville, Mass.: Industrial Cooperative Association.

Ellerman, David P., and Peter Pitegoff. 1980. "Model Bylaws for a Workers' Cooperative." Cambridge, Mass.: Industrial Cooperative Association.

———. 1983. "The Democratic Corporation: The New Worker Cooperative Statute in Massachusetts." *New York University Review of Law and Social Change* 11 (82–83):441–472.

Employee Ownership. 1983. "Majority Employee-Owned Companies: A Survey of Characteristics and Performance." Vol. 3, no. 1 (March):1–2.

Espinosa, Juan G., and Andrew Zimbalist. 1978. *Economic Democracy: Workers' Participation in Chilean Industry.* New York: Academic Press.

Flacks, Richard. 1971. *Youth and Social Change.* Chicago: Markham.

Ford, James. 1913. *Cooperation in New England, Urban and Rural.* New York: Russell Sage Foundation.

Fox, John, and Melvin Guyer. 1978. "'Public' Choice and Cooperation in n-Person Prisoner's Dilemma." *Journal of Conflict Resolution* 22 (September):469–481.

Frieden, Karl. 1978. "The Effect of Workers-Ownership and Workers Participation on Productivity." Washington, D.C.: National Center for Economic Alternatives. Manuscript.

————. 1980. *Workplace Democracy and Productivity.* Washington, D.C.: National Center for Economic Alternatives.

Fromm, Eric. 1961. *Marx's Conception of Man.* New York: Ungar.

Furubotn, Eiric G., and Svetozar Pejovich. 1970. "Property Rights and the Behavior of the Firm in a Socialist State: The Example of Yugoslavia." *Zeitschrift für Nationalökonomie* 30:431–454.

————, eds. 1974. *The Economics of Property Rights.* Cambridge, Mass.: Ballinger Publishing Company.

Gamson, Zelda F. 1979. "Some Dilemmas of Collective Work: The People's Food Cooperative, Ann Arbor, Michigan." Occasional Paper. Palo Alto, California: Center for Economic Studies.

Gamson, Zelda F. et al. 1978. *Collective Work in Small Alternative Enterprises.* Ann Arbor: Residential College, University of Michigan.

Garson, G. David. 1975. "Recent Developments in Workers' Participation in Europe." In *Self Management,* ed. Jaroslav Vanek. Baltimore: Penguin Books.

Grant, Gerald, and David Riesman. 1978. *The Perpetual Dream: Reform and Experiment in the American College.* Chicago: University of Chicago Press.

Greenberg, Edward S. 1975. "Theories of Worker Participation." *Social Science Quarterly* 55 (September):215–232.

————. 1981. "Industrial Self-Management and Political Attitudes." *The American Political Science Review* 75 (March):29–42.

————. 1983. *The American Political System: A Radical Analysis.* 3d edition. Boston: Little, Brown.

Gregory, Denis, and Chris Logan. 1982. "The Wales TUC: On Prospects for Workers' Cooperatives." *Economic and Industrial Democracy* 3 (February):75–78.

Gunn, Christopher. 1980. "Workers' Self-Management in the United States: Theory and Practice." Ph.D. Dissertation, Cornell University.

————. 1981. "The Fruits of Rath: A New Model of Self-Management." *Working Papers* 8 (March/April):17–21.

————. 1984. *Workers' Self-Management in the United States.* Ithaca: Cornell University Press.

Gutierrez-Johnson, Ana and William F. Whyte. 1977. "The Mondragon System of Worker Production Cooperatives." *Industrial and Labor Relations Review* 31 (October):18–30.

Hammer, Tove H., Jacqueline C. Landau, and Robert N. Stern. 1981. "Absenteeism When Workers Have a Voice: The Case of Employee Ownership." *Journal of Applied Psychology* 5 (October):561–573.

Hammer, Tove H., and Robert Stern. 1980. "Employee Ownership: Implications for the Organizational Distribution of Power." *Academy of Management Journal* 23 (March):78–100.

Hirschleifer, Jack, and John Riley. 1979. "The Analytics of Uncertainty and Information—An Expository Survey." *Journal of Economic Literature* 17 (December):1375–1421.

Hoedads Co-Op, Inc. 1978. *Bylaws.* Eugene, Oregon. December.

————. 1979. *Together.* Eugene, Oregon. Summer.

Horvat, Branko. 1976a. "Workers' Management." *Economic Analysis and Workers' Management* 10, 3–4: 197–216.

————. 1976b. *The Yugoslav Economic System.* White Plains, New York: M. E. Sharpe, Inc.

Hosmer, Larue, A. Cooper, and L. Vesper. 1977. *Entrepreneurial Function: Text and Cases on Smaller Firms.* Englewood Cliffs, New Jersey: Prentice-Hall.

Idaho Cooperative Loan Association. 1939. *Self-Help Cooperatives, 1935–1939*. Idaho Cooperative Loan Association.

Industrial Cooperative Association. 1980. "Model Bylaws for a Worker Cooperative." Somerville, Mass.

Inkeles, Alex, and David H. Smith. 1974. *Becoming Modern*. Cambridge, Mass.: Harvard University Press.

Jackall, Robert. 1976. "Workers' Self-Management and the Meaning of Work: A Study of Briarpatch Cooperative Auto Shop." Occasional Paper, July. Palo Alto, California: Center for Economic Studies.

————. 1978. *Workers in a Labyrinth: Jobs and Survival in a Bank Bureaucracy*. Montclair, New Jersey: Allanheld, Osmun and Company.

————. 1983. "Moral Mazes: Bureaucracy and Managerial Work." *Harvard Business Review* 61 (September-October):118–130.

Jenkins, David. 1974. *Job Power*. Baltimore: Penguin Books.

Johannesen, Janette E. 1979. "VAG: A Need for Evaluation." *Industrial Relations* 18 (Fall):364–369.

Jones, Derek C. 1977. "The Economics and Industrial Relations of Producer Cooperatives in the United States, 1791–1939." *Economic Analysis and Workers' Management* 11, 3–4: 295–317.

————. 1978. "Producer Cooperatives in Industrialized Western Economies: An Overview." *Annals of Public and Co-operative Economy* 49 (April-June):149–162.

————. 1979a. "Producer Cooperatives in the U.S.: An Examination and Analysis of Socio-Economic Performance." Palo Alto, California: Center for Economic Studies. Mimeo.

————. 1979b. "U.S. Producer Cooperatives: The Record to Date." *Industrial Relations* 18 (Fall):342–357.

————. 1980a. "Producer Cooperatives in Industrialized Western Economies." *British Journal of Industrial Relations* 17 (July):141–154.

————. 1980b. "U.S. Producer Cooperatives: An Interpretive Essay." Occasional Paper. Palo Alto, California: Center for Economic Studies.

Jones, Derek C., and David K. Backus. 1977. "British Producer Cooperatives in the Footwear Industry: An Empirical Test of the Theory of Financing." *The Economic Journal* 87 (September):488–510.

Jones, Derek C., and Jan Svejnar, eds. 1982. *Participatory and Self-Managed Firms: Evaluating Economic Performance*. Lexington, Mass.: Lexington Books.

Jones, S. C., and Victor H. Vroom. 1964. "Division of Labor and Performance Under Cooperative and Competitive Conditions." *Journal of Abnormal and Social Psychology* 68 (March):313–320.

Joreen, J. 1973. "The Tyranny of Structurelessness." In *Radical Feminism*, ed. A. Koedt, E. Levine, and A. Rapine. New York: Quadrangle Books.

Kanter, Rosabeth Moss. 1972. *Commitment and Community*. Cambridge: Harvard University Press.

Kaus, Robert M. 1983. "The Trouble with Unions." *Harper's* (June):23–35.

Kelso, Louis. 1967. *How to Turn Eighty Million Workers into Capitalists on Borrowed Money*. New York: Random House.

Kelso, Louis, and Mortimer J. Adler. 1958. *The Capitalist Manifesto*. New York: Random House.

Keniston, Kenneth. 1971. *Youth and Dissent*. New York: Harcourt, Brace, and Jovanovich.

Kerr, Clark. 1939. "Productive Enterprises of the Unemployed, 1931–1938." Ph.D. dissertation, University of California.

Kerr, Clark, and A. Harris. 1939. *Self-Help Cooperatives in California*. Legislative Problems, no. 9. Bureau of Public Administration, University of California, Berkeley.

Kreiger, S. 1979. *Hip Capitalism*. Beverly Hills: California Sage Publications.

Kremen, Bennett. 1972. "No Pride in This Dust." *Dissent* (Winter):21–28.

Landes, David. 1969. *The Unbound Prometheus: Technological Change and Industrial Development in Western Europe 1750 to the Present*. Cambridge: Cambridge University Press.

Langer, Elinor. 1970a. "Inside the New York Telephone Company." *New York Review of Books* 14 (March 12):16f.

———. 1970b. "The Women of the Telephone Company." *New York Review of Books* 14 (March 26):14f.

Levin, Henry M. 1980. "Workplace Democracy and Educational Planning." In *Education, Work and Employment*, 2:123–216. Paris UNESCO International Institute for Educational Planning.

———. 1981. "Economic Democracy, Education, and Social Change." In *Prevention Through Political Action and Social Change*, ed. Justin M. Joffee and George W. Albee, 165–184. Hanover, N.H.: University Press of New England.

———. 1982. "Issues in Assessing the Comparative Productivity of Worker-Managed and Participatory Firms in Capitalist Societies." In *Participatory and Self-Managed Firms: Evaluating Economic Performance*, ed. Derek C. Jones and Jan Svejnar. Lexington, Mass.: Lexington Books.

———. 1983. "Education and Organizational Democracy." *International Yearbook of Organizational Democracy*. Vol 1, ed. Colin Crouch and Frank A. Heller, chapter 11. London and New York: John Wiley.

Levin, Henry M. and Russell W. Rumberger. 1983. "The Low Skill Future in High Tech." *Technology Review* (August/September).

Lott, A. J., and B. E. Lott. 1965. "Group Cohesiveness as Interpersonal Attraction: A Review of Relationships with Antecedent and Consequent Variables." *Psychological Bulletin* 64 (October):259–309.

Mansbridge, Jane. 1973. "Time, Emotion, and Inequality: Three Problems of Participatory Groups." *Journal of Applied Behavioral Science* 9 (February/March):351–368.

———. 1979. "The Agony of Inequality." In *Co-ops, Communes, and Collectives*, ed. J. Case and R. Taylor. New York: Pantheon.

Marglin, Steven A. 1974. "What Do Bosses Do?" *Review of Radical Political Economics* 6 (Summer):60–112.

Margolis, Robert. 1978. "Reports on Collectives." Palo Alto: Center for Economic Studies. Manuscript.

———. 1980. "Collectives in Urban Environments: Critical Notetaking." Occasional Paper. Palo Alto, California: Center for Economic Studies.

Mason, Ronald. 1982. *Participatory and Workplace Democracy*. Carbondale, Ill.: Southern Illinois University Press.

McGregor, Andrew. 1977. "Rent Extraction and the Survival of Agricultural Production Cooperatives." *American Journal of Agricultural Economics* 59 (August).

Meade, James E. 1972. "The Theory of Labour-Managed Firms and of Profit-Sharing." *Economic Journal* 82 (March):402–428.

Meissner, Martin. 1971. "The Long Arm of the Job: A Study of Work and Leisure." *Industrial Relations* 10 (October):239–260.

Michels, Robert. 1915. *Political Parties*. Glencoe, Illinois: Free Press.

Mill, John Stuart. 1910. *On Representative Government*. London: Everyman.

Moberg, David. 1980. "ESOP." *In These Times* (October 8–14):23–24.

National Center for Employee Ownership. 1983. "Employee Ownership Annual Resource Guide." Arlington, Virginia: National Center for Employee Ownership. Mimeo.

National Economic Development Law Project. 1974. *A Lawyer's Manual on Community Based Economic Development*. Berkeley.

Nelson, Daniel. 1975. *Managers and Workers: Origins of the New Factory System in the United States.* Madison: University of Wisconsin Press.

Oakeshott, Robert. 1975. "Mondragon: Spain's Oasis of Democracy." *Self-Management,* ed. Jaroslav Vanek. Baltimore: Penguin.

————. 1978. *The Case for Workers' Coops.* London: Routledge and Kegan Paul.

Okun, Arthur M. 1981. *Prices and Quantities.* Washington, D.C.: The Brookings Institution.

Ollman, Bertall. 1971. *Alienation.* Cambridge: Cambridge University Press.

Olsen, Kris, and Olson, Cynthia. 1980. "Commitment, Dreams, and Disappointment." *Scoop* 48 (May):5.

O'Neill, William. 1978. *The Last Romantic: A Life of Max Eastman.* New York: Oxford University Press.

Ornelas, Carlos. 1980. "Producer Cooperatives and Schooling: The Case of Mondragon, Spain." Ph.D. dissertation, School of Education, Stanford University.

————. 1982. "Cooperative Production and Technical Education in the Basque Country." *Prospects* 13:467–475.

O'Toole, James. 1979. "The Uneven Record of Employee Ownership." *Harvard Business Review* 57 (November-December):185–197.

Palmer, John L., ed. 1978. *Creating Jobs.* Washington, D.C.: The Brookings Institution.

Panunzio, Constantine. 1939. *Self-Help Cooperatives in Los Angeles.* Berkeley: University of California.

Panschar, William. 1956. *Baking in America: Volume I. Economic Development.* New York: American Book-Stratford Press, Inc.

Parzen, Julia, Catherine Squire, and Michael Kleschnick. 1982. *Buyout: A Guide for Workers Facing Plant Closings.* Sacramento: Office of Policy, Planning and Research, State of California.

Pateman, Carole. 1970. *Participation and Democratic Theory.* Cambridge, England: The University Press.

————. 1975. "A Contribution to the Political Theory of Organizational Democracy." *Administration and Society* 7 (May):5–26.

People's Cooperating Communities Trucking Collective. 1976. *Beyond Isolation: The West Coast Food System as We See It.* San Francisco: Free Spirit Press.

Perry, Stuart. 1978. *San Francisco Scavengers.* Berkeley, Los Angeles, London: University of California Press.

Pitegoff, Peter. 1982. *The New Massachusetts Law for Worker Cooperatives: MGL Chapter 157A.* Somerville, Mass.: Industrial Cooperative Association.

Polanyi, Karl. 1944. *The Great Transformation.* Boston: Beacon Press.

Rankin, Deborah. 1980. "Stock Plans for Employees." *The New York Times* (August 2):28.

Reich, Charles A. 1970. *The Greening of America.* New York: Random House.

Reich, Michael, and James Devine. 1981. "The Microeconomics of Conflict and Hierarchy in Capitalist Production." *The Review of Radical Political Economics* 12 (Winter):27–45.

Reinharz, Shulamit. 1983. "Consulting to the Alternative Work Setting: A Suggested Strategy for Community Psychology." *Journal of Community Psychology* 11 (July):199–212.

Rishkojski, L. 1977. "North Country Co-op in Crisis." *Scoop* 19 (December/January):6–7.

Ronco, William. 1974. *Food Coops: An Alternative to Shopping in Supermarkets.* Boston: Beacon Press.

Ross, Irwin. 1980. "What Happens When the Employees Buy the Company?" *Fortune* 101 (June):108–111.

Rothschild-Whitt, Joyce. 1976. "Conditions Facilitating Participatory-Democratic

Organizations." *Sociological Inquiry* 46 (Spring):75–86.

———. 1979. "The Collectivist Organization." *American Sociological Review* 44 (August):509–527.

Rumberger, Russell W. 1981. *Overeducation in the U.S. Labor Market.* New York: Praeger.

Russell, Raymond. 1981. "The Viability and Longevity of an American Taxi Cooperative." Paper prepared for the International Conference on Producer Cooperatives, Gilleleje, Denmark, May 31–June 4.

Russell, Raymond, Arthur Hochner, and Stuart Perry. 1979. "Participation, Influence and Worker Ownership." *Industrial Relations* 18 (Fall):330–341.

Sachs, Stephen. 1981. "Running an ESOP Democratically: Thoughts from Fastener Industries." *Workplace Democracy* 9 (Fall):15–16.

Saglio, Janet, and J. Richard Hackman. 1982. "The Design of Governance Systems for Small Worker Cooperatives." Somerville, Mass.: Industrial Cooperative Association.

Sartori, Giovanni. 1962. *Democratic Theory.* Detroit: Wayne State University Press.

Schneider, Donald J. 1979. "The Performance of Self-Help Cooperatives: An Evaluation." Senior Thesis, Hamilton College.

Schumpeter, Joseph. 1943. *Capitalism, Socialism and Democracy.* London: George Allen and Unwin.

Sen, Amartya. 1975. *Employment, Technology and Development.* Oxford: Clarendon Press.

Sheppard, Harold L., and Neal Q. Herrick. 1972. *Where Have All the Robots Gone? Worker Dissatisfaction in the 70's.* New York: Free Press.

Shirom, Arie. 1972. "The Industrial Relations Systems of Industrial Cooperatives in the United States, 1880–1935." *Labor History* 13 (Fall):533–551.

Shostak, Arthur B. 1969. *Blue-Collar Life.* New York: Random House.

Singer, J. E., C. A. Brush, and S. C. Lublin. 1965. "Some Aspects of Deindividuation: Identification and Conformity." *Journal of Experimental Social Psychology* 1 (November):356–378.

Sisson, Rebecca. 1978. "Tequila Mockingbird." In *Collective Work in Small Alternative Enterprises,* by Zelda Gamson et al. Ann Arbor: Residential College, University of Michigan.

Slavin, Robert E. 1983. *Cooperative Learning.* New York: Longman.

Slavin, Robert E., and Allen M. Tanner. 1979. "Effects of Cooperative Reward Structures and Individual Accountability on Productivity and Learning." *Journal of Educational Research* 72 (May/June):294–298.

Smith, Adam. 1937. *The Wealth of Nations.* New York: Random House.

Sockell, Donna. 1978. "Summary of Research on Worker-Owned Firms in the United States." Manuscript, Cornell University, ILR School.

Spence, Michael. 1973. "Job Market Signaling." *Quarterly Journal of Economics* 87 (August):355–374.

Stack, Hal, and Carroll M. Hutton, eds. 1980. *Building New Alliances: Labor Unions and Higher Education.* New Directions for Experiential Learning. No. 10. San Francisco: Jossey-Bass.

Stein, Barry A. 1979. "The Company Family: The Early Years of Andrew Winery." In *Life in Organizations,* ed. R. M. Kanter and B. Stein, 290–301. New York: Basic Books:

Steiner, Claude, et al. 1975. *Readings in Radical Psychiatry.* New York: Grove Press.

Steinherr, Alfred. 1978a. "The Labor-Managed Economy: A Survey of the Economics Literature." *Annals of Public and Co-operative Economy* 49 (April-June):129–148.

———. 1978b. "The Theory of Worker-Managed Economy and Firms." In *Workers'*

Participation in an Internationalized Economy, ed. B. Wilbert, A. Kudat, and Y. Ozkan. Kent, Ohio: Kent State University Press.

Stern, Robert, and Philip Comstock. 1978. *Employee Stock Ownership Plans (ESOPs): Benefits for Whom?* Ithaca: N.Y. State School of Industrial and Labor Relations.

Stern, Robert N., and ReAnn O'Brien. 1977. "National Unions and Employee Ownership." Dept. of Organizational Behavior, School of Industrial Relations, Cornell. Mimeo.

Stern, Robert N., K. Haydn Wood, and Tove Helland Hammer. 1979. *Employee Ownership in Plant Shutdowns*. Kalamazoo, Mich.: W. E. Upjohn. Institute for Employment Research.

Stiglitz, Joseph. 1975. "Incentives, Risk and Information: Notes Towards a Theory of Hierarchy." *Bell Journal of Economics* 6 (Autumn):552–579.

Strongforce. 1977. *Democracy in the Workplace*. Washington, D.C.: Strongforce, Inc.

Taylor, Frank G. 1939. *Self-Help Cooperatives in California*. February. Mimeo.

Terkel, Studs. 1974. *Working*. New York: Pantheon.

Thomas, Henk T., and Chris Logan. 1980. *Mondragon Producer Cooperatives*. The Hague: Institute of Social Studies.

————. 1982. *Mondragon: An Economic Analysis*. Boston: George Allen and Unwin.

Thompson, Dennis. 1970. *The Democratic Citizen*. London: Cambridge University Press.

Thompson, Edward P. 1964. *The Making of the English Working Class*. New York: Pantheon.

Thurston, B. 1980. "South Bend Lathe, E.S.O.P. on Strike Against Itself?" *Self-Management* 8 (Fall):19–20.

Training for Urban Alternatives. 1979. Washington, D.C.: Center for Studies of Metropolitan Problems, National Institute of Mental Health.

Trampcznski, Bosdan. 1973. "Cooperatives of the Disabled in Poland." *International Labor Review* 108 (November):423–437.

United Kingdom, Committee on Public Accounts. 1976. *Sixth Report*. London, H.M.S.O.

United States, Bureau of Labor Statistics. 1933. "Employment Conditions—Unemployment Relief." *Monthly Labor Review* 37 (October):800–802; 844–845.

————. 1936a. "Activities of Federally Aided Self-Help Cooperatives During 1935." *Monthly Labor Review* 42 (March):609–621.

————. 1936b. "Cooperative Self-Help Movement in Utah." *Monthly Labor Review* 43 (August):349–355.

————. 1938. "Self-Help Activities of the Unemployed." *Monthly Labor Review* 47 (July):1–17.

————. 1939a. "Federal Aid to Self-Help Cooperatives." *Monthly Labor Review* 48 (January):111–113.

————. 1939b. "Self-Help Cooperatives for Older Workers." *Monthly Labor Review* 48 (May):1081–1083.

————. 1939c. "Self-Help Organizations in the United States." *Monthly Labor Review* 49 (December):1335–1347.

————. 1941. "Self-Help Cooperatives in Utah, 1935–41." *Monthly Labor Review* 53 (August):438–443.

————. 1947. "Cooperatives in the Pacific States." *Monthly Labor Review* 64 (April):688–695.

United States, Congress, Joint Economic Committee. 1976. *Broadening the Ownership of New Capital: ESOPs and Other Alternatives*. 94th Congress, 2nd Session (June 17). Washington, D.C.: U.S. Government Printing Office.

United States, Department of Commerce, Bureau of the Census. 1942a. *Manufactures 1939.* Washington, D.C.: Government Printing Office.

————. 1942b. *Statistical Abstract of the United States, 1940.* Washington, D.C.: Government Printing Office.

United States, Department of Commerce. 1973. *Long Term Economic Growth, 1860–1870.* Washington, D.C.: Government Printing Office.

United States, Department of Health, Education, and Welfare. 1973. *Work in America.* Cambridge, Mass.: The MIT Press.

United States, Senate. 1972. *Worker Alienation 1972.* Washington, D.C.: Government Printing Office.

————. 1976. *Hearings on the Tax Reform Act of 1975.* Committee on Finance, Part 3, March 29–31, 1976. Washington, D.C.: Government Printing Office.

————, Select Committee on Small Business. 1979. "The Role of the Federal Government and Employee Ownership of Business." Washington, D.C.: Government Printing Office. Jan. 29.

Vanek, Jaroslav. 1970. *The General Theory of Labor-Managed Market Economies.* Ithaca: Cornell University Press.

————, ed. 1975a. *Self-Management.* Baltimore: Penguin Books.

————. 1975b. "The Worker-Managed Enterprise as an Institution." In *Self-Management,* ed. J. Vanek. Baltimore: Penguin.

————. 1977a. "The Basic Theory of Financing of Participatory Firms." In *The Labor-Managed Economy: Essays,* by J. Vanek. Ithaca: Cornell University Press.

————. 1977b. "Education for the Practice of Self-Management." In *Democracy in the Workplace,* by Strongforce. Washington, D.C.: Strongforce, Inc.

————. 1977c. *The Labor-Managed Economy.* Ithaca: Cornell University Press.

Vanek, Jaroslav, and Juan Espinosa. 1972. "The Subsistence Income, Effort, and Development Potential of Labour Management and Other Economic Systems." *Economic Journal* 82:1000–1013.

Virtue, G. O. 1932. "The End of the Cooperative Coopers." *Quarterly Journal of Economics* 46 (May).

Vocations for Social Change. 1976. *Boston People's Yellow Pages.* Cambridge, Mass.

————. 1977. *The 1977 Yellow Pages Update.* Cambridge, Mass.

Walker, Jonathan. 1979. "International Woodworkers of America/Forest Workers Organizing Committee." Eugene, August 14.

Walker, Pat, ed. 1979. *Between Labor and Capital.* Boston: South End Press.

Walton, Richard E. 1976. "Alienation and Innovation in the Workplace." In *Work and the Quality of Life,* ed. James O'Toole. Cambridge, Mass.: M.I.T. Press.

Weber, Max. 1958. "Bureaucracy." *From Max Weber.* Trans. and ed. by Hans Gerth and C. Wright Mills, 196–244. New York: Oxford University Press.

Whyte, William Foote. 1978. "In Support of the Voluntary Employee Ownership and Community Stabilization Act." *Congressional Record.* Also published in *Society* 15 (September/October):73–82.

Whyte, William Foote, and Joseph Blasi. 1980. "From Research to Legislation on Employee Legislation." *Economic and Industrial Democracy* 1 (August):395–416.

Whyte, William Foote, Tove Hammer, Christopher B. Meek, Reed Nelson, and Robert N. Stern. 1983. *Worker Participation and Ownership.* Ithaca: ILR Press, New York State School of Industrial and Labor Relations.

Williams, Mary. 1982. "The Weirton Steel That Was and May Yet Be." *The Progressive* 46 (November):30–36.

Williamson, Oliver E. 1975. *Markets and Hierarchies.* New York: Free Press.

Wyckoff, Hogie, ed. 1976. *Love, Therapy, and Politics.* New York: Grove Press.

Yuchtman, Ephraim. 1972. "Reward Distribution and Work-Role Attractiveness in the Kibbutz—Reflections on Equity Theory." *American Sociological Review* 37 (October):581–592.

Zablocki, Benjamin. 1971. *The Joyful Community*. Chicago: University of Chicago Press.

Zwerdling, Daniel. 1977. "At IGP, It's Not Business as Usual." *Working Papers* 5 (Spring):68–81.

———. 1978. *Democracy at Work*. Washington, D.C.: Association for Workplace Democracy.

———. 1979. "Employee Ownership: How Well is it Working?" *Working Papers* 7 (May/June):15–27.

CONTRIBUTORS

JOYCE CRAIN was a research associate at the Center for Economic Studies in Palo Alto, California. She is the author or coauthor of several essays on worker cooperatives.

DAVID ELLERMAN, PH.D., is cofounder and staff economist of the Industrial Cooperative Association and has worked in the field of workplace democracy for fifteen years. He has received graduate degrees in philosophy, economics, and mathematics, and has taught mathematics, computer science, accounting, and economics in several universities. He is currently teaching in the School of Management at Boston College.

ZELDA F. GAMSON is a professor in the Center for the Study of Higher Education and the Residential College at the University of Michigan. Her publications include *Academic Values and Mass Education* (with David Riesman and Joseph Gusfield) and, most recently, *Liberating Education* (Jossey-Bass). She is also the author of numerous articles on higher education.

EDWARD S. GREENBERG is a professor of political science, and director, Research Program on Political and Economic Change, Institute of Behavioral Science, University of Colorado, Boulder. He is the author of *Understanding American Government* and, most recently, *The Rise and Fall of Limited Government: An Essay on Government and Capitalism in the United States* (M. E. Sharpe).

CHRISTOPHER GUNN is an associate professor of economics at Hobart and William Smith Colleges in Geneva, New York. He is the author of *Workers' Self-Management in the United States*, recently published by Cornell University Press.

ROBERT JACKALL is associate professor of sociology, and chairman, Department of Anthropology and Sociology, Williams College, Williamstown, Massachusetts. He is the author of *Workers in a Labyrinth* and numerous essays on work, workers, and bureaucracy. He is currently completing a book on managerial work, to be published by Oxford University Press.

DEREK C. JONES is an associate professor of economics at Hamilton College, Clinton, New York. He has written extensively on producer cooperatives and is the coeditor (with Jan Svejnar) of the series *Advances in the Economic Analysis of Participatory and Self-Managed Firms* published by J.A.I. in Connecticut.

HENRY M. LEVIN is a professor in the School of Education and Department of Economics, and also director of the Institute for Research on Educational Finance and Governance at Stanford University. He specializes in the economics of human resources and workplace democracy. He is the author, coauthor or editor of nine books and about 125 articles, including *The Dialectic of Education and Work*, coauthored with Martin Carnoy, to be published by Stanford University Press.

DONALD J. SCHNEIDER is a graduate of Hamilton College and Warwick University and specializes in the areas of labor-management relations, employee relations, and organizational analysis and development.

INDEX

Designer: UC Press Staff
Compositor: Publisher's Typography
Printer: Vail-Ballou Press
Binder: Vail-Ballou Press
Text: 11/13 Goudy
Display: Goudy